Multichannel Marketing Ecosystems

Multichannel Marketing Ecosystems

Edited by
Markus Ståhlberg
and Ville Maila

KoganPage

LONDON PHILADELPHIA NEW DELHI

First published in Great Britain and the United States in 2014 by Kogan Page Limited

2nd Floor, 45 Gee Street	1518 Walnut Street, Suite 1100	4737/23 Ansari Road
London EC1V 3RS	Philadelphia PA 19102	Daryaganj
United Kingdom	USA	New Delhi 110002
www.koganpage.com		India

Selection and editorial content © Phenomena Group 2014.
Individual chapters © the contributors 2014.

ISBN   978 0 7494 6962 7
E-ISBN 978 0 7494 6963 4

British Library Cataloguing-in-Publication Data

A CIP record for this book is available from the British Library.

Library of Congress Cataloging-in-Publication Data

Multi-channel marketing ecosystems : creating connected customer experiences / [edited by] Markus Ståhlberg, Ville Maila.
       pages cm
    ISBN 978-0-7494-6962-7 (pbk.) – ISBN 978-0-7494-6963-4 (ebook)   1. Multilevel marketing–Management.   2. Internet marketing.   3. Customer relations.   I. Stahlberg, Markus.
II. Maila, Ville.
    HF5415.126.M843 2013
    658.8'72–dc23
                                                                                              2013026094

Typeset by Graphicraft Limited, Hong Kong
Print production managed by Jellyfish
Printed and bound by CPI Group (UK) Ltd, Croydon, CR0 4YY

CONTENTS

15   Social media romance   118

Justin Gray

16   Changing face of Facebook marketing   126

Kristen James

17   Essentials of mobile marketing technologies   131

David Marutiak

ACKNOWLEDGEMENTS

We would like to thank everyone who explores and tests the dream against the surrounding reality! Everyone who explores in this way needs many supporters. Our best supporters are always our nearest ones: Laura and Valle for Ville; Tia, Mai and Toivo for Markus.

In the multichannel ecosystem everyone needs to iterate from Marketing Plan A to a marketing plan that works. We don't believe in rainmakers – we believe in actionable knowledge.

> 'It is not the strongest of the species that survives, nor the most intelligent that survives. It is the one that is the most adaptable to change'
>
> Charles Darwin

Ville Maila & Markus Ståhlberg
Helsinki, Finland

PREFACE

Consumer marketing is all about impacting the behaviour of consumers. If the basic patterns of consumer behaviour change, that should obviously have some impact on the groundwork of marketing. Due to the advances in technology and software during the past decade we have experienced a huge shift in how consumers interact with brands. In traditional marketing thinking this has meant that it has become more difficult to reach the consumers due to the ever-multiplying range of channels that they use. This phenomenon is often referred to as 'media fragmentation'. Traditional thinking is based on the concept that marketing is fundamentally about broadcasting: in other words that it is one-directional.

As changes in consumer behaviour are usually evolutionary rather than revolutionary, they may be hard to detect. We have set up hundreds of campaigns for the biggest consumer marketers, ranging from PepsiCo to Unilever and Danone, edited the first truly global book on shopper marketing, and eventually built .PROMO, a groundbreaking software platform that automates multichannel marketing. Thus we have had a front row seat from which to observe the slow but inevitable change of consumer behaviour. We have been intrigued to see how difficult it is for marketers to change old ways of thinking, from TV-centric to multichannel and from broadcast to interactive. This is not surprising, since consumer marketing is fundamentally about reaching large numbers of people and having the tools to impact their behaviour in a particular way. Faced with this challenge, most marketers would simply state that they can reach more consumers via TV than any other media and, on the other hand, that efficient tools for impacting the consumer in the multichannel environment are still in their infancy if available at all. Therefore, why all the fuss? Why take the risk of changing an established approach that is delivering good results? Read this book and you will get the answer.

Multichannel Marketing Ecosystems is a book about a new perspective to marketing, focused on actual consumer behaviour and the ecosystem surrounding it, instead of preserving the lens of the status quo and existing traditions of marketing. The book is intended to give you an understanding about why you should change (Part I: From TV-centric thinking to a multichannel ecosystem), how you should do it (Part II: Establishing and successfully taking advantage of the multichannel ecosystem) and how to make it count (Part III: Beyond online: how to translate the multichannel ecosystem into revenue).

The book comprises 30 chapters by various experts in different areas of marketing – from specialists in traditional marketing and media to pioneering interactive marketers. As a compilation book there are many ways to approach it. If you wish to gain a comprehensive understanding or get step-by-step guidance on building and taking advantage of the multichannel marketing ecosystem, it is advisable to read the book from cover to cover. However, if you are interested in a specific topic, ranging from the evolution of the role of TV to understanding how mobile systems should be integrated into your marketing mix, you can just read the relevant individual chapters.

Multichannel Marketing Ecosystems is the first book that takes a holistic view of marketing to the multichannel consumer. We strongly believe that marketing will change fundamentally within the next five years compared with the developments that have taken place over the past five years. Even though marketers and agencies are slow to endorse change, we hope this book may serve as a seed to a change in thinking that can help brands to bypass rivals who don't embrace the change, and that will help them to enhance their relationship with consumers within the new paradigm.

This book is the start of a journey to uncharted territories of marketing and we would highly appreciate readers' opinions. We will be delighted to respond to questions, comments or challenges related to *Multichannel Marketing Ecosystems*. We hope to hear from you so that we can learn something new together, and invite you to visit us at **www.dotpromoinc.com**, or to drop us an e-mail at: **ecosystem@dotpromoinc.com**.

Markus Ståhlberg and Ville Maila

PART I
From TV-centric thinking to a multichannel marketing ecosystem

Introduction to the multichannel marketing ecosystem

01

MARKUS STÅHLBERG

Markus Ståhlberg is the CEO of .PROMO Inc, the app-based marketing automation platform that makes campaign execution as easy as using the App Store. As a leading expert in interaction mechanisms, Markus has helped big brands such as Pepsico, Danone and Nestlé internationally in reaching their marketing objectives. Markus is the editor and co-author of the book *Shopper Marketing* (Kogan Page, 2009, 2012).

Paradigm change

Marketing can be extracted into a fairly simple equation: how do marketers reach consumers and how do the marketing messages impact the consumer behaviour? Both variables in this equation have changed dramatically in recent years due to the rapid fragmentation of consumer media consumption and the emergence of online and mobile interactive media as ubiquitous channels.

To really see the fundamental nature of this change, it is worth taking a look at how the world has changed since 1993. The way consumers communicate has changed dramatically, with 4.5 billion internet users, including more than a billion Facebook users and over 7 billion mobile phones (including more than a billion smartphones). Within the same period, the distribution of content has shifted away from media such as cassettes, VHSs and the paper *New York Times* to Spotify, Netflix and **www.nytimes.com** the online edition. Moreover, the shopping and distribution of physical goods is reaching a tipping point, with shares of online sales breaking records in every consecutive season.

Yet during this period the fundamentals of marketing have not been revised dramatically. TV still dominates the core of marketing strategy for most marketers, while other media, including online and mobile systems, are typically considered as having a supporting or even experimental role.

FIGURE 1.1 A typical 360° approach to marketing

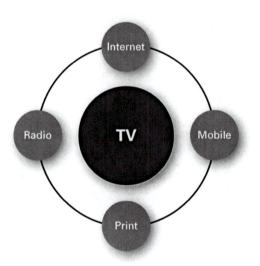

However, we are at the brink of a fundamental change. Marketers must start endorsing what is happening around them and completely rethink their approach. The change means that consumers can no longer be taken simply as passive receivers of marketing communications through a predominantly TV-centric set of channels. Instead, consumers' interactions within a complex marketing ecosystem consisting of various channels and operators must be built into to the very fundamentals of marketing.

The interactive consumer

The interactive consumer is not a new concept. This was one of the buzz-concepts of the late 1990s internet bubble when many strategists were predicting the demise of old ways of marketing in the advent of the 'new media'. At the time, however, this was a theoretical approach that was not reflected by actual consumer behaviour and this is why many marketers, shifting their focus to 'cyberspace', ended up bankrupt or losing a great deal of money and customers. Thus it is understandable that many marketers are cautious about making radical moves and expect concrete proof of results before revising their strategies.

On the other hand, it may not be very clear what kind of actions marketers should take – do they need to shift spending from TV to other media, or to transfer the brand lead-role from the current above-the-line agency to an interactive agency? The answer: neither might be necessary; TV and the moving image format will maintain or increase their importance, and there is no reason to change the agency's focus as long as they agree with the revised approach. The crucial thing is to adapt your overall marketing strategy to the current behaviour of the target audience before it's too late and they jump on the competition's boat.

The first step to revising the thinking is to understand what the 'interactive consumer' means. To start with, interactive means two-directional; it means the consumer being reactive or proactive in relation to the marketing communications. The key difference from the one-way approach is the positive action the consumer takes within the interactive media, in contrast to a passive 'between the ears' effect. Reacting means, for example, the consumer being exposed to brand-sponsored communications and actively discussing it on social media, publishing blog posts or making searches related to the communications. Being proactive means the consumer initiating the cycle without being exposed to any communications sponsored by the brand, for example through reacting a blog post not sponsored by the marketer or to positive or negative feedback related to the brand or product from a friend.

Most marketers are already realizing these changes in consumer behaviour and are taking action to reach the target audience within the various online and mobile environments through being active in social media or using paid online media. This is not enough, however. Instead of simply 'reaching' the consumers, the marketers must be able to take the driver's seat in the entire process of interactions between the brand and the consumer. The process of interaction involves five types of interactions:

- Social interaction:
  A dialogical process, in which the consumer acts as the publisher via social media, forums or e-mail for example.

- Search: The consumer actively searching for something related to the brand, product or service, such as finding product information or making price comparisons, typically by using search engines.

- Click: Consumers click on a hyperlink sponsored by the brand, ranging from text links and online ads to sponsored posts on social media.

- Transaction: The consumer makes a transaction with the brand, product or service, eg making a purchase or giving marketing permission. In contrast to the social interactions and to search and click, the transactions require authentication by the consumer and typically form a relationship between the brand and the consumer. Transactions are sometimes referred to as 'valuable interactions'.

- Relationship interaction: The consumer performs interactions requested by the brand based on an existing relationship, eg providing feedback or inviting friends in response to a request from the brand.

FIGURE 1.2 Categories of interactions

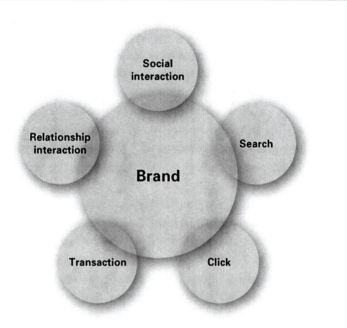

In order to successfully shift the one-directional marketing strategy into an interactive one, brands must have the facilities in place to reach consumers within the different interactions, monitor and measure these interactions, facilitate them and gain ownership of as big a portion of the interactions as possible. However, since brands don't control the internet and the consumers are physical, not digital, a more holistic approach is necessary.

The ecosystem

For the past two decades there has been a lot of talk about fragmentation of media, meaning that the increasing variety of media channels used by consumers is making it more difficult for marketers to reach a specific individual or to segment consumers into major groups based on their behaviour. This change calls for a more dynamic and holistic approach to marketing as opposed to the 'one size fits all' strategy. The traditional view of marketing was to think it is sufficient to broadcast a compelling message that would eventually bring about the desired outcome, be it purchase or brand preference for instance. The '360° branding approach' is an evolution of this approach in which the marketers try to make sure the same message is broadcast on all channels, from TV to shop floor and social media. This approach does embrace a more holistic view that acknowledges the fact that consumers are not only watching prime time TV, but it fails to take into account the progressive nature of consumer behaviour from one channel to another.

Previously the way consumers responded to marketing communications could be characterized as a black box until the desired actions took place. The only way to track their behaviour was to conduct consumer research, which could never give marketers a very conclusive view of the processes nor could it provide marketers with control over the behaviour.

Now things are different: with interactive consumers using the internet to search, to engage in dialogue and in many cases also to purchase, it is possible to track the processes (often with absolute accuracy) from the moment consumers get exposed to marketing to the eventual action that they take, which can thus be significantly influenced by marketers. Unfortunately for marketers, however, the consumer interactions don't usually take place within the brand's sphere of influence but include various different technology-driven service providers that affect the consumers on their way to the eventual action. The crucial change that has taken place is that technology, in the form of devices and especially in the form of software is becoming an integral enabler of the relationship between the brand and the consumer.

Understanding this new, complex environment requires a paradigm shift for marketing. The term 'ecosystem' has been recently embraced by many industries in various contexts, from 'supplier ecosystem', to 'app ecosystem' or even 'Amazon ecosystem', and it does seem to provide a good perspective for approaching complex and dynamic systems with many

FIGURE 1.3 Consumer–brand relationship enabled by technology

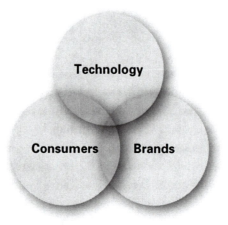

operators interacting with each other. As defined by Smith and Smith (2012): 'An ecosystem is a community of living organisms (plants, animals and microbes) in conjunction with the non-living components of their environment (things like air, water and mineral soil), interacting as a system.'

A definition for the multichannel marketing ecosystem can be derived: 'A multichannel marketing ecosystem is a community of consumers in conjunction with the brands, products and services they are exposed to, interacting as a system enabled by technology.' Viewing marketing and brands' interactions with the consumer as a dynamic and continuous system that is evolving and is enabled by technology changes the role of marketer from broadcaster of communications into the enabler and sponsor of the ecosystem in which consumers interact with each other and the brands.

Harnessing the multichannel marketing ecosystem

A multichannel marketing ecosystem requires a holistic approach that includes all the touch-points between the brand and consumers, from initial exposure to the communications through to purchase and customer relationship communications. Also, even though it would be tempting to simplify the multichannel marketing ecosystem into a funnel with clearly defined hierarchies and mechanisms between the touch-points, the reality is often more complex. The order in which consumers get exposed will vary greatly – consumers might bounce back and forth in the 'funnel' touch-points and the flow will also be strongly affected by the product or service in question as well as the brand.

The biggest mistake marketers can make when extending their reach to the interactive environment is to shift their focus from mass marketing to individual interactions with consumers. In the age of TV it was not really possible to think of communicating individually to every member of the target group, but the emergence of social media in particular, together with concepts like one-to-one marketing, has created the illusion that this is the optimal approach. This is not to say that interactions with individual consumers would be a bad idea, but in terms of marketing return on investment (ROI) it is rarely the best choice – the most fundamental rule of mass marketing should not be forgotten: in the end, only volume counts. High volume must be the main focus in the multichannel marketing ecosystems – otherwise they are doomed to fail.

The marketers should take the driver's seat on defining how consumers interact within the different touch-points and steer them towards the eventual marketing objective. This requires understanding of where the touch-points are and what their roles are within the big picture.

FIGURE 1.4 Holistic view of the multichannel marketing ecosystem

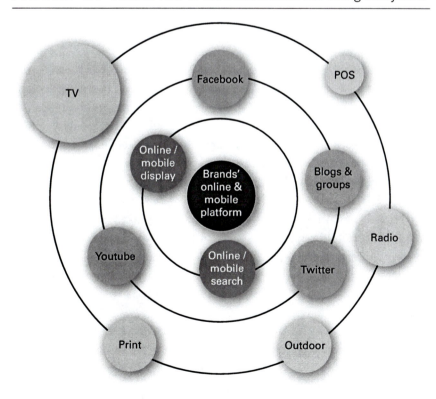

Figure 1.4 depicts a holistic view of the multichannel marketing ecosystem, giving examples of touch-points between the brand and consumer, categorized according to the type of interaction and the brand's capacity to facilitate them. The outer sphere represents traditional broadcast media, based on one-way broadcast-type communications. Understanding the role of this sphere within the ecosystem requires at least basic methods for tracking how consumers are affected by it. This can be done in the traditional way, by using market research, but a more advanced method is to include immediate and channel-specific calls to action, trackable links or QR-codes in the media so that it is possible to track consumers taking the desired action.

Next is the 'social' sphere, most notably Facebook but also other social media, blogs and discussion groups and other media through which consumers interact with each other by publishing, sharing or commenting on brand communications-related topics. Understanding and harnessing this sphere has been the focus of many marketers in recent years, and various service providers, such as Buddy Media (acquired by Salesforce) or Vitrue (acquired by Oracle), have emerged in order to enable tracking and facilitate the social interactions. Many marketers have decided to put the social sphere at the centre of their ecosystem, for example by focusing the brands' entire online and mobile presence into Facebook. The problem with this approach is that the brand is handing out the ownership of the relationship with the consumer to a third party and losing control over it. The social sphere is essential, but it is only one sphere of interaction touch-points in the big picture.

The third sphere is the 'click' sphere consisting of online display and search. With regards to search, the brand must make sure the overall ecosystem is constructed properly – structurally, content-wise and technologically – so that the phrases consumers use in their search efforts, primarily using search engines, match those in the system and direct the interactions towards the ecosystem's centre. With online display, marketers must consider what messaging and what kind of reward mechanisms maximize the clicks with optimal ROI.

The main enabler of the multichannel marketing ecosystem is the brand's online and mobile platform, which consists of the brand's website and mobile site, the mobile apps and the customer relationship management system. The platform is the enabler of the most valuable interactions, the transactions that can take place online or offline, as well as relationship interactions based on consumer permission.

Building a successful multichannel marketing ecosystem may seem a complex and challenging task – and it definitely is. The best strategy for construction is to first define the purpose of the ecosystem, which would typically be to drive consumers towards repeated transactions and into a close relationship with the brand. After this the brand should consider the most relevant touch-points for each of the spheres, and how the brand can track and activate consumers to interact optimally towards the desired goal. Activation should typically focus on motivating new customers to interactions that lead towards the centre of the ecosystem, and on giving existing members reasons act as ambassadors. Finally you should consider the tools needed to run the ecosystem as well as the communications and reward mechanisms used as its fuel.

FIGURE 1.5 Example of marketing automation platform for a multichannel marketing ecosystem

Reference

Smith, T and Smith, R (2012) *Elements of Ecology*, 8th edn, Pearson International

02

The rise of digital branding

SIMON MCEVOY

Simon McEvoy is the Planning Director at Jam, a social media and digital creative agency. He works with brands like Sky, Capital One and Microsoft to help them bring their brands to life in interactive environments.

How the interactive ecosystem is transforming our concept of the brand

What's in a brand? It's a question that has challenged marketers since the popularization of the term in the 19th century and up to the modern day emergence of 'super-brands' like Coca-Cola and Nike. Determining how a brand is comprised, of what, and what makes brands successful is not just an essential part of marketing theory, but also a vital part of business development. Distilling a brand's essence is critical to giving it power and creating a personality that can survive today's modern business conditions.

This has never been a simple matter, however. If pressed we might talk about logos, mission statements, tone of voice and corporate ethics. We might also discuss creative treatments, advertising slogans, style guides and the biblical 'brand book'. These things are, of course, important. They help create brand identity and recognition. However, in the interactive world these assets are no longer enough; the definition of a brand has changed.

According to Oracle, 78 per cent of consumers admit to having interacted with two or more brand channels before making a purchasing decision. Forrester reports that the company's website is the most trusted source of 'owned' information (such as website or TV ad) about a brand. They paint a picture of a world where consumers are demanding interaction, where they are seeking a deeper, more authentic relationship with a brand. And this new relationship is creating complexity in how we define a brand in the first place. Nate Elliot at Forrester writes:

> The way we 'coordinate' our marketing channels right now is broken: Even today, most marketers develop their TV ads first and then hand them to the interactive team and hope they can build a site or a banner campaign that matches. As we've all seen, this rarely works well.

He argues that we need to effectively stop seeing brands as a logo, slogan or TV ad, but rather as a series of interactions. It is not as simple as making sure existing brand values are translated into multiple channels accurately; rather we need to start building interactivity into those values from the start. Brands need to be asking: 'How are we going to put interactivity through digital, social media, or more traditional channels such as customer service, at the heart of our brand values?'

In order to do this we need to understand how this shift has occurred and why. Like many modern social trends it has been caused by the catalyst of technology: the development of a global social marketplace where brands have been exposed to mass praise and criticism in a way never before thought possible. Doc Searls, in his prophetic tome *The Cluetrain Manifesto* (2000) wrote 'markets are conversations'; and with a global marketplace we have, fittingly, evolved a global conversation. Brands are a part of this, intentionally or not, as consumers take to the interactive web to discuss product issues, praise service, complain about rudeness or share interesting brand stories. Essentially all the things they used to do on a one-to-one basis with each other, but publicly, to a global audience of billions, 24 hours a day.

The interactive brand ecosystem has grown out of technology's incredible adherence to Moore's law and consumer hunger for ever deeper connectivity. As the internet has developed rapidly in terms of scale, speed and penetration so have devices that allow for deeper experiences – smartphones, tablets, half-size tablets, netbooks, note-books and e-book readers have all utterly changed the way we consume interactive content. 'Second' and even 'third' screen marketing has become commonplace, with businesses reporting spikes in web traffic during and shortly after TV ads with strong calls to action. Innovations such as Zeebox are channelling the now commonplace viewing behaviour of users tweeting and commenting whilst watching TV, while news programmes have begun to build live social media commentary into their reports, as witnessed during the London riots of 2011.

Alongside this, consumers have started to trust owned, earned and bought online media more than ever before. Nielsen report that 92 per cent of consumers trust earned 'word of mouth' recommendation from friends and family above all other forms of communication, with consumer reviews getting the next best trust approval rating at 70 per cent. Likewise the 'bought' media of online and mobile advertising have healthy trust ratings of 36 per cent and 29 per cent respectively, despite their 'interruptive' nature. This is in the context of a 24 per cent decline in the trust of TV advertising, down to 47 per cent. This clearly makes the interactive brand ecosystem a powerful place to shape brand perception, both positively and negatively.

One of the major differences between this landscape and that of the pre-interactive age is the idea of who 'owns' the brand. This might seem a strange idea, as in theory brands are owned by organizations, shareholders, company directors and the like. However the concept of ownership has changed dramatically. In the interactive world the consumers own the brand, and they shape it. The organization is merely a curator, collecting brand identity from the shared platforms where it exists and reflecting those views as carefully as possible. Much like a movie director who has to painstakingly get every detail right when bringing a much-loved character to life on the big screen, brands need to be aware of loyal fans and how they feel ownership over the brands they identify so strongly with.

GAP struggled to grasp this when, in 2010, they decided to trial their new logo with their Facebook community with no notice or fanfare. GAP may have been struggling commercially, but they totally overlooked the thousands of loyal, devoted fans who had shown their support consistently through purchases and Facebook appreciation. The new logo was horrendously received, with comment after comment posted to their page and across the web criticizing the move. Within a matter of hours the brand felt forced into a turnaround on the logo, returning to the old one and backtracking completely on the rebrand. GAP thought they owned their brand and could do what they wanted with it. They didn't realize that in the minds of their loyal customers, the brand belonged to them.

This incident clearly illustrated the outmoded attitudes to branding that were in place in some of the world's biggest companies: 'If we change the logo then that will be a rebrand.' Of course, for GAP this was untrue. The customers would stay the same, the product philosophy the same, the perception the same, the broadcast 'us and them' relationship with their fans the same. In short, they needed to become truly interactive, not just change a logo, to rebrand.

For most global brands the volume of conversation around the brand generated by consumers far outweighs that generated by the brand itself. Large brands simply cannot hope to 'control the message' any more, they have to let it go, hand it to the consumer and trust that its authenticity and 'truth' will compel the crowds to treat it with respect. Brands are owned by ordinary people now, as Searls puts it:

> 'We are not seats or eyeballs or end users or consumers, we are human beings – and our reach exceeds your grasp' (Cluetrain.com).

So are there any brands that have captured the essence of what it is to be a 'digital brand'? Which brands have adapted to this new model best, 'baking-in' interactivity early in the process and involving their customers in a constructive, two-way dialogue? There are a few, and here are three that have achieved this in an exemplary way: Smirnoff, Nike and Starbucks.

Smirnoff took a bold step in September 2010 to begin it's 'Nightlife Exchange Project' on Facebook, asking users: 'What makes your country's nightlife the best in the world?' For a cornerstone campaign with heavy investment, kicking it off through social media was brave as in 2010 this was still relatively uncharted territory, particularly from an ROI perspective. Likewise, to base a campaign around 'nightlife' rather than a particular Smirnoff product was interesting. It showed a nuanced understanding of the 'global conversation' that Smirnoff were a part of. The number of people online discussing what brand of vodka to drink was far outweighed by those discussing great nights out. Great nights out lead into many other spheres of conversation such as music, dancing, meeting new people and creating wonderful experiences – all of which are at the core of Smirnoff's brand.

Smirnoff knew that by drawing from their fans' and customers' experiences and pulling their likes and dislikes into the brand positioning from the start, they would create a far more compelling proposition. They had begun a two-way dialogue that would propel the campaign forward and give it a 'life' in earned media far more powerful than any bought media they could pay for. It also allowed them to ensure that the campaign would be well received – effectively they were asking their customers to tell the brand what they wanted, and then the brand would give it to them. Simple.

The campaign then lived in a number of interactive spaces online, supported by other social media platforms such as YouTube and Twitter, a website 'hub' of information and online and social advertising. This was then backed up by offline advertising on TV and in print globally, essentially driving traffic to the key interactive hubs. Of course, this campaign was all about nights out, so the ultimate climax for each of the 14 participatory countries was a huge party, with A-list headline DJs and bands, thousands of people and, of course, lots of Smirnoff vodka.

This link between the virtual and physical world was critical, as it made the campaign 'real'. It linked true, memorable experiences to Smirnoff vodka, creating a huge wave of positive sentiment for the brand and delivering a truly interactive experience. In the minds of consumers, Smirnoff was a brand that engaged them early on, listened to them and then delivered. Internally, interactivity had sat at the heart of the campaign; without it the campaign simply could not have happened.

More crucially, the campaign has been an overwhelming success in terms of numbers, with hundreds of thousands of new Facebook fans added during the campaign periods, tens of thousands of ideas submitted and vast numbers of online interactions. Interestingly, brand references to Smirnoff and the Nightlife Exchange Project now substantially outweigh references to Smirnoff products online, showing that by running a campaign that was more relevant to their consumers lives, Smirnoff have captured a far larger share of conversation than they would have simply pushing vodka sales.

Nike is arguably one of the most exciting interactive brands in the world right now, developing a suite of products, online experiences and supporting media campaigns that all put their interactive community right at the centre. Nike+ began with a simple product insight – that people enjoy working out more when they do so with their friends. The Nike+ online community allows customers to connect with friends via existing social

FIGURE 2.1   Smirnoff

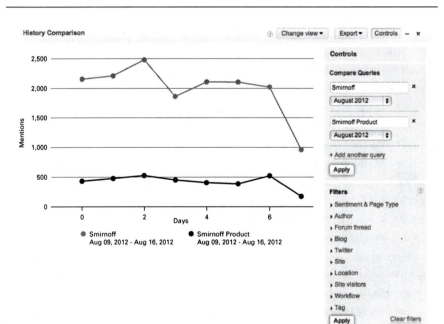

networks, challenge each other and create competitiveness that they would not get from working out alone. This has been infused into products such as Nike Fuelband or Nike+ Training, which track every movement you make and gamify the whole process, converting movement into 'Fuelpoints'. Fuelpoints are the measure of your success, and allow you to compete with friends across the Nike+ network.

What is remarkable about this approach is that it is the interactivity between the customer and their online community that drives the product and marketing strategy. Advertising shows athletes working out alone, but driven to succeed by competitiveness sourced from the Nike+ community. The 'Find Your Greatness' campaign, which revolved around the London 2012 Olympics, focused on the use of hashtags to 'plug it in' to the global conversation around working out and the Games. The idea of sharing scores, boasting of achievements and 'self-actualizing' through sharing were crucial to the media strategy – the more users engaged with Nike+, the more they acted as a hook to pull others in.

The community is then supported by a range of mobile apps and hardware such as watches that keep users engaged and reminded of their involvement. These touch-points keep users logged into the community no matter what they do, so their involvement can be both passive and active. Again all of these devices are built and marketed with one sole purpose in mind: to feed the interactive brand ecosystem. In doing this Nike has said to its consumers: we are a part of your lives and of your friends' lives, we keep you healthy and we reward you for your achievement. Nike transcends being merely a clothing label, and instead becomes a portal into a world of sporting prowess, competition and 'a better life'. As CEO Mark Parker put it last year:

> 'Connecting used to be, "Here's some product, and here's some advertising. We hope you like it." Connecting today is a dialogue.' (*Fortune Magazine*, 2011).

What is hugely interesting about Nike+ was how the platform has evolved over time thanks to consumer input. Initially criticized at launch due to failing apps, a clunky interface and lack of brand support, the platform has grown to become a worldwide phenomenon thanks to repeated iterations and investment. Consumer feedback played a huge part in these developments, not just actively through feedback in online communities, but also passively through data capture on their many apps and devices. Nike's Digital Sport division know when their users log in, how often and for what purpose, and all of this feeds into product development and refinement. The proof of this is in the numbers: a 55 per cent growth in membership of the community last year, a 30 per cent uplift in running division revenues, all while seeing a 40 per cent decrease in US TV advertising spend. Nike+ has translated interactivity into profit in a way that few brands have had the guts or know-how to match.

The final brand to have led the way in interactive branding is Starbucks. Starbucks are a brand with interactivity at their heart, placing huge importance on every sensory interaction a customer has with the brand, from the smell of their coffee beans to the music on their play-lists. And they have put their people, both employees and customers, right at the heart of creating this 'movement' around the humble coffee bean. As Howard Schultz, their pioneering Chairman, is famous for saying:

> 'We are not in the coffee business serving people, but in the people business serving coffee.'

This is not simply marketing rhetoric from Schultz, but an entire interactive ideology that injects the brand with human authenticity. Starbucks believe that a brand is a belief system and, like any belief system, it is only as potent as the devotion of its believers. So Starbucks realize that their 'followers' own the brand and respect them accordingly. In order to do this they have 'tiers' of engagement within the interactive brand ecosystem, which allows them to judge how and when to build consumer feedback into the brand.

The first tier is the corporate website, which aims to be the best exponent of the brand in the online space. Whether you want to know more about the coffee blends, read about Starbucks' values, claim rewards or simply send feedback, this is where to do it. This acts as a springboard to the interactive ecosystem, a hub that connects Starbucks many media platforms together as one seamless unit.

Tier two is their online feedback platform called 'My Starbucks Idea', which directly asks customers for their ideas on how to make Starbucks better. This kind of feedback was usually kept private in the past for fear of embarrassing the brand. But Starbucks realized that by publicly participating in the shaping of the brand consumers become more loyal and more protective, actually insulating the brand better from future criticism. My Starbucks Idea has generated well over 126,000 ideas so far, many of which have been implemented, and feeds straight into their CRM system to make sure regular contributors are being communicated with in an appropriate way.

The third Tier is Starbucks' active social platforms, Facebook, Twitter, YouTube, Google+ and Foursquare. They have over 38 million participants in this community, ranking amongst the largest in the world, and keep it active with conversations around socializing, family and friends, music and, of course, coffee. Value is added to these relationships by pushing offers and discounts through social channels, such as a free latte to launch their new UK 'Stronger Latte' in March 2012. These channels allow for important customer data capture as well as a willing army of sharers and brand advocates that the brand can rely on.

The final tier of interactivity is the cross-channel tier, the active community of customers that frequent their coffee shops every day and use Starbucks mobile apps and loyalty programme to do so. Bridging the gap between digital and physical is important for Starbucks as it is a business that does all of its sales in the offline space. Their mobile apps allow users to find their nearest Starbucks, get information on products, earn loyalty rewards and even pay for their drink using their Starbucks card. This is linked to a loyalty card programme that pays out rewards for loyal customers. All of this data feeds back into their system, allowing them to tailor communications and create a more personal relationship with regular customers. It drives incremental revenue too, with approximately $2.4 billion loaded onto pre-payment loyalty cards globally, $70 million of which is on mobile pre-payment.

By creating this tiered interactive brand ecosystem, Starbucks have been able to evolve naturally with their customers, make subtle improvements without rocking the boat, engage more deeply with the most loyal customers and make their advocates feel truly part of the brand – because they really are. They have done all this and translated it into genuine growth and profit. So when Starbucks decided to change its logo in 2011, whilst they met a backlash, they were able to communicate the reason for change and amplify that through their community quickly and effectively. This helped silence the dissenting voices, allowing the business to move on with this strategic decision and bring loyal fans with it, in stark contrast to GAP's rebrand mismanagement.

These three examples demonstrate how truly interactive brands are reframing the very concept of what a brand is and how it comes into existence. There are lessons here for all brands, no matter what size or scale. Yes, these three have huge resources and some of the best thinkers to guide them into this new, uncharted interactive universe. But what they all have in common is that they have put dialogue with consumers first and put their technology and data people at the head of the table in brand discussions.

The reality is that brands are no longer fixed entities, defined in narrow terms, owned by organizations and dispersed through well-meaning documentation. Businesses can no longer define and control the channels that they engage consumers with. They cannot neatly package their assets, style guide and mission statements in a tidy brand book. Instead the brand 'lives' online, in the minds of consumers and fans, on multiple platforms and in various communities. Brand management is no longer about control and message; rather it is about interactivity, conversation and authenticity.

Modern brands have to adapt. They need to be agile and amorphous, shifting rapidly to align with changing consumer opinion and disruptive technological advances. They have to embrace interactivity, be prepared to engage personally with their customers and let individuals within their business become the voice of their business. As Marshall McLuhan put it beautifully in *The Medium is the Message*: 'Propaganda ends where dialogue begins.'

We are witnessing the end of the 'Age of Propaganda', and an issuing-in of the 'Age of Dialogue'. The question is, are we ready?

Sources

Forrester [online] http://blogs.forrester.com/nate_elliott/11-1-06-6-29-9-how_to_build_an_interactive_brand_ecosystem

McLuhan, Marshall; and Fiore, Quentin (1967) *The Medium is the Message*, Bantam Books, Toronto

Nielsen [online] http://www.nielsen.com/us/en/insights/press-room/2012/nielsen-global-consumers-trust-in-earned-advertising-grows.html

Oracle [online] http://www.oracle.com/us/products/applications/atg/cross-channel-commerce-survey-333315.pdf

Parker, M [online] http://management.fortune.cnn.com/2012/02/13/nike-digital-marketing/

Schultz, H [online] http://www.cbsnews.com/2100-500395_162-20047618.html

Searls, Doc (2000) *The Cluetrain Manifesto*, Basic Books, Cambridge, Mass

Slideshare [online] http://www.slideshare.net/icrossing/the-interactive-brand-ecosystem-putting-digital-at-the-heart-of-your-brand-campaigns

Holistic design for consumer engagement

03

BRAD BRINEGAR

Over the past 10 years Brad Brinegar, former CEO of Leo Burnett USA, has led McKinney to renown as a leader in digital and integrated communications. McKinney, named 'the most effective independent agency in the world' by Warc and Effie Worldwide in 2012, recently joined forces with Cheil Worldwide.

The common wisdom in marketing today is that 'the consumer is in control.' We believe that is a cop-out for marketers still trapped in a TV-centric view of the world, daunted by the very real challenges of bringing ideas into the naturally occurring ongoing conversations between people and brands. This is not to say that your customers lack power. They ignore you now, as they could have ignored you 50 or 100 years ago, if you bore them or are irrelevant to their wants and needs. They are as apt to speak highly of you now through social media as they could speak highly of you then, in what we called word-of-mouth, if you offer more value than you seek in return. And they will turn on you now, as they would turn on you then, if you insult their intelligence or take their values for granted.

But as a marketer you have never had more opportunity to control the conversation between people and your brand. The same tools that allow people to respond faster and to a much broader audience give you the power to listen, amplify your own efforts and become more relevant and engaging. If that's true, why do so many major marketers remain trapped in a TV-centric approach to marketing? Well, there's a price to pay for this power. The process of building brands has become much more interactive, labour intensive and transparent. There is a dangerously simple reason many cling to old habits: because they still can.

What we call TV is changing quickly, and those changes will speed the adoption of cross-channel marketing (more on that later), but for many marketers traditional TV advertising remains the most cost-effective way to deliver an engaging message to people. The scale, the efficiency and the platform for short-form storytelling simply can't be beat. Is there waste in TV advertising? Absolutely. John Wanamaker's lament is probably understated. Our analyses show that only 5–10 per cent of the audience for any TV show represent high value prospects for most brands in most categories. But the cost to reach that that 5–10 per cent still beats other media, none of which are as scalable and schedulable as TV. And there's another factor that's often overlooked: the other 90–95 per cent of the viewers, even if they don't buy the brand, see the advertising and that increases the sense among your best prospects that the advertised brand is a safe choice. Brands gain stature simply by being visible.

But even in a world where TV remains so powerful, any marketer not experimenting with new models of customer engagement is risking the future health of the brand. And we believe that the reason so many marketers find it hard to escape TV-centricity is that they view it as a media issue, when it is really a design and leadership challenge.

The process of developing TV advertising is a very linear approach requiring little collaboration. The pre-testing of TV advertising, while seriously flawed, provides decades-long benchmarked data that marketers use to justify production and media support, trigger bonuses and deflect unwanted attention from senior management and board members.

A cross-channel, conversationally integrated approach requires a very different ecosystem. It is more complex, growing vastly more difficult to manage with each new touch-point. It involves aligning the efforts of a wide range of experts, often from a wider range of organizations. It values collaboration over individual output and hand-offs. It lacks a widely accepted pre-production assessment system, if for no other reason than that no one has yet figured out how to deliver a complex, active brand experience to a consumer, especially one dependent upon social media, until it actually happens. It is hard work.

We know because we made the commitment to this approach nearly a decade ago. We still have some of the bruises. But we've also reaped the benefits. McKinney was recently named 'the most effective independent advertising agency in the world' by Effie Worldwide, sponsor of the Effie Awards for marketing communications effectiveness. And we believe it is because we are able to move quite fluidly online, offline and wherever an idea is best expressed and discussed.

Due to our experience, we have studied the successes and struggles on both the client and agency sides of our business. We've identified what we believe to be the core design issues that must be addressed to change to an idea-centric, conversationally integrated ecosystem.

Integration requires a different view of how people and brands do – and will – interact

The TV-centric view of the world is a marketer-out, one-way communication design for consistency of intended message and takeaway. Because it literally has a beginning (strategy), middle (creative development) and end (broadcast), it is a very linear process requiring limited collaboration.

The conversational model of integration is about seeding and nurturing ideas. It requires the deployment and utilization of a variety of paid, earned, owned and shared media tools to spark, listen and respond to the conversation about your brand.

Marketers who are successful with this approach assume that the fruit of their extra effort – not always measurable – comes from giving meaning to their brands and adding more value to the conversation than they seek in return. Their goal is to develop a relationship between people and their brands that is very similar to any strong human relationship. They are excellent listeners because they assume, correctly, that engaged consumers can become loyal ambassadors – and that every brand critic undoes the good work of many ambassadors.

They also understand a key distinction that many traditional marketers miss: every point of contact with the brand, planned or not, managed or not, says something about the brand. This allows them to avoid the trap of stuffing every relevant piece of information into every contact, instead allowing each tool to do the job is was intended to do.

In this model, a web-centric idea may still rely on television support. But here the role of the TV is to drive awareness and interest in the web event. For categories where there is active evaluation of the tangible properties of the brand (automotive, for example), there are a range of digital tools that help people learn what they need to learn, at the pace they want to learn it. Here, TV's role may be no more complex than to get you to like the brand enough to want to learn more about it.

Succeeding at this game is not in any way linear. It requires a level of collaboration that challenges one to question whether it is worth the work. It requires not just broadcasting, but responding and sometimes changing course. If the TV-centric approach is a hammer, conversational integration is a general contractor.

Integration requires a new culture

When we were trying to decide whether to establish a separate digital practice or take the far bolder and more challenging step of integrating digital into our existing operations, we looked for a relevant example to guide us. We all believed that the web would fundamentally change the world of advertising – this was a tectonic shift, not a little tremor. We also believed that that change would not occur until broadband internet service became pervasive: dial-up presented little opportunity for creative expression.

The only other change in our industry of equal magnitude was the development of commercial television. While the data was hard to find, when we overlaid the growth of household penetration of televisions with the household penetration of broadband, we were shocked to see almost identical adoption curves.

That led to an obvious question: what separated the agencies that rode this explosion in TV viewership to prominence, and to nearly half a century

FIGURE 3.1 TV and internet penetration

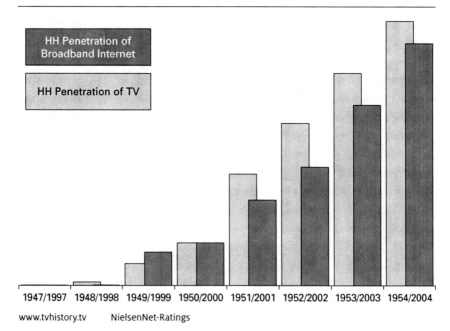

1947/1997   1948/1998   1949/1999   1950/2000   1951/2001   1952/2002   1953/2003   1954/2004

www.tvhistory.tv   NielsenNet-Ratings

of global industry dominance, from those that were left behind to remain niche agency brands? They were agencies that realized that TV would change everything. They forced their print and radio experts to learn this new technology, instead of setting up a separate 'TV unit'.

Whereas TV quickly came to dominate all other forms of media, we believed that the web would complement existing media and offer marketers a far richer, if also far more complex, palette with which to connect people and brands. Those were more reasons for us to make everyone in our agency digitally savvy.

The way we did it drew upon learning from the M&A world. According to a KPMG study, '83 per cent of all mergers and acquisitions (M&As) failed to produce any benefit for the shareholders and over half actually destroyed value'. Interviews with over 100 senior executive involved in these 700 deals over a two-year period revealed that the overwhelming cause for failure 'is the people and the cultural differences' (Gitelson, Bing and Laroche, 2001).

One of the biggest reasons is that the acquired entity conforms to the ways of the acquirer and loses the value that made it attractive in the first place. When two cultures collide, the dominant culture wins.

We recognized the huge cultural divide we had to close. 'Traditional' advertising people believed that digital people were engineering geeks who didn't understand brands. Digital people looked upon the traditionalists as afraid of technology, lacking in curiosity and too lazy to learn new skills. And both were right.

So it was not enough for us to mix up the online and offline people. We had to eliminate that distinction and create a new culture of 'conversationalists', lateral thinkers able to start and carry the conversation between people and brands wherever it needed to go.

Integration requires different physical space and organization

If you have ever been in a Montessori classroom, you know that the structure of the physical space allows a kind of interaction among the students as well as between teacher and students that you simply cannot achieve in a traditional classroom. The Montessori approach to teaching celebrates individual development, discovery and learning by tactile experience, with little direct instruction. For a traditional teacher, a Montessori classroom must look chaotic. And certainly, a Montessori teacher would find it very difficult to succeed in a traditional space dominated by rows and rows of school desks all pointing to the central authority at the front of the class.

Marketing organizations built around a TV-centric view of marketing have their own structural constraints, particularly on the agency side of the business. They are structured for hand-offs, with different departments on different floors (if not in different buildings).

One of the most classic and tragic examples of the difference between siloed organizations and truly integrated operations is what has happened to Sony and Apple over the past decade. We had the privilege of helping Sony launch their last successful line of TVs, the Sony Bravia.

Our relationship began with a letter in the spring of 2005. At that time, the Sony brand was still revered, but a resurgent Apple had achieved nearly the same market value ($35 billion to Sony's $38 billion) despite sales barely a tenth the size ($8 billion to Sony's $71 billion – see Table 3.1).

TABLE 3.1 Sony and Apple sales, 2005

$ Billions	2005	
	Sony	Apple
Revenue	71	8
Market cap	38	35

The letter pointed out the need for Sony, famously an engineering culture, to break down internal silos to become a more consumer-centric marketer. We discovered as we worked with the organization that it was even more complex than we had thought. There were silos within silos. We weren't surprised to see the movie, music, gaming and consumer electronics businesses operated as entirely separate groups, with no shared values or reason for being. But we were shocked to see that the engineers in charge of the venerable Walkman personal audio devices operated independently from – and it appeared at odds with – the engineers in charge of developing the music system that would deliver songs to those devices.

Meanwhile, Steve Jobs had created a fluidly integrated team at Apple. The software and the hardware people collaborated to very elegantly, as

Apple ads with equal elegance promised, 'Put a thousand songs in your pocket.'

Sony had become a series of warring silos, internally focused and hopelessly grid-locked. Apple was a company on a mission to upend the status quo, consistently launching beautifully designed products that were delightfully easy to use.

The result? Today Apple is the most valuable company in the world, with revenue nearly 20 times what it was when we first wrote Sony. And Sony's market value has dropped by two-thirds on sales that have failed to keep pace with inflation (Table 3.2).

TABLE 3.2 Sony and Apple, changes 2005–2012

$ Billions	2005		2012	
	Sony	Apple	Sony	Apple
Revenue	71	8	82	149
Market cap	38	35	12	631

It's worth noting that one of Steve Jobs' final acts was to gain approval for construction of a Norman Foster-designed headquarters building in Cupertino, California. A huge, self-contained perfect circle, it promises to be the physical manifestation of Jobs' belief in seamless integration.

Our own approach to space design and organization, while on a far smaller scale, has been equally dramatic. In 2002, McKinney's new leadership team committed to an industry-redefining approach to integration. One of the first moves, noted earlier, was to break down the barriers between traditional and digital talent, creating 'conversationalists'.

At the time, the agency was spread over five floors of a building with small floor plates, a predominance of larger outer offices and a central elevator core. It was difficult to move from floor to floor and nearly as inconvenient to circle around the elevators. Our 43,000 square foot space allowed us room for no more than 147 people, with a small lobby, one common area and two conference rooms. Our people told us they understood the need for collaboration. But like a traditional classroom for a Montessori school, our space got in the way.

We set out to find and design the most collaborative space in our industry, believing that nothing would be as important in helping us become an integration leader. The first decision we made was to find a building with large floor plates, believing that it's far easier for people to move horizontally than vertically.

We found that space in an old factory complex, The American Tobacco Campus in Durham, North Carolina. We spent the next year researching and designing the space with Duda/Paine Architects and their design partner Alliance Architecture, local firms operating, as we do, on a global stage. We visited the Clive Wilkonson-designed TBWA\Chiat\Day space in Playa Vista, California, then widely known as the most cutting edge of agency designs.

Barely a step or two into the space, our jaws dropped. Our guide rather dismissively acknowledged the beauty of what we were seeing, while insisting that it did nothing to make Chiat the force that they were in our industry. She graciously showed us what she considered the most important design element in the space: install mail slots and stop delivering the mail so people are forced to move through the space, increasing the odds of casual encounters that lead to unexpected ideas.

The more we worked on the problem, the more we understood that a Bauhaus approach (form serving function) was the right way to think about the problem. Just because something looked cool didn't mean it would create a better work environment. We began seeing ideas in unexpected places: sitting with my kindergarten son on the carpeted, terraced rest area at his new school area led to a huge semi-circle of carpeted bleachers for casual encounters and town hall meetings.

We studied organizational behaviour research. Along the way we discovered the article 'Designs for Working' (Gladwell, 2000). This paragraph caught our attention:

> The office used to be imagined as a place where employees punch clocks and bosses roam the halls like school principals, looking for miscreants. But when employees sit chained to their desks, quietly and industriously going about their business, an office is not functioning as it should. That's because innovation – the heart of the knowledge economy – is fundamentally social. Ideas arise as much out of casual conversations as they do out of formal meetings. More precisely, as one study after another has demonstrated, the best ideas in any workplace arise out of casual contacts among different groups within the same company... The catch is that getting people in an office to bump into people from another department is not as easy as it looks. In the sixties and seventies, a researcher at MIT named Thomas Allen conducted a decade-long study of the way in which engineers communicated in research-and-development

laboratories. Allen found that the likelihood that any two people will communicate drops off dramatically as the distances between their desks increases: we are four times as likely to communicate with someone who sits six feet away from us as we are with someone who sits 60 feet away. People seated more than 75 feet apart hardly talk at all.

We had five partners at the time. We arranged the space so that we were all within 60 feet of each other, and everyone else so that they were within 60 feet of one of us. We went from 60 per cent closed offices to over 60 per cent open seating. The offices we retained were a quarter the size of those in our existing space, and in many cases now house teams rather than individuals. We put coffee bars at critical intersections in the space to stop people and give them a reason to meet. It means we now serve 130,000 cups of coffee each year, but even that probably adds to the interaction. In our seating assignments, we mixed up people by discipline and across accounts.

The importance of making it easy for people to bump into each other was reinforced recently in a conversation with a managing director at Google. He noted that Google strive for twice the density of people per square foot of their competitors because they, too, have found that more forced interaction drives far higher levels of collaboration, simply because putting people that close together means everyone learns what everyone else is working on.

We did a hundred other small things, none of which would by itself have made any difference. But they all added up to a radically different working environment that changed the agency the very morning we moved into the new space (Table 3.3).

TABLE 3.3 Transformation of working environment

Old space	New space
43,000 square feet	43,000 square feet
147 person capacity	217 person capacity (+47%)
2 conference rooms and a common area	12 conference rooms, two coffee bars, bleachers and a presentation theatre
A small lobby	A soaring entrance atrium

Smart design does not have to cost more. And we know it made a difference. Within two years, *Advertising Age* named McKinney one of the top agencies in the country, saying our structure and design made us 'uniquely suited to survive – and thrive – in a digital world'.

Based on our experience, it should come as no surprise that in an organization where digital reports to one team, TV reports to another and they are on different floors or in different buildings, integration is difficult at best.

Integration requires new tools and skills

TV-centric thinking persists because it is how people have built brands for over half a century. It persists because it makes sense: If most of your money has gone into creating and supporting a TV idea, there should be some synergy by giving the work in other media the same look and feel as the TV. And it persists because it's easy. If you always start with TV, you pretty much already know where you're going to go.

We realized that to break this cycle and get to idea-based, 'media neutral' integration, the process had to start from a different place. So we became the third agency to pioneer what is now known as connection planning.

Instead of starting with the medium (TV), we now started with the consumer. Through attitudinal segmentation, we sought quantitative insight into what attitudes drove brand choice in the category, and which people had the attitudes most likely to result in the selection of our brand.

Understanding those attitudes gave us a new way to create brand and advertising ideas. Working with online travel provider Travelocity, we discovered that our most promising prospects were far less interested in saving money than in making sure they bought a great trip. So we let the competition stay in the 'cheap tickets' business, and put Travelocity in the 'great travel experiences business', putting a new face on the brand with the now-iconic 'Roaming Gnome' and his promise that with Travelocity, you'll never roam alone.

Knowing that our target cared more about great travel than about cheap tickets also led to our understanding that they recognized six phases to each trip: initiating and dreaming, shopping, buying, getting there, the actual trip and returning. We realized that three of the six phases represented far higher positive emotions than the more transactional parts of the trip in which our competitors were mired. And we were able to model media habits and category attitudes for each phase. From this, we built an experience map showing where and how the Gnome would show up throughout the travel experience.

FIGURE 3.2 Experience map for Gnome

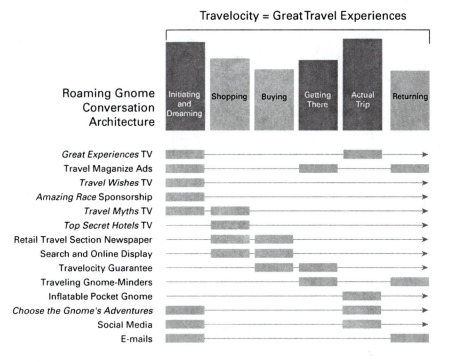

The resulting programme not only reflected an idea built out of media-neutral thinking, but a connection plan built out of cross-channel thinking.

As our programmes have become more complex, and as social media have become central to our marketing efforts, we have evolved the connection plan to what we call the conversation ecosystem. The ecosystem reflects not only the roles for each medium, but how each point of contact interacts with the others to create the overall conversation.

Finally, our media people sit with our creative people and strategists. If the medium is the message, then this interaction promotes the role of media in shaping our messaging.

FIGURE 3.3 Example of an ecosystem

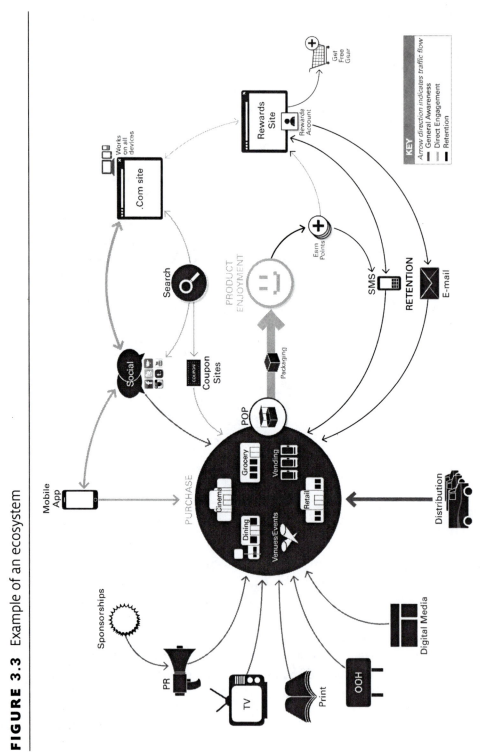

Integration survives through innovation

Many decades ago advertising visionary Leo Burnett said, 'If you think change is painful, it's nothing compared to the pain of standing still or falling behind.' But many organizations endure that pain constantly because they are afraid to give up what has made them successful in the past even in the face of evidence it's no longer working. And it should require none of the reams of data available to say that every day the rate of change becomes faster and the direction harder to predict. Integration is a moving target, and companies who want to succeed at it need to stay nimble.

We consider reinvention a core priority. And we know that the day-to-day press of regular work with our clients tends to reinforce the status quo. So we try to remain open to new ideas, wherever they come from. Two years ago, one of our copywriters asked us to implement Google's '20 per cent time', successor to a similar programme long celebrated at 3M, where engineers get time off to pursue personal projects that might someday result in important new sources of business.

At first, we all though the idea was nuts. Since we don't have official work hours, we would be giving away 20 per cent of nothing. From our perspective, we were promoting innovation with everything we do. But as we dug into the issue further we realized we had a psychological to barrier to overcome. Our people felt so responsible to the needs of our clients that they could not justify taking 'time off' to experiment

So we decided to give it a try. We picked 10 per cent over 20 per cent and launched the McKinney 10 per cent, thinking it might be easier for people to get over the responsibility barrier. In less than a year, it has resulted in two new forms of revenue. As for Google and 3M, it has helped us attract and retain great people. And it's also helped us learn more about the nimbleness of small teams and fluid interactions that we have brought back to our everyday ways of doing business.

Integration requires leadership

I recently had the chance to ask Lucas Watson, the former head of digital at P&G who now heads sales for You Tube, how Procter has managed to get digital so much faster than other large marketers. In his former role, he was at the centre of P&G's dramatic shift in online spending from 2 per cent to 17 per cent of total annual media spend in just two years. He offered a refreshingly simple answer. Since there was no proven rule of thumb for how much money a company should invest online, they developed a simple, measurable goal with obvious face validity: 17 per cent of their consumers' media usage was online, so the goal would be to spend 17 per cent of the budget online. And this goal was sent down from the top by CEO AG Lafley, complete with components baked into compensation.

The fastest way to make anything radical happen in an organization is to lead from the top with clear, measurable goals. It's the only way to make integration happen.

Final thoughts

The move from TV-centricity to cross-channel thinking will happen with or without you. But most important is paying attention to factors that will remain important and even grow in importance over time.

New media proponents, from the direct marketers forward, always seem to feel they need to proclaim the death of all forms of media that preceded them. The fact is that new media have consistently been additive, with the limited exceptions of local newspaper and radio, whose economic model is predicated on the local classified advertising that is much better delivered online.

The right conversation is not what new media will replace, but how the entire ecosystem of media will evolve and what skills must be developed to stay current. Offline TV viewership continues to grow, but it has changed: destination TV is viewed on demand with lots of ad skipping, while sports tend to be viewed live. Programming that targets anyone under the age of 30 is likely to be consumed in a shared media environment, reaching an audience that is simultaneously texting or surfing. The rapid growth of online video presents new ways for people to view programming originally produced for offline viewing, when and where they want to watch it. It has also allowed for the rapid and relatively inexpensive deployment of videos produced for online consumption through owned, earned and shared media.

The skills needed to produce great television advertising (the ability to tell a great story in a compressed timeframe, and the ability to fully utilize sight, sound and motion) are growing in importance as TV evolves and new forms of online video emerge.

Marketers need to put far more emphasis on engagement, emotional connection and, yes, entertainment. They need to understand the role of low-attention processing and how that might affect their copy-testing methodologies (in fact the simple nomenclature 'copy-testing' should be an indication of how far testing services are removed from the reality of how advertising works).

Finally, there is opportunity to think of building brands the way we think of interacting with people. When you are introduced to someone, you know from your first impression if you want to get to know her better (do I like this brand?). Then you might find yourself interested in what she does for a living (does this brand offer what I am looking for?). As you get to know her better, you might wonder about her hobbies (does this brand care about the things that I care about?). You might introduce her to your friends (is this brand doing something worth sharing?). You might be surprised to see her in an unexpected new context (does this brand live in the same world that I live in?). You might see an article about something she has accomplished (does this brand have stature that might make me consider it over another, even if both offer the same basic product?).

These are all considerations about how to use the right media to reach the right people with the right impressions at the right times. And it may very well be that the only thing your TV efforts need to do is entertain your target audience and make them want to get to know you better. Few Super Bowl advertisers admit this publicly, but that is exactly what they are doing when they make that incredible financial commitment – and it is what those who denounce the Super Bowl (or use the investment badly) fail to understand. Our own research, for example, shows a direct correlation between the *USA Today* consumer rankings of Super Bowl car advertising and sustained social media conversation about each brand.

Perhaps if you let this TV focus on this job, you'll quickly see why you need to master the rest of the conversation.

Sources

Gitelson, G, Bing, J and Laroche, L (2001) The impact of culture on mergers and acquisitions, CMA Management, March; online at ITAP International, www.itapintl.com

Gladwell, M (2000) Designs for working, *The New Yorker*, 11 December, page 60

04 TV is dead, long live TV

ROB SMITH

Rob Smith is the Strategy Director at Blueleaf (web, mobile, apps). Rob has been working with great clients like Laura Ashley and Red Bull and adores cars, motorsport, cheese, steak and squash.

The television has been available since the 1920s, and a powerful force in consumer media since the 1950s. After more than half a century of dominating people's media consumption, the TV is undergoing its first major transformation since its dominance started. Many would go as far to say that TV, in its traditional form, is dead.

This transformation had its germination many years ago with the advent of the internet but it wasn't until nearly a decade later that the transformation gathered huge pace and leaves us where we are today.

Traditional TV

In many homes, the TV is traditionally a broadcast viewing model with a central TV in the main living area. You, as the viewer, need to be present at the allotted time for your show. Video recorders and multiple TVs changed that slightly with the ability to set programmes to be recorded for later viewing. They didn't fundamentally change the viewing model though, especially for more popular shows.

Advertising paid for a lot of the business model and adverts were intersected between the show in breaks, allowing for the push of messages to people during their favourite shows. Other services also innovated forwards slightly like Sky, Cable TV and extra channels besides the standard ones such as the BBC (in the UK at least).

The main items of note about the old viewing model that fuel this discussion are:

- Broadcast: generally the viewer needed to be there for the show being broadcast. Secondly though, this is the way people expected to consume TV – at set points in their day and often as a communal activity.

- Advertising: due to the broadcast nature of the medium, advertising was a big way to reach consumers due to its interruptive nature between parts of the show. It was also very effective.

- Technology: TVs were often heavy, tube-based devices for many years, and even until the last 5–10 years were generally one of the most significant technology purchases for a home. They were a centre point of a living space and fights for the TV would be frequent.

Enough of the old viewing model – we all know it well and why you're really reading is to find what's changed and how you can capitalize on this shift.

The changing world

From around 2007, fundamental shifts started to occur in the TV viewing model and consumption habits of the public. The main points to note here are:

- Lifestyles: people's lifestyles have become more 'on demand', tailored, busy and adapted. Smartphones, e-mail, technology proliferation – all this contributed to a faster pace and the transformation of many ways of life, from family interaction to work habits.

- Screens: screen technology has come on leaps and bounds in the past decade. Smaller screens, more detailed screens, better-quality screens, flatter screens, cheaper screens. All have helped revolutionize the role of the screen (and therefore TV) in a variety of circumstances.

- Bandwidth: as the internet has become more widespread and infrastructure more powerful, the capability of delivering rich media and high-quality experiences online has increased exponentially.

- Early adoption: with the changes in screen technology, the age at which we access rich content and experiences without needing the 'big TV' is much younger than ever before.

Combining all of these things together leads us into a very disruptive and exciting time for marketers and the general public as a whole, but it's also the death of TV as we know it.

What TV really means now

So how do people consume the content that we traditionally see as being 'TV'? What are people's viewing habits? Is there any such thing as TV anymore? Let's explore the main points of how TV has evolved:

- No 'TV': increasingly there is no real concept of a TV. The content that used to be on TV now comes from a variety of sources; the devices that produce it are many, and I have even seen young children go up to a TV and call it 'the big computer'.

- Content distribution: with the advent of tablet devices and smartphones, coupled with high-speed internet, TV content can be consumed in many places and on many devices. The content is still the same, but the 'TV' is very different.

- On demand is default: rather than broadcast being the main way of TV content is consumed, increasingly people consume content on demand – services like iPlayer from the BBC and Sky Anytime+ in the UK are powerful systems from TV companies. Add in disruptive players like Netflix and LoveFilm, and you have a plethora of disruptive services changing the ability of people to consume content.

- People want flexibility: people's lifestyles dictate that they want to consume content when they want to, on the device they want in the room they want. Devices allow content to be viewed on tablet or phone, TV or console, small or big screen. On the bus, waiting in a coffee shop or at home.

- Younger audiences: due to phones having easy access to content and no fighting for the TV, younger audiences can be much more readily accessed than previously.

- Advertising is harder: interruptive advertising is much less effective due to the ability to skip through the adverts and people tend to be less tolerant of advertising than previously.

- Innovation is rife: product placement and contextual advertising are getting smarter, experiences are getting more interactive and there's a host of additional services to 'enhance' TV.

This is an incredibly exciting time for marketers and content producers. The ability to create experiences, innovate and engage has never been so accessible.

What does this mean for marketers?

With so much change to understand and so many ways to potentially access audiences, from digital marketing to search engines and beyond, what role does TV play in this brave new world?

Second screen

Second screen is the most fundamental thing to understand about the new role of TV and device interaction. Often, a second screen will be used while also using the TV screen – like an iPad, an iPhone or a smartphone. It is crucial to understand that there is a whole second set of screen space that people can use to enhance the experience of the TV content on the primary screen. I'll run through a few ways now that this is already being exploited, to show how you can capitalize on this opportunity.

Interactive experiences

One use of second screen is to create interactive experiences to make TV content even more engaging. Examples of this are where you may use an online mechanism to vote or give opinions that then can influence the TV show in real time.

This is the way that TV producers can still bring a lot of people together to watch a show and keep them away from their standard 'on demand' lifestyle. This can only be accomplished by making the show add even more value and entertainment than previously.

Enhancement services

This is the most popular and growing area of second screen; it covers apps and information services that augment and enhance the users' experience while they are enjoying the TV content they are seeing.

Examples of these apps range from simple ones such as IMDb (allowing look-ups on films, TV, actors and so on) to more advanced ones like zeebox, which allows you to see the popularity of the show you're currently watching as well as a live feed of people's feedback across social networks.

Others are very show-specific such as the Sky Sports F1 app that allows a viewer to have in-car camera views and audio as well as a driver tracker – all to augment the standard F1 coverage on the 'normal' TV.

These kind of enhancement services make TV a much richer experience, where people can discover and find out much more than by just watching the show. They can take segways and explore the area and entertain themselves more than ever before.

The ecosystem is key

Way before these focused second-screen apps appeared, there were (and still are) two killer second-screen apps that have ruled additional value on TV – Twitter and, to a lesser extent, Facebook.

For a long time, people have been giving live commentary and discussion on Twitter during sporting events, premieres and popular TV shows. This kind of interaction is like gold dust to marketers as it cuts to people's opinions in real time and allows for great opportunities to work with these mechanisms at the right time.

The point here is that for too long marketers have been very channel blind. TV is TV, newspaper ads are just that, and Google Adwords is digital marketing only. The key though is linking these together as a complete ecosystem.

During a show where your product may be placed, you should be on Twitter monitoring and interacting; your Adwords should be powered up to gather significant traffic from unusual terms ('car in fringe' for example); and your offline marketing could be increased the following day reminding viewers of what they saw. Never before has it been so possible to wrap TV in such a rich and engaging set of experiences that maximize the use of the interactive ecosystem, instead of seeing it as separate activities.

Content is still king

Having made all of these points about enhancement and richer experiences, there is no substitute for the right content to start with. People won't watch boring shows, much less interact with them or dive deeper into enhancements. You still need those killer pieces of content – documentaries, dramas, sports: they all draw in the audience to use the ecosystem, and are the root of all interaction.

Five golden rules for marketers and the new 'TV'

Remind yourself of these golden rules to make TV work for you.

You don't need to be big to influence

With the guerrilla use of e-mail marketing, Google Adwords and social media, marketers can take much better advantage of TV than ever before. Influencing the conversation and aligning your offer and brand with killer content doesn't need to be in the form of big TV advertising. It can be as simple as a well-placed PPC advert or re-tweeted offer timed just right.

There are more opportunities than ever before

Big and small, opportunities are everywhere to interact with TV. From apps that allow product placement to be flagged and searched (what was that mirror in the hotel in the latest Bond movie?), to getting people to dictate the actual direction of a TV show – there is a huge number of opportunities to use TV as a key part of your ecosystem.

People still love TV

They really do. There's a reason why people have been glued to the tube for well over five decades – it's entertaining. The addition of these enhancements will only further cement this relationship. The only difference now is that TV is the content, not the device.

Interaction environment is not reliable

People could be on a bus or a plane, moving or stationary, viewing on a big or small screen, doing something else or not. The multiple ways that people can consume content is huge and should not be underestimated.

Everything is changing

The final golden rule is that everything is changing. New opportunities are emerging, others fading away. The one thing to take away from this is that marketers need to be constantly testing and tweaking, and doing so within an ecosystem, not a channel. The understanding of how all the pieces fit together has never been more crucial.

05 Multichannel ecosystem toolbox

KYLE LACY

Kyle Lacy is a direct response and digital marketing professional with extensive experience in utilizing social media, e-mail and mobile marketing for business. Kyle is a senior manager of content marketing & research for ExactTarget, a leading global provider of interactive marketing solutions, and has authored three acclaimed books, *Twitter Marketing for Dummies*, *Social CRM for Dummies* and *Branding Yourself*.

There are many of us in the marketing world that are just getting started in fully implementing interactive marketing. This means we are going beyond the strategy and discussions surrounding tools like e-mail, social and mobile. It means we are implementing real strategy with measurable results. Welcome to the shift.

If you're just getting started with interactive marketing and want to learn how you can use it to strengthen customer relationships and boost ROI, this guide will help you ensure your systems are ready for interactive marketing, and give you tips on how to get started so that you can be freed from the burden of tedious tasks and can focus your attention on strategy and optimization. Sound familiar? Keep reading.

To build a truly effective interactive marketing programme, it's essential that you integrate your e-mail, mobile, social, CRM and web analytics systems so you can gain a holistic view of your marketing activities. Then you can use interactive marketing to automate traditionally manual processes such as customer segmentation, customer data integration and campaign management for increased efficiencies and better results.

Believe it or not, you should be pretty excited about the road ahead. Why? Because by automating your e-mail, mobile, social, CRM and web analytics systems, you can create tremendous growth opportunities for your interactive marketing programme – without additional costs or resources.

As with any well-executed project, it's best to measure twice and cut once. For those new to interactive marketing, that means taking an honest look at the way you currently use your e-mail, mobile, social, CRM and web analytics systems before trying to jump ahead to the most complex level of interactive marketing.

If you're just starting out, your current approach to interactive marketing probably looks a bit like what is described below.

E-mail marketing

Some of you may be entirely new to e-mail marketing. But most beginners already have access to an e-mail marketing solution and have sent some form of user-initiated (ie not automated) messages to opt-in subscribers.

Preferring to keep costs low and ease-of-use high, you might have purchased entry-level e-mail marketing solutions. These solutions typically have a lower price tag, basic functionality and features, and WYSIWYG e-mail editors. More adventurous beginners may have also tried some simple audience segmentation. But chances are they haven't leveraged more advanced interactive marketing tools like automated interaction management to aggregate data, trigger messages and manage messages across all digital communication channels automatically.

Mobile marketing

You might not have ventured into the world of mobile marketing yet, typically because resources are limited and you may not have the funds to invest in a mobile marketing provider or a more robust marketing platform like ExactTarget's Interactive Marketing Hub that can manage all forms of interactive messaging. Coupled with the 'unknowns' that come with relying on SMS as a marketing channel, you may be a bit weary of trying something new, especially without adequate resources to support your efforts.

Social marketing

You certainly can't ignore the importance of having a presence on social media networks. However, your presence is typically limited to only a few select social networks (eg a single Facebook page or Twitter account). And due to resource constraints across the organization, you spend much of your time managing your social network presence yourself. Automating social media efforts is something you may not have yet considered.

CRM

If you're new to interactive marketing, you may already capture some customer and prospect data in a central, home-grown database or commercial CRM system like Microsoft Dynamics CRM or Salesforce CRM. You may need to work with other teams like IT or sales to access your CRM data, but sales pipeline, customer service and existing client data are often accessible if you're willing to do a little digging.

However, beginners like you tend not to have tried using CRM data to power more relevant, timely e-mail communications automatically. At most, you use your CRM system to pull lists of subscriber e-mail addresses for sends. Messages tend to be manual and do not feed performance metrics back into individual subscriber records in your CRM systems.

Web analytics

Inexpensive (or free!) web analytics tools like Google Analytics or Click-Tracks are frequently used by those at the beginning stages of interactive marketing. Others may use more robust solutions from providers like Adobe or Coremetrics. Regardless, you may tend to gravitate towards the most basic web analytics solution offered, thus avoiding the higher costs and sometimes overwhelming complexity associated with more advanced products.

You commonly use web analytics solutions to monitor website traffic metrics and behaviour. Out-of-the-box reports provide a baseline look at overall metrics like website visits, page views, popular pages and traffic sources. You focus on aggregate site performance and popularity as you ask, 'What happened on my site, why, and when?'

Due to time, resource or monetary constraints, often little to no interactive marketing exists for novices. Some may use basic web analytics reporting for specific e-mail marketing campaigns, but aren't tracking their e-mail campaigns and web analytics performance holistically and then using this data to take action.

If these scenarios sound familiar, take heart. We understand how difficult it can be to get started with automating your interactive marketing programmes. Here are just a few of the challenges that you – and a ton of other beginning marketers – probably face daily:

- Time constraints: you're swamped, right? From last-minute projects to your chatty cube-neighbour, the incessant demands of your day job make it hard to find a moment to yourself. Much less to carve out time to learn how to automate your existing systems.

- Limited human resources: dedicated data analysts and technical resources are rare at this level. In fact, you're probably juggling the creation and deployment of your messages, along with whatever data you use to power and track them.

- Tight budgets: investing.in the proper e-mail, mobile, social, CRM and web analytics technology takes money. Sadly, your budget's tighter than ever, and you have to constantly find ways to do more with less.

- Low technical enterprise: if you had ample time and money to automate your systems, would you technically be able to? Chances are, you're trying to play catch-up and figure out how all the new online marketing channels impact your business. Plus limited technical expertise often makes you wary of attempting more advanced interactive marketing.

- Incomplete information: making marketing decisions based on incomplete information is dangerous. Not only do you risk wasting valuable time and money, but you have no way to measure why things go wrong. When e-mail, mobile, social, CRM and web analytics systems aren't fully integrated, you only see part of the puzzle. Without a 360° view of subscriber engagement, you're left throwing darts in the dark.

Here are a few ideas to help you get ready for interactive marketing:

Free up valuable time by *streamlining your e-mail marketing processes*. Attend online training classes to learn how to use your e-mail marketing solution's automation tools. Or seek out web-based tutorial training options to learn at your own pace.

Automate your welcome e-mail. As a critical component of any interactive marketing strategy, your welcome e-mail is the one message your subscribers anticipate the most and is consistently the e-mail that is most-opened. Since your welcome e-mail is a message you will send again and again as you gain new subscribers, it's a perfect opportunity for you to take a test swim in the interactive marketing waters. Check with your e-mail marketing provider to see if they offer an easy way to automate the sending of your welcome e-mail without the help of a development resource.

Chances are, they do!

Try some simple e-mail personalization techniques like using substitution strings for pre-set subscriber attributes. Or go a step farther by upgrading to a more advanced edition of your e-mail marketing solution, and start personalizing your messages with subscriber-specific content and offers using tools like dynamic content and dynamic subject line.

Monitor data cleanliness. Your interactive marketing processes are only as good as the data powering them. Work with internal key players to streamline CRM system access and processes so your data stays clean.

Think about what subscriber data you need for your interactive marketing programme. Always wanted to start a birthday club? Make sure you're gathering the data you need to make it happen. Or if you'd eventually like to try your hand at automating a mobile campaign, make sure you've got subscriber permission to do so and their mobile numbers. A well-thought-out communication plan will help organize your goals and data needs.

If you haven't already, *research more robust CRM applications* like Microsoft Dynamics CRM or Salesforce CRM. See if your e-mail provider offers productized automations with leading CRM systems that allow you to get up and running quickly and smoothly.

Similarly, determine if your current web analytics provider can provide the metrics you've deemed necessary to evaluate performance. If not, it's time to research leading web analytics providers like Adobe or Coremetrics.

Create a Twitter account – if you haven't done so already. Tools like ExactTarget SocialEngage™ make it even easier for you to maintain and – more importantly – automate certain aspects of your Twitter presence. For example, ExactTarget SocialEngage lets you schedule tweets, so you can keep your presence strong even if you're out of the office for a few days.

Planning a big company announcement? Schedule your tweet ahead of time and cross that off your to-do list for the big day. But remember: while scheduled tweets are helpful for specific situations, don't let that be the only way you communicate on Twitter.

Set up a basic integration between your web analytics system and your e-mail marketing provider so you can consolidate metrics into a single system. For example, your e-mail provider may offer a tool like ExactTarget's Web Analytics Connector that lets you integrate quickly and seamlessly with virtually any web analytics package. If you're already using Adobe or Coremetrics, a productized integration can make this process even easier.

If you're only gathering aggregate data, *start laying the foundation for behavioural analysis on a segment level.* Eventually, you'll need this more granular data to predict behaviour and response to your interactive marketing campaigns. Look for pre-defined or customizable visitor segmentation reports and begin analysing how different segments of your audience react to different offers or areas of your website.

Create a set of unique reports and metrics for each of your interactive marketing initiatives. More specific reporting will let you compare the performance of campaigns across different mediums like e-mail, website, paid search, organic search and more.

Intermediate marketers who charge ahead to the expert level can anticipate high returns as their once-manual programmes are automatically created, delivered and tracked through multiple systems. So work through your goals one by one – always making sure your data processes are streamlined and reliable so there are no false starts when you turn on your new one-to-one interactive marketing machine for the first time.

06 Conversational customer journey planning

FELIX VELARDE

Felix Velarde started one of the first digital agencies, Hyperinteractive, in 1994, later founding pioneering agency Head New Media – where he co-created one of the world's most influential websites, Head-Space. Velarde is an educator and writer, and is CEO of Underwired, a leading customer engagement agency (**www.underwired.com**).

U ntil now, marketing has been about brands. In fact, how brands see themselves. Marketing is about how this view of one's brand can be expressed, sometimes loftily and without care for what goes through the consumer's mind – Apple is a good example here – and sometimes so thoroughly researched that customer insight defines product design and brand definition outright. We talk about brand architecture, brand synchronicity, brand presence, acceptance, preference and evolution. I believe the era of brand marketing, born in print, accelerated through television and understood through research, is over.

I was fortunate to have been involved in the very early growth of the internet as a marketing channel. I have watched while marketers have discovered a new medium, realized that it provides a medium for consumer conversation. What has been most critical however is that it is a medium in which it is actually possible to monitor, record and analyse people's conversations amongst themselves. Until now, what people thought about our brands was anecdotal, hearsay or the output of qualitative research.

What people think today can be quantitative, facilitated by social media monitoring, peer scoring and reviews in e-commerce environments, and near-real-time behavioural data. We can create highly sophisticated behavioural models for our customers and validate them live. We have moved from marketing based on what we want our brands to do, to marketing based on what our customers want to do. The role of marketing strategists has changed from one where we have a brand and try to find things that resonate with customers when we talk about it, to one where we understand our customers and need to try to adapt the brand to meet them where they are.

This demands that we shift our focus to the consumer, and let the brand sit in the background, subject to bokeh (the blurred depth of field in the background of a photograph), only brought into sharp clarity when viewed through the lens of the customer themself. In this way the brand becomes pliable, depending on which customer is experiencing it and when they are doing so.

In this way, gone is the solipsistic 'Brand Onion'. If you can understand the customer's journey, and can manipulate the customer's relationship with your brand by using it as a medium, then you have moved from the old world to the new. Welcome the Brand Union.

So where do you start?

I am going to outline a highly practical way of approaching the new strategy. It revolves around a framework designed to put the emphasis on the customer. It has several component considerations, in order of priority:

1 how to get customers to change behaviour;
2 phasing of customer journey elements;
3 planning the journey;
4 channel selection;
5 unified briefing.

This approach brings together a number of elements with which we are familiar – nudge, the customer journey, touch-point planning and agency briefing. The last becomes a very different process, and requires a common understanding of the end goal by each component supplier. This demands clear instruction and generalist, rather than specialist, management, and perhaps this will be the most challenging aspect. This framework however does make it easier to get the right result, and the right result brings benefits to suppliers in turn.

Getting customers to change what they think

It is always a tall order to ask people to change their minds. Advertising traditionally starts with a blank slate, introducing a brand as a fait accompli, fully formed and self-contained, and to an extent that is why it works so effectively when introducing new products. It has always, as we know well, been a very difficult medium for changing consumer perceptions of a brand. Once established, a brand's values and position are fixed. If it falls from favour because mores or circumstances change it is often irrecoverable.

Digital channels make it much easier to encourage change, although again as we know there is a significant risk that, when custody of a brand is subject to consumers' rumour, negative comment and hijacking can cause considerable and occasionally irreversible damage to both reputation and sales. Social media disasters are a feature of the new landscape.

There are two principles that need to be brought into play here:

- Nudge
  Depending on who you believe, Albert Einstein, Keynes or an ad man famously said: 'Compound interest is mankind's greatest invention.' For our purposes, it allows us to make transformation changes easy to achieve. If your sales team (or your CEO) were asked if they could double turnover in two years, most would claim it to be difficult or impossible. Yet increasing turnover by 3 per cent in the next month is easy. Whoever's quote it is, compound interest says that 3 per cent a month, every month for two years, more than doubles turnover. If you can apply this notion to changing consumer attitudes – and in turn translate this change into modified behaviour – then we have an enormously powerful principle for leveraging marketing budgets.

- Relevance
  Peppers & Rogers taught us how one-to-one marketing could revolutionize response. We are all practised in using data to transform marketing accuracy (through understanding who our customers are) and efficiency (by understanding how they have behaved and therefore may be likely to behave in future). This can be translated into step changes in results through segmentation, of course, and timing. Getting a relevant message to the right person at the most appropriate time is what makes direct marketing, whether digital or traditional, so wonderfully effective especially in recession or post-recessionary times.

As far back as 1972 the idea that need states could be exploited to add a third dimension – motivation – to segmentation also crossed marketing boundaries into the retail experience (Tauber, 1972). Multichannel marketing gave us the discipline of Customer Journey Planning, a term which has been shamelessly re-appropriated by the (online) CRM consultancies. Understanding why a customer might find a message particularly relevant at a given moment may mean the difference between genuine brand loyalty and transient brand selection. B&Q, the British home improvements retailer, uses need states in a very practical way to create positive feeling: their stores employ semi-retired people to stand at the entrance to act as welcomers as customers walk in. They can see if the customer is in a hurry, with their family, in decorators' overalls or with dust in their hair, and can infer a tentative need state. By asking a simple welcoming question they can quickly direct the customer precisely to what they need. This makes the customer feel several things:

- welcomed;
- that B&Q cares;
- that B&Q is tuned to their needs right now;
- that B&Q always has exactly what they want.

It's an almost subconscious impression that is formed, but it is a powerful one that discourages even considering going to a competitor next time.

By combining these two ideas, nudge and relevance, we can create powerful journeys towards change, albeit by definition slower and requiring more thought and coordination than the succession of campaigns that traditional advertising and marketing is designed around.

FIGURE 6.1 Three-dimensional segmentation

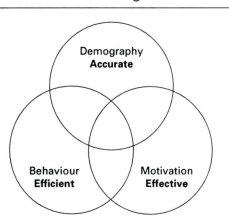

Let me illustrate this by invoking Suzy, a young mum with two young children, and a frozen potato products brand, McCain Foods. What can we say about Suzy? We know (for example) that she went to college and has some education, is concerned about her children's well-being, but is time-poor. Like most of us, she thinks that oven fries are bad for you. In the old world, we'd try and change Suzy's mind by trying to tell her what to think; but 'Fries are good for you' is not a credible message, especially not a credible advertising proposition. Today we apply nudge. And we do it by understanding Suzy's needs.

So Suzy gets an e-mail. The e-mail is a print and colour-by-numbers picture of a farmer and his tractor. The promise is that we will tell the children about farming by using engaging activities. The corollary of course is that Suzy gets half an hour of peace while they colour at the kitchen table, doing something safe that supports their education. Next week the e-mail shows the farmer ploughing a field. The next how a potato grows – with its component parts. The next how it is harvested, and the next... McCain peels it, adds sunflower oil and that's it, farm to table. With a voucher. Suzy has had a modicum of value, and in return she has given us her permission to communicate a message. By the end of the process, her kids have learned something, she has had a bit of quiet, and everyone knows that McCain's fries are, in fact, healthy.

When this principle was put into practice, McCain UK saw an increase of 3 per cent in average purchase frequency within the core segment over six months. Brand consideration went up by 11 per cent versus the TV-watching universe. This is a simple, low-impact principle, but it can have enormous results when applied well.

FIGURE 6.2 A process to drive measurable change

21000
17500
14000
10500
7000
3500
0

Pre-Campaign Registrations
Post-Campaign Registrations

FIGURE 6.3 Archetypal phased customer journey

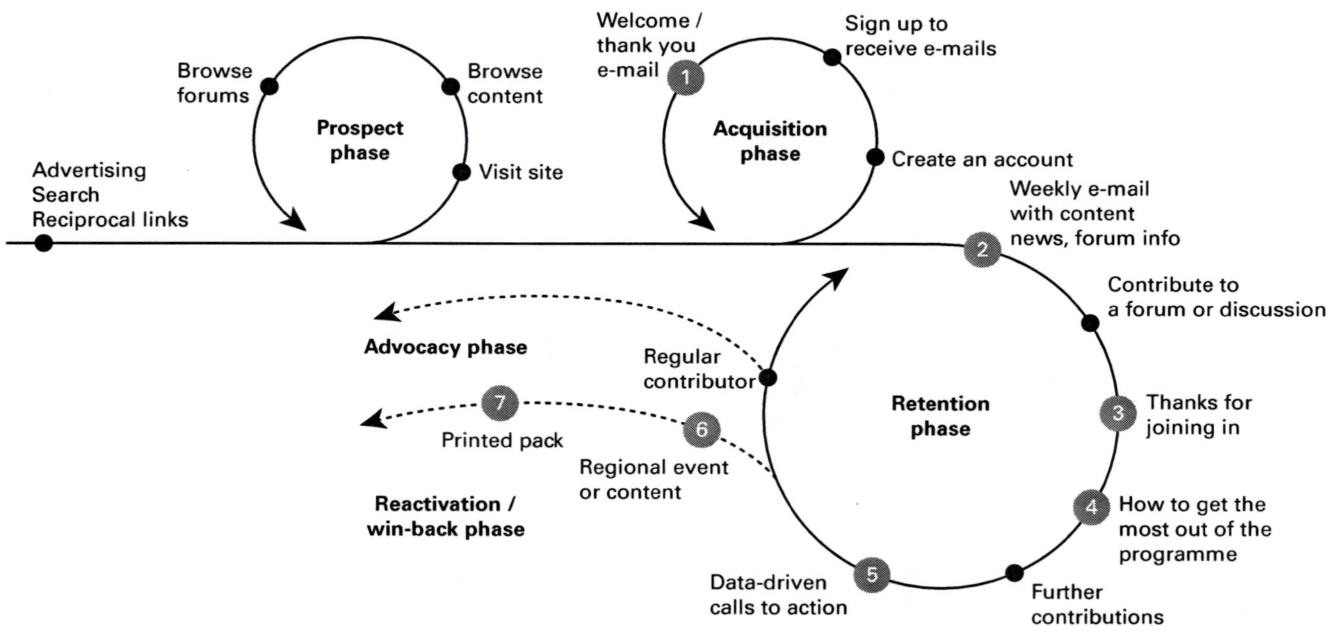

Advertising
Search
Reciprocal links

Prospect phase

Browse forums

Browse content

Visit site

Welcome / thank you e-mail

Acquisition phase

1

Sign up to receive e-mails

Create an account

Weekly e-mail with content news, forum info

2

Contribute to a forum or discussion

3 Thanks for joining in

4 How to get the most out of the programme

Further contributions

Retention phase

5

Data-driven calls to action

Regular contributor

6

Advocacy phase

Regional event or content

7 Printed pack

Reactivation / win-back phase

Relevance applies not just to the customer's need state, demographics or behavioural propensities; it also applies to channel. Meeting the consumers where they are now or will be when we reach out provides us with a venue that is essentially in the control of the customer and not the brand. For far too long marketers have sought to control the location, and this has led to such oddities as a 'social media strategy' that sits in isolation from the marketing strategy. We can work out where to reach and engage customers using broad spectrum research like Forrester's Social Technographics, or by doing specific research within our own customer segments. And because we can do this we can take a customer-centric view rather than a channel-based view.

This is critical. This approach requires us to define a customer journey by positing a sequence of customer touches or nudges that take the customers (representing our three-dimensional segment) on a low-impact journey from today's attitude towards the brand to the one we wish them to have in a year's time. We use this sequence of nudges, broken down for convenience into phases (engagement, conversion, retention, advocacy – and if it all goes wrong, churn reduction and win-back; see Figure 6.3), to give us an actions matrix.

The actions matrix

This actions matrix has several aspects and outputs:

- what to say when;
- channel selector;
- benchmark for improvement.

What to say when

This is simple. Taking a specific phase you can easily create a series of incremental messages that will take a customer from one point in their journey to the next. By planning the journey using a blank tool (Figure 6.3) it provides a straightforward, easily established sequence of logical pro-positions that, when looked at on a message-by-message level, never says anything too controversial and never asks the customer to make anything more than a single small step at a time.

From this it is easy to see that you can create a communications brief. In fact, this leads neatly to channel selection.

Channel selection

Once the steps have been mapped out (even roughly), you can then decide which venue or channel is the most appropriate one in which to deliver the message. For example, getting a customer from A to B might be most readily achieved on a landing page, B to C by sending an e-mail, C to D on a micro-site, D to E with an e-mail follow-up, E to F on Facebook, and F to G with an SMS reminder.

FIGURE 6.4 Customer journey sequence showing appropriate channel selection

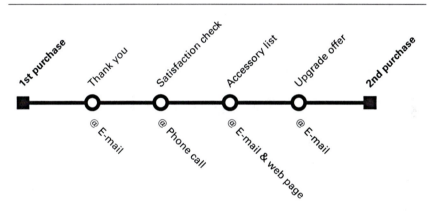

By definition you have created a customer journey that is independent of any individual channel strategy. That said, it means the briefing process has become extremely easy, as it is now executional and functional rather than strategic. The brief is: 'Get the customer who arrives here (who will have the journey thus far in their mind) to do X and go to Y with Z in their mind.' An agency or supplier worth their salt will quickly realize that they are required to cooperate with the other agencies in your employ.

Benchmark for improvement

Finally, by taking this step-by-step approach, you get a simple way to quickly optimize the programme. At any given point, all you have to do is move the customer to the next point. So if any given point is proving to be a stumbling block in the customer's journey, you can quickly work out what is going wrong and change it. You can test messaging, channel selection and calls to action very quickly (using split testing for example), unblock the step and move to the next blockage. This offers an iterative approach to continual improvement that is again executional rather than strategic and therefore easily dealt with, without much expense.

Ultimately you will have a plan of action, from which branches supplier selection, internal resource requirement planning, technology requirements, communications planning and – at the end – revenue generation. This means that rather than having a brand strategy you have a customer strategy. This makes you infinitely flexible, as opposed to intransigent, rigid and vulnerable to societal change. By focusing on the customer, multichannel becomes a distinct and practical reality. And that in turn means you can create not just incremental steps for your consumers, but step changes for your business.

Reference

Tauber, EM (1972) Why Do People Shop? *Journal of Marketing*, October, pp 46–49

Emerging mobile dynasty

07

DIMITRIOS KONTARINIS

Dimitrios Kontarinis is the VP of Innovation at Velti, the leading global marketing platform, connecting brands with consumers around the world. Dimitrios has over 15 years of experience in innovation management (concept to market) including new business development, start-up founding and management, venture capital and product development.

The past two decades have undoubtedly changed our social behaviour more radically than the whole of the past century. The way we interact with information and knowledge as well as with other people has been enriched in many cases and impoverished in others. There is a great depiction of

FIGURE 7.1 Rate of participation in social institutions (% of households)

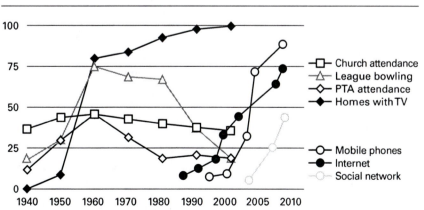

this discontinuity in social behaviour in Putnam's *Bowling Alone* (with some additions by yours truly).

The introduction first of TV and now of digital means for social networking has clearly influenced our social behaviour and activity: we go to church less, we attend PTA meetings less and we certainly go bowling alone; however, we 'live' in the internet, we communicate through social networks at exploding rates and we certainly have at least one mobile phone that is always on and that we carry at all times. Mobile devices have become an integral part of our everyday outfit; we carry them on our belts at work, in fashionable covers when we are out, in armbands when we jog. Dependence and ubiquity will become even more pronounced with wearable devices. In this new era mobile is king. It is the cornerstone of communication because it is not just another medium: it is the communication channel where all other media converge. It is the glue that holds together the new social and knowledge infrastructure and at the same time the remote control of life for people to choose their preferred social and knowledge engagement anytime, everywhere.

In this article we will consider the central role of mobile in the interactive and social ecosystem, its growth and persistence and the implications in the digital ecosystem.

Why is mobile the connecting medium?

Mobile phones' utility by default makes them the device that can be the crossing point of convergence: they have computing power, screens, interaction interfaces, network connection, voice, messaging and data services. These capabilities have existed for years but the timing to enthrone mobile came this past year due to the simultaneous blossoming of disruptive technologies:

- HTML 5 maturing;
- Smartphones' explosion & tablet era

HTML 5 has converged desktop and mobile internet, mobile web and apps in a way that makes the mobile landscape more rational. HTML 5 enables technological harmony and business agility and delivers superior user experience.

HTML 5 is a new technology that is used to develop rich media applications over the latest generation devices, across all screens (PCs, handsets, tablets, connected TVs), and resolves mobile landscape fragmentation. It brings together online and mobile internet, sites and applications and it is essentially the cornerstone of the new rich media internet superset. Such

FIGURE 7.2 Desktop vs digital crossover

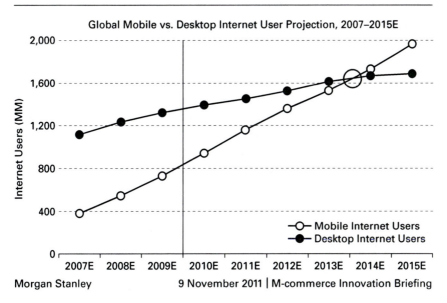

Global Mobile vs. Desktop Internet User Projection, 2007–2015E

Morgan Stanley   9 November 2011 | M-commerce Innovation Briefing

technology gives sites 'application-like' characteristics such as caching, which enables a site to function even when offline or access to GPS and other phone sensors, enabling location and context relevant functionality.

Proprietary and esoteric barriers from one platform to another are becoming obsolete and more developers and creators now have access to more end users through different platforms using the same technology: HTML 5. This will become even more apparent in the next few years.

The rich interactive content that can be delivered with HTML 5 (tailored to mobile needs) along with the development of new interaction devices (smartphones and tablets) have moved us to the point where mobile is the superset of desktop internet.

Summing it up, the mobile phone fills its 'natural' niche in the interactive ecosystem because of its technical capabilities, the ending of the fragmentation in the mobile technology and the aggressive uptake of mobile internet.

Mobile is a way of life

For any disruptive technology, easy as it is to take off, it is just as easy to fall flat on its face or not do as well as its technological superiority would promise (examples of such technologies are Minidisk, Newton PDA, Video Phone, the Wankel engine). For every individual case there is a different set of reasons that can explain their failure to become broadly adopted (like timing, competition etc) but the main cause for short-lived, otherwise competent if not groundbreaking technologies was that they did not blend in with the culture and social utility. The mobile phone today has become an integral part of culture and economy (digital lifestyle). It is extensively used as a tool for journalism. Mobile phones have also provided means of communication where landlines and other telecommunication networks are not accessible, for example in underdeveloped countries. In some of these countries this form of communication is now used to facilitate the spread of social happenings such as weddings and births. Mobile phones have penetrated society and religion deeply enough that even a 'kosher' phone is now available (Hirshfeld, 2012).

This dominance has also created ample economic opportunities for people to maintain and service mobile phones (Denison, 2009). Mobile banking has also proved to be an emerging and rapidly expanding sector, capturing a big chunk of the economy in some countries. For example half of the world's mobile banking users are in sub-Saharan Africa generating $0.5 billion worth of monthly transactions (Greenwood, 2012). Overall, mobile phones have deeply penetrated society, sometimes filling in gaps that landline telephony could not serve and in other cases providing novel paths of communication. As such, mobile telephony is not a technological progress that exists in vacuum but rather an integral part of the social communication layer.

Riding the technological wave

Consumers are engaged to a number of interactions through their mobile devices throughout the day. This places mobile phones in the centre of personal communications. As such it leads and leverages on parallel technologies. For example, the development of low-power-consumption processors, batteries and high-fidelity small screens for mobile computing devices has provided the ability to develop smartphones that offer unprecedented user experience, which in turn has unleashed the potential for advanced mobile applications and mobile internet. At the same time the evolution of networks and GPS coverage has upgraded (and will continue to do so) the sluggish response of mobile devices to useable and seamless.

Perhaps what is more interesting is the fact that changes in traditional dominant media also assists in strengthening mobile dominance. For example, the rapid changes in the TV sector with VOD, streaming TV but even more interestingly second screening put the mobile channel as the 'natural' continuation of traditional media. This means that mobile is not here to overtake the status quo and rival those media that have shaped our social behaviour and have led us to go 'bowling alone'. It is here to take existing trends to the next level, most probably enhancing physical social interactions and ensuring longevity for the mobile medium.

Mobile content is king

The era when content for mobile phones was the secondary product derived from content produced for other media is now over. Most users accessing content are now accessing it through their mobile device. For example Facebook, now serving a billion users, is becoming mobile (Heussner, 2012). The number of mobile TV users will reach 240 million by 2014, while 10 per cent of TV revenues will come from tablet devices by 2016 (PRNewsWire, nd). It is evident that content for mobile devices will not be the by-product any more. It will be the main focus of content producers. Combine this with the fact that the mobile content market was $6.5 billion in 2011 and is projected to grow at $18.6 billion in 2017 (e-Marketer, 2006), and one can see the mobile content dominance in the near future. Online and traditional presence is now driven by mobile, leveraging not only on the penetration of the medium but also on the unique capabilities of modern technology mobile phones.

Mobile user experience: multi-sense, multi-interaction

Another unique characteristic of mobile devices is the fact that they exploit the full spectrum (well, almost, considering smell and taste interactions have not yet been implemented commercially) of the human sensory system. TV, landline phones, print media even desktops (for the most part) have heavily addressed vision and hearing as the dominant communication channel with the human, though lacking, at the same time, interactivity. This results in over-burdening individual senses, resulting in fatigue and loss of the potential communication bandwidth. It also results in a uni-dimensional representation that is far less exciting and informative. Modern mobile phones can alert us to an incoming call or message via vibrations (extended body sense of touch) while we are attending a meeting and cannot be accessed otherwise. We can communicate commands to our phone via speech while engaged with some other task. The latest developments (and more is yet to come) allow us to interact with multi-touch interfaces, 'feel' the virtual keys, and soon we will be able to control our phones using gestures. Furthermore, the multitude of sensors that our mobile devices are equipped with nowadays automates, and thus facilitates, their adoption in different conditions.

Conclusion

Mobile is becoming the medium of preference for the internet and will soon become the superset of all media. It is overcoming the initial fragmentation resulting in a 'joint task force' that progresses and rapidly evolves. It has become an integral part of society and in several cases has initiated economies that did not exist. Mobile is a complementary and not a rival technology. It assists other sectors and draws traction from those. The unique and differentiating capabilities of mobile devices provide a more 'natural' interface and an eager canvas for creativity. All of the above ensure that the growth of the mobile sector will be sustainable and spectacular and progress in this field will be the spearhead for many important advances in the fields it engulfs.

Sources

Denison, N (2009) *Discovery Channel*, 2 February 2009, '10 ways cell phones help people living in poverty'

e-Marketer (2006) [online] study of internet penetration in US households from e-Marketer 2006 study [http://thebankwatch.com/ 2006/10/26/ emarketercom-canada-online-growth-rates/

Greenwood, J (2012) *Financial Post*, 24 July 2012, 'Kenya dominating global mobile payments industry, posing monopolistic threat: World Bank'

Heussner, K M (2012) 'AdWeek Facebook moves closer to becoming a "mobile company"', Juniper Research Report, May 2012

Hirshfeld, R (2012) 'Introducing: a "kosher phone" permitted on shabbat' [online] israelnationalnews.com, 26 March 2012

PRNewsWire (nd) 'TransparencyMarket research mobile content market – global and US industry analysis, size, share, trends and forecasts 2011 – 2017

Putnam, R D (2000) *Bowling Alone: The collapse and revival of American community*, Simon & Schuster, New York

For mobile handsets in US households, see the study by SNL 2007, available at: http://www.marketingcharts.com/interactive/mobile-phone-penetration-84– wireless-revenue-155b-by-years-end-1371/snl-kagan-cell-phone-penetration-usjpg/

For social networks users as a percentage of internet users, see the study reported in eMarketer (2012), available at: http://www.emarketer.com/Article.aspx?R=1007712

Cross-channel analytics

ROBERT CATAFORD

Rob Cataford is the Vice President of Analytics at Ignitio, a software company with customer intelligence solutions. With over 20 years of experience in data analytics, Cataford has worked for several web analytics vendors and other software vendors and built up an in-depth knowledge of the data and analysis techniques required in the industry.

The move from traditional advertising to supplemental digital advertising, and now to the ecosystem where interactive marketing is leading your brand, is establishing new challenges for measurement and analysis. The old adage of 'I know I waste half of my marketing dollars, I just don't know which half' still rings true.

Traditionally it was difficult to connect the marketing to the value. The reach of TV and print ads could be measured with statistical samples and the connection to value was measured and analysed with focus groups, statistical correlations and sometimes just intuition. The onset of digital marketing was a dream for many marketers in terms of measurement and analysis. Now a specific marketing initiative could be linked directly to an outcome. This provided very precise measurement on a channel-by-channel basis.

The new ecosystem recognizes that your brand and value are communicated through many channels, and that individuals perceive your brand based on their exposure to all channels, whether they are online or offline. The engagement of an individual or a company with your brand becomes a 'journey' along exposure from different channels. How do we effectively measure this journey and understand each channel's role? This is a complex problem. Certain marketing activities can be linked to specific individuals with specific outcomes while other marketing activities cannot be linked to individuals and can only be analysed as an aggregate.

Digital advertising: a marketing analysis dream

In traditional advertising it has always been difficult to measure the effectiveness of the marketing. Television, print and radio reach a broad audience. The audience itself can be estimated and measured in terms of size and demographics but understanding the impact the marketing has had on the audience has always been a challenge.

The internet provided an alternate sales and marketing channel for many companies. There are companies that have only a small portion of their marketing budgets focused on online channels while other companies have most or all of their marketing budgets dedicated to online.

The use of the internet as a sales and marketing channel solved many of these analysis challenges. At least for the portion of the budget spent online. The early methods of online marketing – mainly e-mail, display and search leading prospects to your website – were all easy to measure. Web analytics systems started by reading log files and decoding a user's behaviour and have advanced to sophisticated marketing measurement systems. Most web analytics systems will tag campaigns and organic traffic to your website, and measure conversions to website activities that are considered of value: either a sale or indicator of interest leading to a sale. In addition, most analytics systems will apply some sort of attribution modelling so the credit for value is spread out appropriately between the marketing campaigns in which the prospect has interacted.

Tracking an individual's behaviour and having a direct connection between marketing and a specific outcome has enabled marketers to truly optimize and finally answer the question of which half of their marketing dollars are working. All this sounds too good to be true and that's probably because it is. Just because there is a clear and concise metric, that doesn't mean that it is the correct metric. We have all relied on our online marketing conversion metrics and haven't necessarily stopped and asked if that measurement is really telling us what is working and what's not.

Measuring the success of a campaign

In the digital marketing world a lot of weight is put behind the 'conversion' metric. An individual reacts to a piece of marketing (a banner ad, a sponsored link in a search or an e-mail) and then converts on a call to action. This is the ultimate measurement of success but only a very small proportion of people follow this path. I recently heard Avinash Kaushik (a well-known web analytics 'guru') speak and he touched on this point. He asked: 'Are you really going to optimize your site and marketing based on the actions of 1 per cent of your audience?' He raises a good point: what about the other 99 per cent of people that engaged with your site and your digital marketing?

Digital marketing has become more and more sophisticated and people no longer react based on a single digital channel. They are exposed to your brand and value proposition everywhere. Your website, your ads, references to you on other websites, your Facebook page, your Twitter messages, blogs, reviews – and it goes on and on. Just because they used search to find you before they bought or filled out a lead form doesn't mean search was responsible for making them aware of you.

Tracking an individual through these marketing touch-points is not always possible. Sometimes part of the journey has to be measured using an aggregate, and the eventual connection of an individual to a call to action cannot be made. Add into this the concept of the marketing ecosystem where all your online and offline marketing efforts create your brand and the measurement of success becomes even murkier.

The reality of the new ecosystem

The new ecosystem relies on all marketing (online and offline) building a brand and a message for your company. Each channel provides some awareness and information for your potential customers, and channels are actually encouraging those potential customers to use the other channels. The marketing becomes a journey for each prospect with many multichannel marketing touch-points along the way.

I recently worked with a customer where we determined – through analysis – the effectiveness of their social media marketing. As a single channel measured just on conversion, it appeared that social media marketing was a waste of money but the data told a different story. Behaviour patterns came out of the data where social media was found to be a 'nurturer' of sales. The combination of search, e-mail, display and other traditional channels driving awareness and social media then nurturing the prospects provided the highest correlation to success.

In deciding where to spend your money, you must understand how the channels interact and when they stand alone. Which combination of channels is effective in turning a prospect into a customer? Which channels create initial awareness? Which channels support the education of the prospect? Which channels are effective at driving a call to action? If the analysis can provide answers to these questions, then the best decisions will made. The new ecosystem almost demands analysis with these concepts in mind. Measuring each channel separately – offline channels measured traditionally and online channels measured using primarily conversion metrics – isn't enough any more if you want to truly understand how your marketing is working.

'Big data': can it provide the answers?

The data to answer the questions posed above mostly exists and is scattered throughout different systems. Digital impression data is typically held by your display provider; web analytics data contains the click-throughs and web behaviour; marketing nurturing systems contain marketing activity data; your CRM contains all the customer data and tools; agencies and vendors have access to other data such as social media monitoring, search rankings and many other sources of data. The concept of 'big data' is to bring as much of this data together as possible and analyse it.

This is typically a very large challenge but even if you can combine and link a few of these data sources together it's better than looking at it in individual silos and can often provide marketing insights that you didn't see before.

For example, connecting your web data to downstream marketing activities and CRM data can give you a better measure of success than the web data alone. If your website's main purpose is to generate leads or registrations, then much of your digital marketing success measurement is most likely based on conversion to leads. What about the quality of those leads? What about people who consume website content, don't fill out a lead form and then engage with you over the phone? Using the downstream data, you can create more meaningful success metrics.

The same goes for the top of the funnel. If you rely on just the web data, you start measuring based on the first action taken. What about the display ads that have been viewed but not clicked? What about your print or television marketing? It is possible to account for things like 'view-throughs' and link offline advertising to online behaviour?

Connecting the data

One of the requirements for analysing the data together is to connect the data wherever possible. If there are no keys in the data from one source of data to the other, then putting it together doesn't provide much benefit over analysing it in the silos where it originated. For example, your web data is keyed by a cookie and contains all the data from acquisition to conversion point, while your CRM data is keyed by a lead ID or customer number. If you can't link the cookie to the CRM key, you can't take advantage of measuring the digital touch-points that led to a lead and an eventual offline customer sale.

In the ideal case you would be able to connect all data to a master key that identifies an individual. Take the case of a person who watches a TV commercial, searches and visits your website, and then performs an offline sale. It's not possible, but imagine linking those activities together for everyone and the insights you could gleam from the analysis.

Now take the case where a person watches a TV commercial, is directed to your site via a vanity URL, a search key word related to the commercial or via a Facebook site aligned with the campaign presented in the commercial. On the site, the person downloads a coupon or is registered and then presents that information at the time of the offline sale. Now these channels are linked together and you can see the marketing journey and optimize appropriately. Of course it isn't possible for all campaigns and channels to be linked explicitly for all prospects but any connection in the data can provide incremental insights to your analysis.

Once connections are made, either by passing keys from one system to another or tagging campaigns between systems, they can be referenced together, bringing the data together, and segmenting for analysis becomes possible. Even if you don't bring the data together the aggregate reporting from each system can be compared.

Measure based on intent

Another thing that can assist in understanding your marketing impact and optimizing your market spend is to create metrics that measure a marketing activity based on the intent or objective of the activity. Earlier I discussed how a conversion metric may be misleading when evaluating the impact of marketing. Most companies create one or two metrics to measure all things the same way. Marketing activities, campaigns and programmes are designed with different objectives in mind. Some are designed to create initial awareness and introduce your company, products or solutions to new prospects; some are designed to provide information and create thought leadership; and some are designed to initiate a particular call to action for a prospect. All these campaigns should not be evaluated with and optimized to the same metric.

If a programme is designed to create awareness or establish a brand message then measure it that way. Perhaps a television commercial that is designed to introduce a new slogan or messaging and drive people to engage with social media designed for the campaign should be measured with social media traffic or brand messaging searches. Marketing content that is designed to educate prospects should be measured with metrics like time on site and return visits.

Using metrics that align with the objective enable you to optimize to that objective. If all the marketing campaigns are optimized to their design, the yield should also be optimized. Obviously, attempting to measure the end value and tie it back to the marketing campaigns is always desirable, but when it's not possible measure and optimize to a mid-point success factor.

Putting it all together

The points discussed here will help us get closer to the answer to: 'I know I waste half of my marketing dollars, I just don't know which half.' A question that is getting more and more difficult to answer in the new marketing ecosystem where offline and online campaigns are linked, and together are responsible for creating awareness, establishing brands, educating prospects and driving action.

The data gathered from the different channels and along the sales funnel needs to be connected wherever possible and analysed together. The journey of a prospect needs to be determined through analysis and all campaigns optimized keeping this journey in mind. Optimizing channel by channel with a silo-driven approach just doesn't fit with the requirements called out for in the new ecosystem.

The good news is that there are techniques to connect the data and 'big data' is getting some attention, with many solutions coming forward that can deal with this data challenge. This, on top of some different techniques to measure and optimize to success, can get you on the correct path to having your analytics meet the measurement challenges posed by the new ecosystem.

Software-driven marketing ROI

SCOTT BRINKER

Scott Brinker is ion interactive's President and Chief Technology Officer, and leads the company's product development and technical operations from the firm's Boston office. He has over 20 years of experience in developing and marketing commercial online services and software.

Marketers have always been quick to embrace new technologies. The Ancient Egyptians invented one of the first media technologies – papyrus – thousands of years ago and they were also the first to pioneer using it for advertising. Sales messages and wall posters have been discovered in the ruins of their civilization.

As technological innovation accelerated over the centuries, the speed at which new media were co-opted by marketers kept pace as well. Radio broadcasting began in the United States in 1920. By the beginning of 1922, the first paid radio commercial aired.

The first real web browser, Mosaic, was launched in 1993. One year later, the first banner ad, an advertisement for a Silicon Valley law firm, was sold on a commercial website. Given the anti-commercial nature of the early web, that was a bold move at the time. But by 2011, an estimated $25 billion worldwide was spent annually on web-based display advertising of that kind.

Nowadays, when a new web service emerges – such as Google+ or Pinterest – we end up hearing within a matter of days about some innovative marketer using it to get their message out.

Looking at these points on the curve, you'd reasonably conclude that marketers are evidently quite tech savvy. The technologies change, but marketers' relationship with them has remained the same. Or has it?

From communications to experiences

In truth, the relationship that marketing has had with technology up until now has actually been relatively narrow. Marketing has used new technologies primarily for communications.

Arguably, a marketer's main job has been to craft messages – to tell stories – that would resonate with their target audience. 'Marketing communications' became the majority of what marketing did, taking up the bulk of the marketing budget with advertising and promotion. It's certainly what most people picture in their minds when they hear the word 'marketing'.

Technological innovations have offered new ways to express and distribute those messages, but they didn't disrupt the marketer's job of storytelling. Whether you were expressing your brand through direct mail, TV spots, PR or new search engine-optimized content on the web, the marketer's main job ended with the distribution of such stories. But two major shifts in technology and customer behaviour over the past few years have disrupted the formerly insulated bubble of marketing communications.

First, digital has evolved rapidly from a place where people merely consume content to a place where they actively use products and services online. It's nice that a brand has a website where prospects can read about their offerings, but increasingly what matters is the actual experience customers have when they inquire, demo, purchase, use, troubleshoot, update, renew, extend and interact in all kinds of ways with those products and services via the web and mobile devices.

Second, social media has hacked the narrative that revolves around most brands. Marketing is no longer just what you say about yourself, but what other people say about you. Prospects are always one Google search away from a wealth of reviews and opinions published by your customers and a broad spectrum of other market influencers. Twitter, Facebook and community forums let them see first-hand the praise and criticism that people have for you – and how well (or not) you handle those interactions.

These two major shifts are intertwined. The experiences people have with you – good or bad – are echoed back into social media, where they influence others who are considering doing business with you. Delivering amazing experiences to your prospects and customers is the best way to build a stellar brand narrative in social media.

As a result, marketing has become about delivering compelling experiences, not merely telling compelling stories. And that's changed the relationship marketers have with the technology on which these experiences are built.

Architecting brand experiences

For marketers, moving from telling stories to delivering experiences is a big change. It's like switching careers from being a painter to being an architect. A painter's imagination and eye for design will be a valuable asset for a career as an architect. But that talent must now be augmented by an understanding of forces, materials, engineering and construction.

Likewise, a marketer's storytelling skills are still as important as ever – experiences are tangible incarnations of stories. But now marketers must understand how such experiences are designed, developed and deployed.

Instead of painting the image of a brand experience, marketing must architect the actual brand experience. It's important to recognize that 'experience' in this context is quite broad. It begins at the very first touch-point a prospective customer has with you.

For instance, think of a prospect who does a search on Google and sees one of your keyword ads. If they click on it, does the web landing page fulfil the expectations set by the ad? Is it telling a consistent story? That sounds simple at first, but remember, you conceivably have hundreds or thousands of different ads on Google at any one time. Making sure that the right ad is matched by the right, up-to-date landing page is a non-trivial challenge. If there's a disconnect, you can instantly lose people's interest and trust.

But that's just the start. Are the promises made by that first touch-point upheld throughout the rest of the purchase funnel? Does your e-commerce system honour the offer of that original ad until checkout is complete? What if the prospect drops out – say, to run to an appointment – and then comes back to your regular website later? Is it easy for them to pick up where they left off?

What is the experience like if they reach you using a mobile web browser? If they interact with your brand on Facebook or Twitter? If they call you or visit a physical store location? Do you maintain continuity in subsequent e-mail nurturing, website personalization, online ad re-targeting, even good, old-fashioned direct mail?

All of this is brand experience – each of these touch-points individually and the flow of all of them collectively. And this is even before the prospect's first purchase!

Ideally, the progression of these touch-points will appear graceful and connected in the eyes of your customer. The alternative is that an experience appears disjointed or sloppy, which can trigger feelings of annoyance, frustration, or mistrust.

Either way, such experiences will define your brand.

Software powers the modern brand experience

On the web, on mobile devices and increasingly in physical retail locations, software powers these brand experiences. From your website to your CRM, from your mobile apps to your e-mail platform, software either directly interfaces with your customers or enables your sales and customer service staff in their interactions with them.

Software determines what brand experiences are possible.

There are now many different kinds of software in marketing's ecosystem. There are commercial software packages that you buy – or, increasingly, rent in the cloud as software-as-a-service. These include web content management (WCM), marketing automation, social media management, campaign management, customer analytics, digital asset management, ad management, landing page management and more.

Today there are literally thousands of commercial marketing software offerings out there, from large public companies such as Adobe and IBM to innovative start-up ventures as small as a couple people with a brilliant idea. Reinventing marketing in the digital age has proven to be a fertile ground for software entrepreneurs.

In addition to all those commercial packages, there is another significant category: software that brands, or their agencies, build themselves. This can be as simple as an interactive feature on a web page or as advanced as a full-blown iPad app. In digital and interactive agencies, a whole new group of professionals known as 'creative technologists' produce such software, most visibly for big, splashy and hopefully viral digital promotions.

But the vast majority of internally developed marketing software is deployed quietly behind the scenes. Excel spreadsheets, custom databases, scripts to automate tasks on other software platforms, proprietary ways of analysing and mining customer data. A lot of this software simply serves as 'glue' to connect multiple commercial packages together and to integrate with a company's other IT systems or third-party services.

Although customers don't directly interact with such back-office software, it often has a significant effect on their experiences. It feeds data into many front-facing experiences, determining how useful or sophisticated those experiences can be. It also feeds data back from those customer experiences, filtering it and framing it to help inform marketing's tactical decisions and evolving strategic vision.

Look around: software is now ubiquitous in marketing and customer service.

In a very real sense, software has become marketing's eyes, ears and hands in the digital world. Monitoring and analytics software lets us 'see' and 'listen' to what people are doing and saying across mobile and web experiences. And the software that interfaces to customers – websites, mobile apps, landing pages, interactive ads, etc – is how we 'touch' them.

Even with in-person and over-the-phone interactions, customer-facing staff often serve as proxies for the software that supports them. It's software that gives them the ability to answer questions about an account, engage a loyalty programme, or take action to rectify a problem.

A great customer service representative can have a sympathetic tone of voice and a friendly demeanour, but if they're saying things such as, 'sorry, I don't have a way to do that on my computer' or 'please wait, our systems seem to be taking a really long time today', software is ruining that brand experience. It can make or break you. It gives you appreciation for a remark that Marc Andreessen made in a *Wall Street Journal* editorial about a year ago: 'Software is eating the world.'

Marketing's new role in software leadership

As soon as you recognize that marketing has become about delivering experiences, and that software drives those experiences, the conclusion is manifest: marketing must embrace software leadership as part of its modern identity.

That doesn't mean that everyone in marketing needs to become a software engineer. The CMO does not need to become the CIO. However, everyone in marketing, from the CMO on down, should become knowledgeable of the dynamics of software and be comfortable harnessing it to shape brand experiences.

Consider an analogy with graphic design. Not everyone in marketing needs to be a graphic designer. But an appreciation for graphic design, the knowledge of how to leverage it, is integrated deeply into marketing culture. Marketers work naturally with graphic designers and can easily share a common vision.

So must it be with software.

Whether working with a software vendor, a creative technologist at an agency or a project leader from the IT department, marketers must learn the language of their technical partners. They must willingly incorporate some of the DNA of technology culture into marketing culture.

But while not every marketer will be a software engineer, software engineers will, with increasing frequency, work directly in the marketing department. Similar to the creative technologists in agencies, there is a growing profession of 'marketing technologists' arising in marketing departments. They select, configure and operate commercial marketing software platforms. They create and manage much of the glue that binds the disparate pieces of marketing's technology ecosystem together. And they design and build proprietary, technical components of brand experiences.

In some companies, these marketing technologists live organizationally in the IT department, while spending their days working with marketers. But more often, these marketing technologists are native to the marketing department.

The advantage of native marketing technologists is that they're true hybrids: they think of marketing and software holistically. They're constantly experimenting and learning about new technologies, but always with an eye towards how they can be applied in a marketing context. When a new marketing idea is raised, they're quick to brainstorm ways that software can help. They think laterally between the two domains. Nothing is lost in translation, as can sometimes happen when marketers and technologists are separated into different departments.

But to manage technologists – even marketing technologists – it helps to have a technical background yourself. Since in most organizations that won't be the CMO, one solution is to create a new senior marketing role: a chief marketing technologist.

This person, a marketing–technology hybrid, can serve as the right-hand of the CMO for the technical facets of marketing's mission. This includes managing the team of marketing technologists, vetting technical products and services from vendors and agencies, coordinating software integrations with multiple parties (including the IT department), and implementing good marketing technology management practices around software security, reliability, maintainability and scalability.

Most importantly, this role serves as the CMO's technology *consigliere* – showing how software can achieve the CMO's strategic vision, and helping to inform that vision with the latest advancements in technology.

Software is the new fabric of marketing

Without doubt, marketing's new responsibilities for delivering experiences – and leading the software that makes those experiences possible – presents significant new challenges.

Marketing must have a much deeper relationship with technology than ever before. It requires new kinds of members on the team and new organizational structures and processes to incorporate their capabilities into marketing's expanded mission.

For most marketing groups, this evolution will take time. However, the market is moving quickly, and customer expectations have already shifted to judge brands by their digital experiences. Marketers are well advised to prioritize their adaptation to a software-powered discipline.

Although this mission is clearly a bigger challenge – experience design and delivery is far more complicated than marketing communications – this new responsibility vaults marketing into an even greater strategic role to the business as a whole. It opens up new opportunities for competitive advantage and marketing leadership.

Software is the new fabric of marketing. What will you create with it?

PART II
Establishing and successfully taking advantage of the multichannel ecosystem

Why do big companies fail in the multichannel ecosystem?

ALEXEY ANDREEV

Alexey (Lexa) Andreev has been one of the most prominent Russian internet activists since the 1990s. He has been the chief or deputy chief editor in a number of print magazines about internet and numerous parental and medical websites. SUP Media is an international online media company that owns and operates Russia's biggest blogging platform, oldest online newspaper and top sports website among others.

Before the collapse of the Soviet Union and the onset of market economics, the concept of product advertising was practically alien in Russia – and as anyone who grew up in the defunct Union will tell you, that was – in many ways – an advantage. The first 20 years of my life were devoid of any advertising. My American peers have no such life experience. The abundance of distracting highway billboards, of meaningless spam letters in their mailboxes and intrusive offers on TV and the radio are an intrinsic reality for them, just like Santa Claus and his troop of red-nosed reindeer.

We have been fortunate enough to experience a different reality. So it should come as no surprise that the profusion of advertising in the 'wild' 1990s created a backlash: we were used to the idea that the written word is an instrument used for the transfer of useful information. At school we were taught that 'A book is a source of knowledge.' We thought that advertising had to work in the same way. There is a consumer of the product and there is the product's producer – they have to find each other somehow. Advertising as an information service had to fill that niche, connecting producers and consumers. Why did it then become a symbol of trash and spam?

Mass advertising came to Russia along with the internet – a system that allowed the exchange of information to become even more targeted and useful. And this really did happen... but not with advertising. The paradox only deepened. Online you could find friends with most uncommon interests, recruit employees with very special skills, get expert advice about some rare disease or order a product from halfway around the world. But there was one thing that these wonderful informational communities had in common – they were operating in the shadows of huge banner ads peddling unwanted cosmetics. Somebody kept on spending their money and our attention in vain.

Later, after working for over 10 years as the editor-in-chief of a number of parental community sites, I discovered a number of other oddities that were putting advertising on a track that was completely opposite to the general internet trend towards a more sensible exchange of information. In 2004 I was working at Eva.ru – a large internet portal for women. Two major diaper brands were in competition for the main banner spot on the site's home page. They kept refusing any other kind of promotion even though we kept telling them that nobody stays on the home page, that the community was congregating at other pages, in the forums, which should be the main locus of their campaigns. We were ready to show them the exact forums where their target audience was hanging out. But the advertising specialists from both companies kept brushing such suggestions aside as heresy. They wanted to show their diapers to everyone – even to those who had no plans to have kids.

Later, when the idea of running ads in blogs, forums and social networks began to make sense to the large brands, new oddities became apparent. It turned out that individual doctors with private practices thrived in such environments, quickly growing their client base. The same was true for small medical centres. But there was also a certain size limit and the social network effect was lost once that threshold was crossed. A large clinic is incapable of communicating with internet users even though it would seem that it has more specialists and resources to do that. What was the problem?

Zoological model: elephants and anthills

When such questions snowballed, I realized that I was in the grip of a popular delusion. We think that if a company employs a lot of people and has a highly hierarchical system, then in its everyday actions such a company is governed by something akin to divine wisdom.

But the reality is different. We are confusing size and complexity. It is well known that a large, dense crowd behaves like a liquid. No matter how complex its individual members, in a dense crowd they are no more than water molecules. If you don't believe this, take a subway ride at rush hour. Or go to a football match and look out for the 'wave' when football fans jump up in their seats to make a wave around the stadium.

In the same way a large company made up of many people does not behave as wisely as it could. We wouldn't compare it to water of course; a more fitting comparison would be to a large animal. Observing the behaviour of animals, one can develop correct strategies for interaction.

Yes, in the beginning I myself was appalled by such an unrefined 'zoological' approach. But soon I discovered that it has some serious proponents. Oxford Risk Research and Analysis – a firm established by real zoologists – was consulting for large companies on how they did their business: for example, they advised an oil-producing company looking for new deposits to adapt the same risk assessment strategy that is used by starlings looking for worms. Scientists from the University College London used the 'ant' model in planning the carnival at Notting Hill, which allowed them to choose the safest route for the carnival crowd.

But let us get back to the advertising in internet communities. The zoological model can easily explain the oddities mentioned earlier. Advertising is something that is used by companies to 'mark' their territory, and the marketing department has a very specific role in this regard. If we use the 'animal' model of a company, the marketing department plays the role of a specific organ and, of course, it is impossible to explain to the animal's organ which places should be 'marked'. Especially when it comes to international companies whose brains, their headquarters (you see, they themselves refer to it as a 'head'!), are located in a different country, while one of their not-so-creative tentacles is spread our way.

It is no less clear that the foot-dragging at large companies, their excessively long chain of decision making and the outdated habit of treating the audience as passive TV viewers (in this day and age of active and interactive communications!) give a greater advantage to smaller animals that are more mobile and agile. This is why a small start-up can become very popular among the social network audience while the attempts of some large corporations to make it in that environment remind an observer of an elephant trying to climb into an anthill.

Of course this doesn't mean that the elephant has no other advantages. It does. The question is what it should do with an anthill. Should it even attempt to get it? Should it stick to its own ecological niche of TVs and billboards? Or are their some other ways of interacting with new environments?

Symbiotes and parasites: why brand communities fail

Just recently I was fortunate to read two good books about new research in the sphere of evolutionary biology. Both books deal with the interaction between different animal species. *The Birth of Complexity* by Alexander Markov contains many examples of symbiosis, a mutually profitable co-habitation. It talks, for example, of a grass that survives in a very dry desert thanks to the fact that this grass is home to a special kind of mould, which in turn is contaminated with a particular virus – separately none of them would survive the arid heat. The second book – *Parasite Rex* by Carl Zimmer – talks about something different: parasitical relations. Primitive micro-organisms such as toxoplasma easily control the behaviour of higher animals (and people) to their advantage: they modify the owner's character and habits and in some cases can even programme the sex of their offspring.

I think that both books should be required reading for those who want to understand why large companies spend large amounts of money on useless advertising. This is especially true for the new fad of the day – anything with the magic word digital.

Earlier I mentioned the story of two diaper brands that back in 2004 were fighting for the banner space on a home page and ignoring forums. But a couple of years later both these brands decided to organize their own internet communities. These two websites are very much alike: the pregnancy and first years of life calendars, guidebooks, consultations and a forum. They have been around for over five years... but they play no noticeable role among the parental communities of the Russian internet. Why is that? Let us look at how it actually works.

The main problem is that such projects come about because they are fashionable, not because the companies understand what the audience needs. After one of the elephants has given an example, the rest rush to do the same thing. But they don't do it by themselves. For starters, having raised its head (from the headquarters) the corporation finds an international advertising agency that speaks English and has already worked with one of the elephants. The agency organizers a tender and finds local providers of the magical digital content. These agencies in turn don't understand a thing about the internet, but they also hire developers, editors and other contractors. Consequently the tentacle of the corporate animal is overgrown with a long chain of symbiotes acting as intermediaries and only the very last link actually makes it to our internet anthill.

It is difficult and costly to support such a chain, as all of its links are trying to hog the blanket. In other words, symbiotes are in constant danger of turning into parasites.

Back in 2006 one of the top two soft drink brands came to the Russian internet with a very interesting project for their diet version. In one of my presentations I cited them as an example, lauding their expert combination of the brand's and consumers' needs: the community had united people wishing to lose weight around a low-calorie soft drink. The community's participants exchanged diets and compiled ratings of fitness clubs. Later the same group of developers began to work on the main brand website, once again creating a community around a popular topic – athletic events and games. But today you won't see that community on the drink's website. Now the only thing to do there is to submit codes from bottle caps in hopes of winning a prize. Last year I spoke to the marketing specialists working in one of the companies of this soft drink empire. I asked them why they abandoned the internet communities. They said: 'There was no connection with the product! What does it have to do with losing weight?'

By the way, the parasites can be found not only on the surface of a corporate animal, but inside as well. Back in 2010 a Russian dairy and juice producer hired an advertising agency to create an internet community for the promotion of branded infant food. The website that the advertising agency created used 'all the latest technologies' in the area of community building. In addition to the common set of functions such as blogs, forums, online consultations, personal ratings and photo competitions, it had such novelties as maps (search for companions for long strolls with children) and even some sort of 'internal currency' (active participation on the site was rewarded with Moneybox points that could be exchanged for real presents from the brand).

After a year of successful operation the client company... outsourced its support to the competitor ad agency. It was completely illogical from the point of view of the project's development, since this very development was cut short right away. But the reasoning becomes clear once you understand the yearly cycle of advertising budgets and other aspects of the operations of marketing departments of large companies: long-term projects are simply unprofitable for them since every year they have to show something new.

Mimicry of butterflies and nutrition of locusts

Once upon a time I was playing tennis with a friend on a campus of an American university. The sun was setting. Getting ready to hit back another ball I saw some woolly creature with huge eyes flying at me from the dark. My instincts told me to duck. The creature fell down on the court. It was a peaceful butterfly, Antheraea polyphemus. What I thought were the eyes turned out to be a pattern on her wings. It is believed that such patterns help the butterflies to scare off birds.

Mimicry is a widespread phenomenon of the animal world. It thrives in marketing as well. In the end, if the clients believe only in big banners, 'branding' and other outdated modes of promotion, why waste energy on trying to convince them to try something new? It's easier to try mimicry: turn the site's home page into a storefront that looks like either a TV screen or a glossy magazine. This is what many sites of internet communities look like today. The real life is taking place somewhere inside the site, but the external front is made for big clients to collect advertising.

It was Philip Dick who noted that 'fake realities can create fake people'. Modern-day digital promotion includes fast-track creation of large-scale groups on Facebook and its Russian competitors vKontakte and Odnoklassniki (Russian version of classmates.com). Thousands of Twitter feed followers are added to the list of KPIs. Wouldn't you call it a community? Wouldn't you say that this is a direct line of communication between the brand and its consumer? But there is a difference. In 2006 the head of Eva.ru project Vladimir Voloshin suggested a very coherent and also biological analogy for such pseudo-communities in his article 'Locusts and ants':

> Large swarms of insects are not always communal. A single grig in a locust swarm simply lives next to other grigs, it is only concerned with its personal well-being. But other communal insects, such as ants, demonstrate a complex social organization.
>
> The locusts are only capable of propagating and devouring cabbage fields, which leads to the increase in the swarm's biomass. If the weather conditions

are bad, the locusts are miserable. If the conditions are favourable – warm summer and plentiful harvest – the size of the swarm can grow catastrophically and locusts will completely destroy the environment around them.

The ants on the other hand are extremely eco-friendly: they peacefully coexist with their neighbours, they can withstand the bad weather and they demonstrate civilized forms of behaviour such as waging wars, building and ranching 'cattle'.

The lifespan of a locust is short. Once the food is gone and the air temperature is down, the swarm dissipates. Until the next investment boom.

The above excerpt describes what several years later became the classical mode of digital campaigns in social networks, which seem to be specifically tailored for such promo actions. Plentiful 'feeding' of quickly created groups with special viral content, competitions and gifts allows the agencies to present the clients with large numbers of registered participants... and it makes no difference that soon after that the locust swarm will take off for a new feeding ground: the next annual cycle of the advertising industry will bring with it new budgets and new locusts.

I do not exclude the possibility that such approaches really help to promote goods that are characterized by spontaneous consumption – beer, potato chips, football tickets. But if the product demands bigger spending than that, it is clear that it will demand a more thought-through informational support, something that you won't find in the 'locust' groups.

What's next?

All of the above may create an impression that this author does not believe in the possibility of effective, eco-friendly and informative large-brand advertising on the internet. But this is not so. When my notebook broke down, I went to the forum on the manufacturer's site – and received advice that wasn't half bad (instead of an offer to look for the winning promo code under the keyboard). The majority of large IT companies are successfully and 'naturally' using internet communities for their promotion. New services by Google and new smartphones by Apple are actively discussed in blogs and social networks without any special 'dirty pressure' from the brands themselves.

Maybe the secret here is that IT companies inherently understand the importance of 'information' better than most and know the correct methods of working with it in the modern world, where internet-based consumers are more independent than TV viewers. They are capable of compiling information from alternative sources and expert communities and are not susceptible to primitive marketing tricks.

Another driver of eco-friendly advertising is the active consumers. Not all of the product groups have them, but if a product group does, the producer of the product should seriously consider changes in marketing strategy. This is where research of internet communities comes in handy: the communities can show the producers the real needs of the audience.

For example, parental communities at LiveJournal not only show that Russia is experiencing a baby boom, but they also demonstrate a growing fragmentation of this audience. There aren't that many large parental communities: there is however a sizable 'long tail' of various groups and micro groups that are united by children's age or place of residence, preference for certain educational methods, joint purchases, joint travel and other parameters. This is a completely new structure, a self-organized fractal instead of the planned portal. Clearly this audience requires a smarter marketing strategy.

References

Markov, A (2010) *The Birth of a Complexity: Evolutionary biology today, the unexpected discoveries and new questions*, Astrel, Moscow
Zimmer, C (2001) *Parasite Rex*, Free Press, New York

How e-mail defines, builds and leverages brands

11

ANTHONY SCHNEIDER

Anthony Schneider is President of Mass Transmit, a New York-based multichannel marketing firm, and author of *Tony Soprano on Management*. Follow him @anthonyws.

Many heads and long legs

It has many heads and long legs. It's slippery, strong and very fast. It's already in your house, on your computer, inside your cellphone. And it's got an extremely long tail. No, we're not talking about a horror movie monster but a pervasive and hugely powerful marketing force that sits right in the middle of the new interactive brand ecosystem: e-mail.

E-mail isn't just a way we talk to our friends using our phones and computers. It's a ubiquitous marketing tool that both defines brands and changes the way brands evolve and spread. E-mail is the *lingua franca* of the internet – and the primary connector of the interactive ecosystem. E-mail is a vital part of the new brand mix and an important yardstick for measuring brand leverage across different sectors and channels.

FIGURE 11.1

The medium is the multifarious message

In days of yore brands were fairly static things, communicated from the top down via one-to-many media, like television or print advertising. Marketers owned brands. Today's brands are fluid, crafted by advocates and customers, communicated via all manner of media, from e-mail and websites to social channels and mobile apps (and of course TV, print and billboard advertising). Customers own brands. The medium is the message, and today's brand media are multifarious.

For today's customer and communications mix, this brand ownership begins – if not ends – with e-mail. According to a 2012 study, fully 77 per cent of users prefer to get permission-based marketing messages via e-mail (ExactTarget). (And by the way, this preferred marketing channel is on the rise, up from 72 per cent in 2008.) Of course e-mail doesn't define brands; e-mail disseminates brand information, feelings, facts, opinions and data. Some of those e-mails come from the brands themselves; others come from third parties; still more e-mails go directly from customer to customer, friend to friend.

The long-tail of e-mail begins in the inbox but extends across social channels, online and offline media, into our hearts and minds.

First and fast

Whatever a brand is doing, it's probably being communicated via e-mail. Company newsletters, sales announcements, product updates, white papers, new videos, surveys and so forth are a brand's most consistent and constant forays into their customers' inboxes – and minds. Then there are customer rants and raves, third-party reviews and media coverage of new products and services, all contained in a variety of e-mail transmissions. These e-mails spread the brand, disseminate news and also work to evolve the brand. Why? Because they are both first and fast. How do marketers announce a sale, kick off a new product line, respond to a crisis? How do customers forward information to friends? There are other elements in the mix but e-mail is often the first salvo.

It's important to differentiate between brand mechanism and brand meaning. E-mail and social media may be where customers interact with brands first and where they see brand activity most often, but the meaning of the brand – what it is, how it works, how it can be leveraged – needs to be worked out before the brand hits the channel.

Brand personalizer

E-mail is the advance team of the brand that takes it from generic to specific, from 'mass' to 'me'. E-mail newsletters allow brands to reach a large group in person. We get to know a brand, or already like a brand, then sign up for their e-mails and, presto, they're talking to us directly, and possibly sending customized e-mails, based on our location, shopping history or other attributes. Thus begins a personal, evolved and unique communication stream between the consumer and the brand. And, in a way, that's exactly what a brand is: a conversation.

Brand builder

Technology changes the very DNA of today's brands. First, technology transfers ownership from company to customers. Second, technology affords the brand and the customer a more proximate, personal relationship, albeit a digital one. E-mail is (or should be) a personal, one-to-one communication. It follows that the essence of today's brands is (or should be) personal: a complex and constantly evolving conversation.

Pervasive yet intimate, e-mail brings brands into our *sanctum sanctorum*, our inbox. Marketing e-mails sit in our inboxes along with notes from girlfriends, sports events, company reminders. And even if we don't go further than the preview pane, we see their logos and inviting images of fleece slippers or cool gadgets, building brand recognition and strengthening these brands. E-mail has a 'nudge effect'. Even if we don't open an e-mail we still register it and may still engage and transact with the brand in another channel.[1] That's because even an unopened e-mail contains a brand name, URL and subject line (and often logo images and some text), making the unopened e-mail a tiny but powerful brand beachhead in the inbox.

Measurable media

Unlike print or TV advertising, e-mail is both personal and measurable. We don't know who watches a TV ad or reads a print piece. But e-mail is immediately measurable. With e-mail, marketers know in real time how many e-mails have been opened, what has been clicked and by whom. Many e-mails include conversion tracking so that marketers can see even more than that: they can follow a user from e-mail opening to shopping cart checkout.

Real-time tracking allows marketers to refine their message and offer, continue what's working, and if something doesn't succeed, scrap it or reconfigure it. And the result? As a marketing tool, e-mail has no equal. The Direct Marketing Association puts e-mail marketing's ROI for 2011 at $40.56 for every $1 invested. It's no surprise then that a recent study of business executives found that e-mail was the highest performing advertising channel (Direct Marketing Association).

Bounce factor

Just about every e-mail you get from a marketer has a 'forward to a friend' link. That simple link is one of the places where brand ownership shifts: from marketer to customer. Marketers give up control but gain brand advocates, influencers and sharers.

Studies show that e-mails that originate from marketers get shared (via e-mail) two to three times. One retailer found that for every for every e-mail shopping cart sale, they see 3.76 other, typically non-tracked, sales due to the e-mail.[2]

Social starter

That bounce extends beyond e-mail-to-e-mail, moving in swift digital waves across social channels, video sharing, apps, mobile messages, even word-of-mouth. The best way to start social media engagement with your audience is through e-mail. According to a Harris Interactive study, 96 per cent of online adults are willing to share e-mail addresses with a brand, while only 12 per cent are willing to share social networking information. And the two aren't mutually exclusive or cannibalistic. On the contrary, e-mail helps social media and social media help e-mail.

Web and app launchpad

Our inboxes are repositories of information, e-mail addresses and URLs. E-mails are powerful open systems: we read an e-mail, then we go to a website, look up that restaurant, check out that online video, or locate that store.[3] These open systems also function as de facto digital repositories. We save (or don't delete) e-mails and go back to them to find a phone number, enter a contest or order a product.

Search enhancer

E-mail provides the results for a great many online searches. With the increasingly ubiquitous web archive of e-mail newsletters, automated-then-Tweeted composite newsletters, not to mention RSS feeds and social sharing, a lot of e-mail content ends up being indexed and searchable. That means e-mail content is a frequent result in keyword query results on search engines. And, like other elements of the new brand mix, it's a two-way street. E-mail informs search results while smart marketers use search analytics, blog comments and user feedback to build e-mails that resonate with and engage audiences and, in turn, inform the brand DNA.

Recently Google began extending online search to the e-mail inbox. If you so desire, Google will search e-mails from your mum along with the trillion or so websites and blogs that the search giant indexes. This dual searchability and longevity of e-mail points to an intertwining of personal and private, e-mail and web – a big online mix-up. It's a mashup of information and channel, authorship and chronology and, somewhere in there, brands.

Mobile mover

We use our smartphones to access applications, check out Facebook... and of course to check e-mail. E-mail is the bridge between web and mobile. Marketers are starting to pay attention to mobile social platforms, mobile marketing opportunities and, of course, mobile-friendly versions of e-mails.

As mobile devices become more prevalent, the humble e-mail gains access to a new device, new channels and apps and gains more presence, literally in the customer's pocket. Nearly half of all e-mails are opened on a mobile device, and that number keeps rising.

The future: the medium is in motion

Brands are changing, and the channels where customers interact with brands are themselves in constant flux. The medium is in motion.

Like media and technology, the new brand ecosystem is evolving rapidly, shaped by innovation and demand, shifted by trends and demographics and buffeted by economic fluctuations. E-mail is one of the more stable elements in the brand and marketing mix, but even e-mail is evolving, as automation, personalization and new technologies change the way we build, transmit and use e-mails.

Brands – and businesses – move at warp speed. It's vital that brand managers and marketers stay ahead of the curve. The brand rules of last year won't apply next year; e-mail, social media and other channels will continue to evolve rapidly. So brand vision means having an eye on the future and a yen for speed. Innovation means embracing the new and erasing the old. Tom Peters warns of 'the perils of polishing yesterday's apple', and this advice applies to brands as much as it does to products, services, financials or management.

Technology is implicated in the very notion of the brand, and that relationship will remain close even as it changes. As Sir Martin Sorrell, CEO of WPP Group says, 'You can have innovation without branding, but you cannot have branding without innovation.'

Where is branding going? Check your inbox.

Measuring the long tail

- More than 294 billion e-mails are sent each daily (Radicati Group).
- Well over 100 trillion e-mails are sent per year (Radicati Group).

- 43 per cent of all e-mails are opened on a mobile device (Litmus).

- 57 per cent of personal e-mails are opened on a mobile device (Relevency Group).

- 44 per cent of all Americans age 12 and over own a smartphone, representing half of all cell phone owners (Edison Research).

- 69 per cent of online adults use social networking sites (Pew Internet).

- 96 per cent of online adults are willing to share e-mail addresses with a brand, while only 12 per cent are willing to share social networking information (Harris Interactive).

- 669.5 million people used mobile e-mail; this is expected to grow to 2.4 billion by 2016 (Portico Research).

- In 2012, companies spent $1.5 billion on e-mail marketing (Forrester).

- E-mail marketing generates $40.56 ROI for every $1 spent (Direct Marketing Association).

Sources

The Direct Marketing Association 'Response Rate 2012 Report', with data from Bizo and Epsilon, June 2012

Edison Research [online] http://www.edisonresearch.com/home/archives/2012/06/the-smartphone-consumer-2012.php

Exact Target [online] http://www.exacttarget.com/email-marketing/best-practices/consumers-prefer-email-marketing

Forrester [online] http://blogs.hbr.org/cs/2012/08/why_email_marketing_is_king.html

Harris Interactive [online] http://pontiflex.wpengine.netdna-cdn.com/wp-content/uploads/2012/04/AcquiringUsersForYourEmailandSocialCommunities1.pdf

Litmus E [online] http://litmus.com/blog/emails-opened-on-mobile-start-designing-for-fingers-and-thumbs

Pew Internet [online] http://www.pewinternet.org/Reports/2013/Civic-Engagement/Main-Report/Part-2.aspx

Portico Research [online] http://www.portioresearch.com/en/major-reports/current-portfolio/mobile-messaging-futures-2012-2016.aspx

Radicati Group [online] http://email.about.com/od/emailtrivia/f/emails_per_day.htm

Notes

1   The 'nudge effect' refers to the indirect influence of e-mail, whereby the e-mail encourages an action without actually initiating one. An unopened e-mail in an inbox can influence a recipient's behaviour by creating awareness or acting as a reminder. Where a user's e-mail client contains a preview pane, that nudge effect may be stronger because even without opening the e-mail, the recipient is exposed to more elements of the brand and some details of the e-mail.

2   Obviously non-tracked sales are difficult to measure. The unnamed retailer cited here appears in Arthur Middleton Hughes' article 'Why e-mail marketing is king' in the *Harvard Business Review* [online] http://blogs.hbr.org/cs/ 2012/08/why_e-mail_marketing_is_king.html (August 21, 2012)

3   The theory of open systems was developed by Ludwig von Bertanlanffy, a biologist, in 1956. But the theory was almost immediately applied to other disciplines. Von Bertanlanffy defined the concept of a system, where 'all systems are characterized by an assemblage or combination of parts whose relations make them interdependent'. The new brand ecosystem is very much an open system, and successful marketers will exploit the many parts and relations rather than trying to maintain complete control of their brand or the media across which it travels.

How to win your Zero Moment of Truth

12

BRICE BAY

Brice Bay, CEO of EnVeritas Group (EVG), is a pioneer in the content marketing industry. For over a decade, his firm has helped Fortune 500 companies power their digital initiatives with engaging content and communications. EVG features over 2,000 writers worldwide who can create content in 34 languages.

There is no doubt that today's shoppers are digital consumers, with over 80 per cent first searching our interactive ecosystem for information that shapes their buying decisions. With just a few swipes of a smartphone, consumers can compare prices, read reviews, watch a demonstration, send product photos or locate a store. What was once a one-way marketing plan that funnelled the consumer from stimulus to purchase inside a bricks-and-mortar store is now a multi-person, interactive dialogue, with consumers often leading the conversation as they search for local goods and services online.

Google calls this the 'Zero Moment of Truth' (ZMOT), and it's defined as the moment when first impressions are made and an individual becomes aware of and forms an opinion about a company's brand. Historically, marketers such as Procter & Gamble have understood that the FMOT (first moment of truth) is when an individual encounters a product on the store shelf and decides to buy one brand or another, and the SMOT (second moment of truth) as when she uses the brand at home and likes it or doesn't.

In a 2010 Google Consumer Packaged Goods (CPG) Blog entry, Jenny Liu pointed to IRI's Economic Longitude 2009 Study, which showed that 83 per cent of shoppers made purchase decisions before they entered a store, a striking increase from 60 per cent in 2007. That number has continued to rise each subsequent year since the IRI study was released.

FIGURE 12.1 Zero Moment of Truth

Stimulus

ZMOT

First
Moment of Truth
(Shelf)

Second
Moment of Truth
(Experience)

SOURCE: Lecinski, Jim (2011) *ZMOT Winning the Zero Moment of Truth*, Google.

It is critical for brands to be part of this conversation and provide prospects with real value instead of just another marketing message. This new paradigm requires that brands become publishers and deploy strategies that address audiences' needs for relevant content across the interactive ecosystem throughout the purchasing process.

Innovative brands are now focusing on this purchasing process, instead of the selling process, and becoming an integral part of it by creating relevant content that solves their prospects' problems, answers questions and engages them with their brand through all phases of the buying cycle.

Join the conversation

The exponential growth of the internet and interactive platforms has turned the web into a digital shelf for shoppers thanks to 24/7 access and global reach. That means that no matter when or where consumers first encounter your brand's stimulus, they can immediately begin their conversations and search for more information. It's why local and regional companies, like King Arthur Flour in New England and Nebraska's Oriental Trading Company have seen their businesses grow thanks to the internet. The 220-year-old King Arthur Flour Company transformed itself from a local business into a global one. The company issued its first mail-order catalogue in 1990 and in 1996 launched its first website.

Today, the website offers forums, baking advice, videos, blogs and education as well as a hotline for bakers, in addition to shipping baked goods and items around the world. According to internetretailer.com, the King Arthur Flour Company keeps its fingers on the pulse of consumers by using short, online surveys to gauge brand recognition and assess future product development. The result is an e-commerce retailer that is ready with the information before potential customers even ask the questions.

If your prospects are actively seeking information about your brand and product, what are you offering them in return? Take this test: open up a Google search page and begin to type in your product or brand name. Before you complete it, Google offers up phrases it thinks you're looking for. That's what your prospects see when they search. Is your company name or product there? Are your competitors listed? How hard are you making it for consumers to find out what they want to know about your company or products? How easy are you making it for them to turn to your competitors instead?

To join the conversation, you can begin to meet the needs of consumers as they engage in their non-linear quests for data. The ZMOT Macro Study notes that 70 per cent of consumers look at product reviews before they make purchases and 83 per cent research products they see on TV. Those numbers may be impressive, but this behaviour isn't new. Before the digital age, Consumer Reports, Zagat and Kelley Blue Book, were supplying product reviews in hard copy. The only difference is that now smartphones and other digital platforms provide instant access to the same information, eliminating the need to go to the corner store or library to read the latest issue.

In 2010, consumers consulted an average of 5.3 sources online before purchasing, and in 2011 that number has nearly doubled to 10.4 sources according to the April 2011 ZMOT Macro Study by Google/Shopper Sciences. Each of those 10.4 sources represents a chance for your company to offer credible, reliable and trustworthy information that can influence the purchase decision. So what sources are being consulted?

- word of mouth from friends and family;
- communal sites such as Facebook, Pinterest and Twitter;
- product reviews by users;
- blogs;
- articles;
- user guides;
- forums;
- your company website.

Answer questions

Search engines are proven game changers, whether you are using Google, Bing or another engine. We turn to a favourite search engine similarly to the way we once used the Yellow Pages, encyclopaedias and the library. The search engine is now the first place people turn to for information. According to Rishad Tobaccowala, Chief Strategy and Innovation Officer at VivaKi, in an op-ed piece last August for inma.com, search engines should be called 'connection engines' because they let people everywhere interact, transact and express themselves. Brands need to think in these terms.

The hotel industry has kept up with the changing landscape because they know that 99 per cent of travellers, according to the 2011 ZMOT Macro Study by Google/Shopper Sciences, admit to being influenced by online content during the ZMOT. Hotels have used search engine optimized (SEO) keywords within their content to help their websites move to the first pages of search results.

But what many have missed is that the ZMOT has changed what consumers are searching for and how they're searching. Previously, travellers planning a trip to North Dakota's capitol might have searched for 'hotel in Bismarck', and that drove hotels to write copy interwoven with those fundamental keywords. But, according to a recent article on wihphotel.com about the change in hotel search, broad queries for hotels have been declining steadily, and keyword searches for 'hotels in [city]' are down 70 per cent in the past six years. To support this claim, the authors looked at three examples: 'hotels in New York', 'hotels in Paris' and 'hotels in London'. While each keyword currently has roughly 2.7–3.3 million monthly searches, the overall trend between 2004 and 2011 has been downward. The authors point to Google Insights to bolster their argument with graphics like the one shown in Figure 12.2.

Today, consumers are turning to a broader range of sources to answer their questions and make their decisions (remember they're using 10 or 11 sources per ZMOT), and when they're ready to hit the FMOT and purchase they are going to use everything that they've learned to make the purchase, whether it's online or in person. That means they may walk into a car dealership armed with list price, dealer's price and a roster of the specific features they want on their Mercedes S550 Sedan in Diamond White Metallic. Or they've chosen a hotel and pull the website that offers the best deal to book their room.

That's why Hilton hotels is shifting its focus from where travellers book to all the touch-points involved in their decision process, said Paul Brown,

FIGURE 12.2 Changes in hotel search

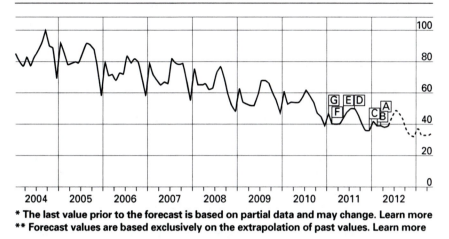

* **The last value prior to the forecast is based on partial data and may change. Learn more**
** **Forecast values are based exclusively on the extrapolation of past values. Learn more**

SOURCE: The change in hotel search (Google insights for search graph) [accessed 16 December 2012]
<**www.wihphotel.com/mag/2012/the-change-in-hotel-search**>.

President of Global Brands and Commercial Services for Hilton during his keynote address at the 2011 PhoCusWright conference. The result is a new digital initiative to ensure that direct channels are the ultimate truth with the best rates. In order to accomplish this, Hilton will increase spend on direct channels by more than $100 million and has formulated a four-pronged approach to distribution:

- Direct channels must be ultimate truth and offer the best rates.
- The entire portfolio of hotels must operate as a single system, otherwise the brand will appear schizophrenic.
- Suppliers can't be 'penny wise and pound foolish' about channel economics.
- Third parties will be given inventory 'once the hotel has its own house in order'.

Carlson, one of the world's leading hospitality and hotel companies with approximately 1,070 hotels operating in 77 countries, also understands the value of content for its own brands and direct channels. The company has five distinct brands, including Radisson, Country Inn & Suites, Park Inn, Park Plaza and Regent. Creating and managing content for each brand and every hotel property microsite is not only challenging, but also critical to driving traffic to individual hotel websites and increasing overall bookings. Since many marketers do not have the internal resources for large-scale content production they often outsource to firms that specialize in this field. EnVeritas Group created a dedicated team that manages and updates digital content for over 750 individual hotel branded websites. The branded content includes custom, comprehensive overviews about each hotel, focusing on location and unique selling points, rooms and suites information, hotel dining and lounge facilities/services, hotel wellness services/facilities, amenities, local area information and nearby attractions. The results have been dramatic, with online revenue increasing from 28 per cent to 35 per cent for each brand.

Whether consumers are looking for a Mercedes or a hotel room, the process takes time, and Google's ZMOT study found that they spend time thinking about purchasing and actually researching separately. Time frames for both stages vary according to the type of purchase being considered. That means that brands must have long-term strategies to offer reasons to research and answers to immediate questions. And this is not limited to big-ticket items like cars, vacations and electronics. Almost all types of businesses and products have some form of information on the web, a handful of videos on YouTube and a website.

Consumers even research low-cost purchases like Scotch tape, which is why there are 2,120,000 results for it on Google. Smart companies like 3M know this and make it easy for consumers to do just that. They're even giving away prizes to encourage consumers to post reviews about their tape, glues, adhesives and other products. Consumers want to talk about the products, their experiences and what they think others might want to know, which leads directly to the second moment of truth (SMOT).

Listen to your users

Humans are, by their very nature, social beings, and that's one of the reasons we want to share our experiences and interact with others. The SMOT reflects users' experiences with the product:

- Are they happy with it?
- Would they buy it again?
- Did it live up to its claims?

In the past, they might have told friends about a trendy new winery, advised colleagues not to waste their money on a bad film or shared the name of an exceptional mechanic. Recipients were grateful to get actual hands-on info; that's the same mechanism at work today on the web.

Whether or not you're actively participating in your brand's ZMOT, the conversation is going on and others are stepping into the breach to share their information in your place. Reviews by actual consumers are among the most important components of ZMOT, so when one person posts a post-purchase/experience review, it forms another link in the ZMOT chain as a source for the next person searching. But too many brands are afraid of negative reviews and simply try to avoid them by not providing such a forum on their websites. They ignore the fact that the conversations and reviews are ongoing, and most often happening on a third-party site, as in the case of hotels being discussed on TripAdvisor.com and restaurants on Zagat.com and Yelp.com. Brands that fear engaging in an open, up-front dialogue with consumers either get left out of the conversation entirely or end up playing goalie as they respond to deflect negative feedback from consumers.

Brett Hurt of Bazaarvoice points out that, worldwide, 4.3 out of 5 reviews are positive reviews. More importantly, 80 per cent of the reviews are written by a company's top 20 per cent of customers. Hurt says that sometimes bad reviews can be helpful rather than harmful and negative reviews can actually increase conversion rates because consumers are convinced they are in a truthful environment. Seeing a well-rounded group of reviews by 'people just like me' encourages consumers and influences them to take action. Bazaarvoice is also pointing to new research that 'millennials' (those between the ages of 18 and 30) rely on user-generated content in purchasing decisions 84 per cent of the time compared to 70 per cent for Baby Boomers.

Beyond reviews, other forms of online content add to the SMOT: tweets, Facebook, Google+ and blogs candidly discuss topics, products and experiences inside and out. Historically, marketers tend to focus on selling their products to the 'heavy users', who in turn influence their followers to use the same products. For example, a celebrity wearing a designer's gown on the red carpet can sends sales soaring for that designer.

A new twist in this strategy is the rise of 'heavy influencers' with a large network of followers in the social media ecosystem. Now, celebrities and other heavy influencers are being paid to blog and tweet about products in an effort to influence their numerous fans and followers. According to a *New York Times* article (29 January 2012), celebs and wannabe celebs are paid upwards of $10,000 per tweet to promote a company or its products. High-end earners include Kim Kardashian, who pocketed that much from Shoedazzle.com; Paula Abdul, who earns about half that; and the $50,000 per tweet raked in by Charlie Sheen from internships.com.

Is it worth it? Charlie Sheen's tweet generated 95,333 clicks in the first hour and 450,000 within 48 hours. That translated into 82,148 applications from 181 countries and boosted site visitors by a million. That's pretty powerful for only 140 characters.

Start with seven steps to win your ZMOT

If you're ready to win your brand's ZMOT, you're probably wondering where to begin. You can start with these seven steps that will put you on the path to delivering real results for your bottom line.

1 *Empower*. Put someone in charge of ZMOT for your company. Be specific and acknowledge the time this person needs to spend working on it. Then support those efforts with a budget. Be prepared to see results long term, not overnight.

2 *Discover*. Find out where your brand's ZMOTs happen. Ask users how they go about learning about your products and/or company. Then, when you have identified where and how they search, as well as what they're looking for, look at the information that is and, more importantly, is not available.

3 *Listen and learn*. To answer the questions people are asking, you'll need to spend some time listening to the conversation, both in online communities and by talking with your customer service staff. What questions are they routinely answering? What do you know about your company that you think consumers already know? What should they know so they'll be happy with their experience?

4 *Optimize for the ZMOT*. Now that you know where consumers are researching and what they want to know, decide on what content you'll need to provide to assist consumers in their ZMOT. Then make it a priority to provide the content in a trustworthy format. Learn to think like your consumers and develop channels that serve their needs without the hard sell.

5 *Join in*. These consumer conversations are happening right this very second, so it's time to join in. Someone, somewhere is talking about your brand, telling a friend about a cool new tech gadget or complaining about your product's warranty. Be there for them, and they'll be there for you.

6 *Be fast*. Things happen in the digital world 24/7, and ideas go viral at the drop of a hat. Stay on top of the ZMOT experience and be

prepared to adapt and adopt quickly. Don't dig in and keep something just because you've invested time and money. Be ready to move and react so that you can take advantage of the moment, because if you don't, there are others who will.

7 *Visualize.* The internet is, above all else, a visual medium. Sometimes it's easy to forget that and get caught up with the words. But the visual component may be more powerful than words alone, and a helpful video demonstrating how to do something, showcasing your products in 'real life' or otherwise engaging potential users really validates the old adage: 'a picture is worth a thousand words.' Just consider the fact that the 'Old Spice: the man your man could smell like' viral video received over 42 million hits on YouTube.

According to Google, $428 billion is spent on products and services that are researched online and purchased offline. That money is being spent by 97 per cent of consumers who turn first to their laptop, tablet or smart-phone to find out more about your company, brand and products. When they ask questions, when they join the ZMOT conversation, are you ready with the answers?

Sources

Tobaccowala, Rishad, August 2011, International News Media Association, *Ideas Magazine*, http://www.inma.org/blogs/
The Zero Moment of Truth Macro Study, Google/Shopper Sciences, United States, April 2011, www.google.com/think/insights

13

360° direct response marketing

MIKE TEASDALE

Mike Teasdale is Planning Director at Harvest Digital, a specialist online marketing agency. Harvest Digital helps clients to exploit online marketing opportunities, including e-mail, online advertising, search engine marketing, microsites and tracking/reporting. Current clients include Tesco, Sage, Stannah and The Economist.

Much has been written about the marketing ecosystem for brand marketing, but the changes in the direct marketing ecosystem have been every bit as dramatic. In just a few decades, direct response has moved from being paper-based (clipping coupons, completing forms in direct mail), to phone-based (driving traffic to call centres) to the current situation where the call to action of almost every television commercial features a website address.

Clearly we are now in an age where the website sits at the heart of direct marketing activity for many businesses. But to describe this as purely 'drive to web' marketing is to miss a lot of the complexity that actually exists in the current ecosystem.

In this chapter, I want to focus on three areas that are at the core of direct marketing – targeting, gaining permission and ongoing relationship marketing. Each of these areas has been the subject of rapid change – and in many cases the situation is still very much in a state of flux.

What does the interactive direct marketing ecosystem look like?

This is a fascinating time to be working in direct marketing. Over the past 10 years, the rise of digital marketing has created an entirely new way to interact with customers. In fact over that decade digital marketing has grown from virtually nothing to be the largest single marketing channel – bigger in marketing spend terms than press or TV. The change has been remarkable – and yet I believe the biggest changes within the channel are yet to come.

The vast majority of marketing spend on digital is in pursuit of direct marketing goals. In the UK, 80 per cent of digital spend goes on paid search and online classified advertising, which are essentially focused on the direct acquisition of customers. Even within display media, a very small percentage of spend goes on the kind of interruptive, interactive formats that are used to support brand campaigns.

To show how things have changed and are about to change still more, I want to focus on three key areas for digital direct marketers – segmentation, permission and e-mail marketing – and look at how they have changed and are changing.

Segmentation and targeting

The gold standard of offline targeting and customer segmentation is demographic targeting, where target audiences are defined in terms of age, sex and socio-economic group. Demographic targeting is also used in the digital world, but generally plays a subsidiary role to behavioural targeting. In fact much of what we do from a planning point of view can be summed up in a simple philosophy – don't ask, observe.

In its purest form, choice of search terms is a brilliant indicator of purchase intention. Search marketing then lets you overlay keyword selection with other factors like time of day, day of week, location and – belatedly – demographic information. But demographic information can be a false friend. The office manager and the company director will have very different characteristics – yet the director's fancy foreign trips may be being researched and booked by the office manager. Search marketing avoids these issues – if you are searching, you are potentially researching and purchasing.

Display media is where targeting gets really interesting. When you land on a web page, before a banner is served there is a 'data exchange event' –

a real-time conversation between your web browser and multiple adservers to work out which banner should be displayed.

While all this data is anonymous, it is still incredibly rich. We can potentially target on some or all of these factors:

- *Demographic data*: age, gender, income, etc.
- *Environment*: device, operating system, type of browser, bandwidth, ISP.
- *Behaviour*: recent visits to a website, recent search history.
- *Context*: content on the page where the banner is being displayed. Targeting could be by relevant section – say the finance section – or targeted to specific keywords appearing on a page.
- *Time and location*: time of day, day of week, computer location.

To add a further level of complexity, some of these criteria could be used to target a specific audience and others could be used as triggers for 'dynamic creative'. For instance, Harvest Digital has created campaigns for Interflora using dynamic creative based on time of day. If the banner is displayed before 3 pm, the call to action is: 'Order now for same day delivery'; after 3 pm, the banner automatically switches to 'Order now for next day delivery'.

To give another example, Orbitz in the United States realized that visitors to their website using Apple computers tended to have a higher disposable income. So when their banners are shown on Apple devices, they automatically show hotel rooms that are 30 per cent more expensive than the norm.

The rise in web browsing from smart phones and other mobile devices is now giving us yet another segmentation opportunity – user location. For instance, we can bid more to display ads on the mobile phones of consumers who are physically at certain locations – for instance, within walking distance of a particular retail outlet.

These are all exciting opportunities for direct marketers. We have moved from an essentially static form of targeting based at its core on physical location – ie demographic data derived from postcodes – to fluid, real-time targeting based on the changing patterns of consumer behaviour.

Gaining permission

This is a really interesting area because change has for once been driven by legislation and consumer action. Permission in the narrowest sense refers to explicit data capture – normally in digital marketing the acquisition of an e-mail address. As I go on to argue, this kind of permission and the value exchange that supports it are more important than ever.

However, particularly in Europe, we are seeing the development of a secondary level of permission around the acceptance of cookies. Marketers have generally seen this requirement to get some form of (in practice quite weak) permission to use cookies as a major inconvenience. However, I'd suggest that it can be viewed in a positive light.

The 'permission landscape' now looks like this. The inner circle comprises customers where you have transaction-related e-mails alongside marketing e-mail. Beyond that are prospects who have given you permission to e-mail them, perhaps in exchange for a software trial, a free offer or an informative newsletter. And now there is an outer circle, of consumers who have visited our website and given us permission to deploy a range of tracking cookies.

This final category can be reached through re-targeted display advertising. We can't personalize communications since the cookie data is anonymous – but we can infer quite a lot from the other data associated with that cookie. From a content point of view, re-targeted advertising has got a little bogged down on simply replaying the last product you looked at on a website. That's OK on an e-commerce site – although as the same fridge follows you round the internet it does get tedious quite quickly.

However, there is much more that could potentially be done via re-targeting. It is possible to drive re-targeting strategy off rich web analytics data.

E-mail marketing

Finally, e-mail marketing. E-mail is important to digital marketing as the primary channel we use to deliver CRM programmes – but the rise of mobile devices is turning e-mail into a much more powerful channel.

According to MailChimp research, in the UK some 30 per cent of e-mail is now delivered to mobile devices. In the United States, that figure is over 40 per cent and in Japan it is approaching 60 per cent. So e-mail is no longer a way of reaching customers on a desktop computer during work hours – it is a way of reaching customers in real time wherever they are.

This is already making profound changes to the way we create e-mail marketing campaigns. Creative needs to be adapted to work on smaller screens operated by fatter fingers. Conventional thinking about e-mail delivery times needs to be revised.

But beyond this, mobile e-mail will need to adapt to the capabilities of its environment. We can see the possibilities by looking at mobile search marketing, which in addition to offering a conventional click-to-website functionality also offers click-to-call and click-to-view-map.

Thinking further into the future, the mobile phone will become the primary payment mechanism – a kind of mobile wallet. At that point, e-mail becomes an extremely powerful channel to deliver vouchers and offers direct to the consumer, direct to their payment device.

The interactive direct response ecosystem

These add up to really important changes in areas that are the bedrock of the new direct marketing. So what does this do for our diagram (Figure 13.1)?

I have left offline media off this diagram, because I just want to focus on the digital journey. The big changes here are identifying re-marketing and e-mail as separate channels. Here's another way of looking at these

FIGURE 13.1 Interactive direct response ecosystem

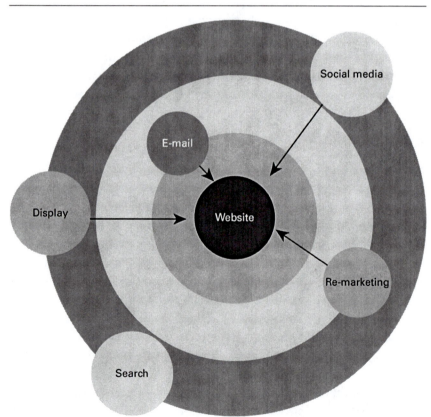

FIGURE 13.2 Channel strategy and a typical customer journey

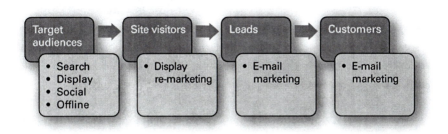

relationships, which shows how channel strategy lines up against a typical customer journey (Figure 13.2).

So where are we heading? Across targeting, gaining permission and e-mail marketing, the potential is there for digital direct marketing to be even more effective than before.

However, it is vital that we bring consumers with us on this journey. We have seen from resistance to text marketing that consumers are very protective of what they see as personal spaces – and hence people may become even more resistant to e-mail marketing as it moves from desktop to mobile.

The key to success will I think come down to the central concept of permission marketing – the value exchange between customer and company at the point at which permission is granted. For this to be a value exchange, we need to have something of value to offer – relevant content, great offers, exclusive information. If we don't offer value, this will become a sterile conversation that consumers will turn their backs on.

The future: opportunities and threats

Permission is quite a dry concept, but what it really comes down to is trust. Will customers trust you with their contact information? If they don't, they are highly unlikely to hand over credit card information!

Earning trust is of course partly around brand reputation – but within digital there is a strong sense that trust is earned through the overall experience you offer online. This is conveyed through technical issues – speed of page downloads, ease of navigation, etc – but also through being clear about the value exchange and dealing directly with any perceived negatives.

However, the fascinating thing about digital marketing from a direct marketing perspective is that even before customers offer personal information to you, it is still possible to infer a great deal of data about them. We potentially know their geographical location, their computer's operating system, how they connect to the internet, their browser type, their screen size, what time of day they tend to come online, what search terms they used, what pages of our website they dwelled on.

One of the arts of this new direct marketing is blending this kind of observed information with the personal data that the customers finally offer when they register. It's obvious that a combination of the two will give us a much fuller picture and allow us to predict future purchasing needs more accurately.

These are exciting opportunities – but what of the threats? In Europe and the United States, there is clear consumer-led pressure against the kind of casual data collection I have described above. The industry will argue that observed data tracked through cookies is not personal data because it is not personally identifiable – but this is an argument that may not be robust enough to survive the next wave of data protection legislation.

So we live in interesting times. At its best, digital direct marketing can offer consumers incredibly relevant, time-sensitive information that will make it easier to take informed decisions in their busy lives. At its worst, it will be seen to be abusing consumers' trust and will fail to reach its full potential.

Creating relevant conversations

SUNDEEP KAPUR

Sundeep Kapur has been assisting organizations with their converged channel marketing strategies since 1990. From direct marketing to digital to converged, he is a passionate teacher who works with businesses across multiple industries, helping them to enable technology and services to brand, personalize and speak to consumers more effectively.

Two personal stories

A very good friend of mine owns a restaurant in London. His patrons enjoy the food and love the personal treatment. Rather than just recognizing the patron, my friend remembers what his customer ate on the previous visit. He begins the conversation with a greeting, tells the customers what they ate the last time, and then asks them if he can make a recommendation. His patrons enjoy this level of recognition and are always open to what my friend recommends.

Contrast this with how my bank treats me. My bank has known me for over 27 years yet the same scene is repeated over and over. I walk up to their ATM, insert my card and am asked to select a language. Next I must choose a transaction, after which I am presented with an exclusive offer. How can you create an offer when you don't recognize me, or for that matter remember my last transaction? How can you create an exclusive offer for me when you still do not know that I speak English?

Create relationships through relevance

Brands need to realize that they can create relationships with consumers through relevant messaging. The right way to build upon this relevant stream of messaging is by listening across all communication channels. While the web makes it easier, the opportunity lies in leveraging this listening across other channels.

By inundating consumers with irrelevant messaging, brands begin alienating the consumers and are only able to get them to pay attention when they need something from the brand.

Brands have three open opportunities to build information about their consumers. The first is when the consumer first arrives – asking the consumer to provide preferences. The second is while interacting with the consumer – observing the consumer's preferences. The third is through testing, segmentation, control groups and associations – basically trying to find what the consumer might respond to.

Provided preferences

Think about asking the consumer some basic questions so you can create a better experience for them while interacting with your brand. Brands start by asking for a name, an address and an array of basic preferences. A men's clothing retailer could ask its consumers to provide it with information about size, clothing preferences and the consumer's preferred medium of communication. An airline might ask you for your e-mail address, mobile number (so they can text you flight changes), home city, preferred destinations and information on other family members. Some financial institutions and retailers even ask you about other family members so they can begin the process of 'householding' the consumers into like groups.

Observed preferences

Brands need to keep track of what they are communicating with their consumers. What is even more important is that they observe how their consumers are reacting to these offers. You, as a consumer, might receive multiple e-mail and mobile messages from your airline. The first e-mail message is their newsletter, which you might ignore. The second message is an offer on domestic flights. You open this e-mail and happen to 'view' or click on two mountain destinations. You receive two confirmation messages from the airline – one by e-mail and one by mobile. You ignore the mobile message and click on the e-mail message. Could it be that you only look at mobile messages when they are important? The next e-mail from the airline might feature round trip fares to New York; you simply open this e-mail. The final e-mail from the airline for the month features two things – its credit card and offers from local restaurants. You open the e-mail and click on the restaurant offers. On the day of your flight you may get two messages – an e-mail and a mobile message; you open the mobile message. What the airline needs to do is make a list of what campaigns the consumer has viewed or opened, as well as a list of everything that the consumer has clicked on. This way the airline can observe what the consumer likes and what the consumer may not like.

Implied preferences

Every consumer interaction can you give you insight into what might be of interest to a particular consumer. If a consumer were to purchase infant shoes, it is very likely that the consumer would be looking for another pair within three months. A purchase of a French cuffed shirt can be enhanced by an offer for cufflinks to the consumer. CRM systems house a lot of data on what can influence a consumer, and it is up to brands to keep testing out implied interactions to see what might be of value. The important thing here is to think about testing your implied offers to a control group before making them available to the entire list. Also, keep in mind that you can use every interaction opportunity to test out what your consumers may be interested in. Think about putting together a list of what your consumer might need from you, prioritize this list and begin communicating.

Asking questions

Surveys continue to be an important way to communicate with consumers. The success of a survey depends on three things – how many people respond to the survey, how much information they provide about themselves, and how honest they can be with the brand. You have to be timely when you ask for feedback from your consumers and try to make the questions as relevant as possible to the interaction. Rather than forcing the consumer to fill out a form where the consumer ranks a product or a service, consider putting out a survey that is top heavy. Start by asking the consumer for information about the interaction. Next, move over to the standard questions such as 'rank my product' and 'rank my service'. A few other keys to successful surveys are brevity, relevance and your ability to translate the survey results into something meaningful for the consumer. Also, here are three additional things to consider so you do not mess up the interactions: first, don't wait a whole year to survey your consumers; second, do not badger your consumers at every interaction for their input; and the third thing is not to ask obvious questions.

Here are three examples of surveys that can alienate a consumer. The first one is a survey from my financial institution. Every year they send me a 46-question survey. The survey is a way for the financial institution to evaluate their business performance. Even if I have a concern, it usually takes them more than three months to get back to me (that is if they do). The second example is a survey by my airline. Every time I call them, I am told about taking a survey so they can improve their performance. It is irritating to continue to be badgered by them at every interaction and so I tend to hang up or avoid them every time I see a survey coming. The third type of survey is the one that does not work properly or where the questions are poorly thought out. Imagine renting a movie and getting a survey from the brand that begins with the obvious question of what movie I rented.

The value of surveys is your ability to build up a relationship with your consumers. Think about my friend's restaurant: if you went to eat at his place, he certainly would want to know if things did not go well. He would also like to use this interaction opportunity to tell you something new about his brand. The value of a well-executed survey is immense; you basically build up your relationship with the consumer.

Is your consumer real?

Sometimes consumers may assume identities to test out the types of offers that a brand may have for them. The recent announcement by Facebook that there are more than 80 million fictitious accounts gives credibility to the fact that a consumer might be willing to assume an identity to get an offer or to see how the brand may treat them. You can avoid issues here by trying to be as transparent as possible with your consumers. Also, think about doing a little research on your consumers to make sure that they are real.

Grabbing your consumers' attention?

Consumers are willing to share information about themselves or their interaction. Brands tend to use three approaches to coax the consumers to interact. One approach is to offer the consumer an incentive, the second approach is to offer some kind of 'intrigue', and the third approach is to try to time it around an interaction. Incentives are successful in getting the consumer to interact with our brands. The challenge lies in sustaining the interaction with particular consumers as you may not be able to receive feedback if they are not offered any incentive. If you are giving away a prize, ask yourself if the consumers are filling out the information to win the prize or are they participating in the survey to tell you more about themselves?

Intrigue gives you the possibility of finding consumers who might be compatible. A company that sells flour used to offer consumers the chance to win $1,000 shopping sprees. They now offer their consumers two or three recipes to choose from. Consumers who are interested in the recipes are consumers that might be interested in purchasing flour from that brand. The third approach is to grab the consumers' attention when they are interacting with you. You have to be careful about timing here because if you do this before they interact, you may slow them down or drive them away. A credit bureau schedules their communications immediately after the consumers have visited their website or completed a transaction. They are successful because they leverage the consumers interaction history and because of their timing – 'striking while the iron is hot'.

Perfecting transactions

HDFC Bank in India has won the Asian Banker of the Year award for being innovative and staying connected with their consumers. The bank started down their road of success by speeding up transactions at the ATM by remembering the consumers' past transactions. The bank now simply greets you with a message that says, 'Hi Sundeep, do you still want Rs 5000?' The time that the consumer has saved is a gift for letting the bank know more about them. Financial institutions and other businesses can now use this interaction history with the consumer to message them across multiple channels. Why not offer the consumer a receipt on their mobile device after an interaction at the ATM? When the customer gets their receipt, give them an offer and allow the consumer to talk about their experience on their social networks.

E-mail is a very personal form of communication. Your goal as a brand is to use this channel to send important information to the consumer. Consumers keep their mobile devices with them at all times and brands need to leverage this channel to ensure that their messaging is timely. Social is a channel to boast or to vent – so brands need to leverage this channel by encouraging the consumer to talk them up. I do realize that there are many brands that are concerned about negative feedback on social media; such feedback is not all bad as two things happen – first, it gives the brand an opportunity to clean up their act. Second, it makes the conversation on social media look real.

Building an intelligent preference centre

Assume you were a concierge at a hotel and were tasked with knowing all your guests so you can serve them better. You would recognize your guests, look up their preferences and try to be as proactive as possible. So if you saw Mrs Jones at 11.00 am, you could ask her about her daughter's college and offer her a taxi to the airport. You might meet Mr Takahashi and ask him if he wants a reservation at the steak house. The important things here are to recognize the consumer, remember what they did the last time (this helps build trust) and anticipate their next transaction – you need to do all this while being extremely personal.

I have an approach that has been very effective as I help businesses build these relationships. I make a list of use cases of how I might serve different consumer segments and only then do I try to use technology to serve these consumers.

Recognition on digital channels is easy; it is the following steps that are very important. Instead of just telling the consumer you have a deal for them, remind them that you know what they did last time and that you hope your recommendation will be appreciated.

Leveraging mobility

Brands also need to think about the idea of mobility. The smartphone is a device that is with the consumer at all times. Why not use this device to engage consumers – you can e-mail them and you can get them to interact on social media. Brands can interact better with mobile consumers by knowing their preferences, knowing their presence, and being as personal or relevant as possible.

Many restaurants provide the consumer with a receipt on which half of the receipt dedicated to soliciting the consumers input through a survey. The same brands also want the consumer to become their friend on social media. Why can't brands start off the interaction by offering a digital receipt – this is convenient for the consumer and also very informative for the brand as it allows them to create real-time offers for the consumer. Next, the brand should seek consumer feedback on social media – allow the consumer to interact on the social network in real time.

Creating interactive conversations

Digital offers us a way to know where our consumers are and also to be very strategic as we interact with consumers. The idea is to think about offering a personal concierge-type service to truly show the consumer that you care. Like a good concierge, you don't want to bore the consumer by asking them to tell you all about themselves in one sitting. Instead, you need to be interactive and keep amassing intelligence about that consumer.

The future of marketing lies in anticipating what our consumers desire, and the best way to do this is by having short conversations that are interactive. Yes, creating interactive conversations is what it is all about.

15 Social media romance

JUSTIN GRAY

Justin Gray is the CEO of LeadMD, a preferred Marketo partner, which specializes in the core functions of a marketing department through either on-demand solutions, consulting or both. Justin is a strong voice and thought leader for the marketing industry, and is frequently called upon to speak and write on a variety of marketing best practices.

Within the tender heart of the interactive brand ecosystem, social media beats on. As companies continue to be converted to a web-centric model of marketing, more and more are discovering that, if used well, social media can play a vital role in driving demand and ultimately building sales. There are hardly ever truly perfect analogies to be drawn, but if there were one, it would be that the art of mastering social media is analogous to the life cycle of a romance. In order to establish the interactive ecosystem, and move it past the 'puppy-love' stage, social media is critical as a support to other efforts as well as a beast all its own. Whether you're a social media junkie or still waiting cautiously in the wings to see how worthwhile it really is, you should know that social media strategy and tools can create deeper customer relationships, and can lead to higher conversions. Here is how to integrate social media in a way that is smart and impactful, and ultimately brings about the fruition of your goals.

Courting social media: what marketers can and can't expect when integrating social with other marketing platforms

When romance initially takes flight, two people are usually feeling giddy about the new relationship. Most companies have experienced this kind of 'newness' excitement when starting a social media campaign. While top executives' hearts have surely not fluttered at the mere sight of the Twitter bird, the idea of having yet another avenue to maximize engagement can be enough to make the most stoic marketer feel dizzyingly interested. Who wouldn't want an (essentially) free way to reach a limitless number of customers? As time has progressed since the business world first discovered that Facebook wasn't just for socializing, and businesspeople have grown wary of the promises they believed these mediums could fulfil, the rapid heartbeats surrounding the concept have cooled a bit. Marketers know by now that they need social media in order to meet their buyers, but they're still not quite sure how to make a connection on the various social platforms. This lesson needs to begin with proper expectations.

One of the most difficult parts of a romantic relationship lies in unfulfilled expectations. With social media, it's imperative to tackle the monster of expectations upfront. No one is going to tell you that social media is going to cure world hunger or single-handedly take your company to a billion dollar net worth. But there is a lot of misinformation about the power of these tools that can be deceptive and set your business up for disappointment and unrealized expectations. To combat this, be realistic.

Invest the time in the beginning to really understand each of the social media tools you're going to engage, and how they can be best utilized. Don't plunge right into your social media strategy by obsessively trying to become the mayor in Foursquare – maybe start by taking the current mayor to coffee (hypothetically of course). It's important to get your feet wet and comprehend why certain platforms work for specific buyer personas, while others don't at all. LinkedIn is not Twitter, and Yelp! is not Facebook. While some social media tools are, in fact, redundant, the big players hold their own and are designed to perform differently from one another. Learn about this. Find out their histories, like you would on a first or second date. You can't know if someone – or a particular platform – is right for you, until you know how your target buyers use that platform. Are they there to research business solutions and expand their network (LinkedIn) or are they there to deepen relationships with people and businesses they identify with (Facebook)? Get digging.

Once you've established the role of the different tools, it's easier to set reasonable expectations. Reasonable expectations for your company will differ from those of another company or even a different department, based on your individual strategy and goals. There are some baseline expectations about social media that are applicable to everyone, though, and useful to keep in mind. Here are a few of the 'givens' for any company:

- You can expect extra work. Someone will have to own the tasks of content creation, consistent monitoring and engagement with customers. Ongoing strategic direction with each tool will be necessary.

- There may be a fairly long lead time before you see results. Few things in life are quick fixes, and social media is no exception. It will take time to build a following, time to win the trust of your prospects, and time to see ROI.

- Social media will rarely drive direct sales on its own. No marketing strategy works without multiple layers, and the interactive ecosystem corroborates that. Layer in the social media, and use it to complement other efforts. Make sure your goals for social are clearly defined – and measurable.

When used appropriately, social media can offer your company a host of bonuses. The various channels allow for quick and fluid conversations with customers, and real-time market research. If your business faces a potentially damaging situation like a PR disaster or misstep, you can immediately take to the social outlets to quell the destruction that's already occurred and give your customers the answers they seek. Even using tools within social media, like the search resource Twitter offers, can give you an idea of what people are saying about you and provide you with a chance to respond accordingly. Instant feedback and communication with your buyers can go a long way in improving your company's standing in the eyes of your audience, which is precisely where it matters most.

Ongoing flirtation: how social media fits into the marketing automation plan and platform

As marketing automation continues to garner attention and become a commonly used tool for millions of businesses, the crossover between social media and automation resources must be delineated. When marketing automation first started gaining traction, social media was not touted as a piece of the puzzle. CRM, e-commerce and e-mail marketing were the main focuses initially, leaving many to wonder if social media would even make sense within the platform of automation. Naturally, things have evolved and there are numerous social media management tools that either fall under the umbrella of marketing automation as stand-alone tools, or integrate with existing marketing automation platforms. The importance of this lies more in how you view the relationship, rather than which particular tool you use. There are many upsides to playing Cupid and pairing up your social media and marketing automation, but also notes worthy of caution.

For instance, if you automate your social media content and it's obvious, your brand will appear lazy, untrustworthy and unengaged. The whole engine behind social media is the nature of conversation. Scheduled tweets, for example, just aren't quite the same as a conversation with a real, live person over Twitter. There are plenty of tools that allow you to automate your social media content and make it sound genuine. And in some cases, such as a news announcement or a scheduled promotion, it's actually okay. But don't make the mistake of thinking your audience can be fooled and that they'll tolerate canned, scheduled interactions every day or even every week.

Designate a real person to interface with customers and prospects who are reaching out to your brand through social channels. The trust that will be established this way will transcend a transitory 'like' on Facebook and result in a deeper relationship and more loyal following. Connections made through social channels should be ported into the nurture funnel and end up driving prospects back to the website. When they reach the website, it's important they are met with encouragement to further the conversation by engaging with webinars, e-books and other content. This is where the conversion engine starts. Marketers should focus on striking the right balance between authenticity and automated tools for time management, all while directing customers back to the hub of the B2B marketing experience – their website. One example of a brand that captures this hard-to-reach but very powerful balance is Salesforce.com. The company (most likely) automates the majority of its social media output, but keeps its interactions real with a lot of involvement from the company's CEO.

Last year when Salesforce CEO Marc Benioff was suddenly ousted from the annual Oracle user conference keynote, with Oracle citing timing issues, Salesforce took to the twittersphere. Over the next 24 hours they organized their own 'keynote' session across from where the Oracle conference was being held. The promotion for the event was held completely online, mainly over Twitter and Facebook. The event took a grassroots, almost protest-type, vibe and in 24 hours Marc's own keynote was delivered to a standing-room-only venue and broadcast live via the company's website – reaching more than the original keynote would have. The Salesforce brand was epito-mized through every piece of conversation; the revolutionary tone used on its social mediums and the creative ways the company magnetically draws an audience create relationships. There's a lot to be learned from this notable company about how to make social interactions count, while still taking advantage of the ease provided by marketing automation.

Chasing the ideal: current best practices for integration and where we'd like to eventually end up

When falling in love, you tend to idealize your significant other in your mind and conjure up images of that person as perfection incarnate. The truth is, no one can be the perfect partner. But, through intentional effort and figuring out how to make the relationship work to its fullest potential, it is entirely possible to attain an ideal partnership. Again, read into this the parallels with social media integration. There isn't one way, or even an ultimately perfect way to use it, but eventually an ideal integration can be obtained with enough analysis and hard work.

Many marketing automation companies offer social media products as well, like Salesforce.com's Social Marketing Cloud or Marketo's offerings of interactive B2B social media applications. Before jumping on the band-wagon of using any product just for the sake of using it, figure out how your overall marketing automation strategy is set to work. If social media falls into the plan (and it most likely will in some capacity or another), deter-mine the best platform to use so integration with your current marketing automation can be seamless. You may already be using Salesforce.com, for example, but may discover through honest analysis that all you need for your social media tool is something like Hootsuite. Don't feel you need to match brands to brands unless the synergy between products is unparalleled; focus instead on finding the social media tool whose hand fits yours.

The eventual ideal integration that will hopefully show its face down the road will be an even more customizable tool. As each brand is different, social media automation and management tools should have a more modular makeup, so companies can handpick the elements necessary for a successful integration with their existing strategies. The integration would be straightforward and blend in with whichever marketing automation platform the business is using, and preferably track social media efforts on the same dashboard where other marketing efforts reside. This sort of ideal integration is not going to materialize in the imminent future, but it'll evolve to this point sometime over the next few years. In the meantime, keep chasing the ideal and making the best of where things stand presently.

Nurturing the relationship: how to make social media part of the nurture funnel

Once a relationship is established, the work sets in. Often taking the place of the banter and excitement is the work of nurturing. With marketing automation, nurturing is one of the most essential parts of a solid customer-brand relationship. Having multiple touches of a carefully selected variety along the nurture funnel keeps a company on the customer's mind, and keeps the customer apprised of new products and new ways to interact with the company. You can very easily make social media a piece of the nurture funnel, and it's a very good way to meet people where they are. After all, 62 per cent of adults worldwide currently are involved with social media. With that massive number of people being accessible in an online, easily reachable environment, it stands to reason that businesses engaging through these outlets make sense.

Social media is a highly effective platform for inquiries, and that's a good place to start with the nurture funnel. Most buyers need some time to understand your company and your products or services, and they will probably have questions. Allowing an open forum for asking questions and learning more will make a more informed prospect and a more likely buyer. If a customer inquires about something on a social channel, be sure there is someone there to answer them thoroughly – and quickly. Time is of the essence with this age of instant gratification, and if you lose the instantaneous interaction you may lose the prospect. Once a slightly deeper relationship has been forged through simple Q&A, you can use social media to learn a lot more about your leads. See what content they share, and give them incentives to share your content as well. Find out what their pain-points are, and proactively offer them resources (read: not sales pitches) to help them out. As the prospect progresses through the nurture funnel, maintain the conversation through social channels and utilize social media analytics to gauge how the interaction is going. When you think about it, socializing and nurturing really are cut of the same cloth and made for one another.

An important part of making nurturing powerful is being sure you're giving value to your prospects through the most fitting channels. One company that has done its homework on how to use the different social media tools is the retail giant Zappos. A glance at its Facebook page, and you'll notice numerous customer-centric campaigns built around lively and interesting graphics. Customers on Facebook aren't looking for in-depth articles, for instance, and if you try to serve them something out of the realm of what they're there for, they will disengage. If you check out Zappos' Twitter page, you'll see that the content and overall vibe is different than that of its Facebook presence. On Twitter, Zappos showcases its customer service people by using its wallpaper to display their pictures, making them relatable. Its Twitter is used more as a customer service tool, and a way to respond to customers' needs. Twitter is a better forum for brief questions and concerns, and Zappos hits the mark again by using it accordingly. It's tempting to try to force a one-size-fits-all shell onto all social media platforms, but you're best served following Zappos' example and customizing each one to make the best use of its unique purposes. Your prospects are more likely to receive what you're trying to give them, and will move along the nurture funnel more quickly.

Reward of the relational investment: what points best indicate social media ROI

Ultimately, when all the flowers and chocolates and heart-shaped plush gifts are stripped away, a relationship is only invested in if there is something deeper and more rewarding to get from it. The same goes for social media. If there could never be ROI established for social media efforts, there would be absolutely no point to doing it, aside from giving customers a few warm fuzzies and feeling like you're a basically nice company. Depending on who you speak to, ROI can be calculated very scientifically based on your costs to execute your strategy and various values, or it can be something as simple as contrasting your sales and revenue before implementing social media with your sales and revenue after it's been in use for a set period of time. It's up to you and your company to determine how your business best determines ROI, but there are a few giveaways to whether or not you are getting a healthy ROI with your social media strategy.

First, if you can directly attribute spikes in website traffic (regardless of conversions) to links or directives on your social channels, this is already a great start. Adhering to the principles of the interactive ecosystem, getting prospects to your website is the number one goal, so anything helping to support that is worth its while. Second, if you start to have customers actually engaging with your brand beyond complaints or product-related questions, you will most likely end up with solid ROI. It's been said that time is money, which is true, but it's also the only resource everybody has that is incredibly limited. Time cannot be extended, and we all are given the same amount on a daily basis. If a prospect is choosing to spend their time on fun or interesting engagement opportunities with your brand, you can nearly guarantee you will see sales as a result. And the more happy customers you have, the more buyers you will ultimately have. People believe their friends 10-fold over advertisers, so loyal customers equate to brand advocates that will do your work for you (and, dare I say, better than you since their credibility is already established with their friends). Lastly, you really should find a way to measure cold, hard metrics as best you can. When the time comes to prove whether social media is really worth the costs to your company, you will need more than some approximations to make your case for a continuing budget. If you handle the tools intelligently, you will almost always see a substantial ROI, so give it your best shot.

The interactive ecosystem needs thrumming innovations to survive and thrive, and social media is one of these. Using social media is akin to a romance, with many of the pitfalls and hardships, but all the positive memories and ultimate rewards as well. It's up to you to decide if the latter outweigh the former, but if you approach social media with rational expectations and understand its role within your unique company, you are sure to end up in a satisfied marriage of evolving technology and customer loyalty.

16 Changing face of Facebook marketing

KRISTEN JAMES

Kristen is a professional writer and editor and has over 20 published works. Her e-books have hit the top 100 Bestsellers in Kindle, Number 1 in free and many different categories. She freelances a wide spectrum of writing, from business to fiction to web content.

In every language and in every part of the world, people talk about the weather. It's something that's universal, affects everyone and changes constantly. In today's rapidly changing world, we can almost say the same about Facebook: most people connect on Facebook, making it a marketing gold rush. More and more, this central social connecting site wields as much marketing power as TV, especially when used together with it. Facebook needs to be a vital asset in your overall marketing strategy because:

- Facebook is not only interactive, it offers your customers the opportunity to share your business with their friends.
- You can target users by their interests, location and even friends.
- You can attract fans through 'common interests' as you share relevant, fun, helpful information or current news.
- You are competing with many start-ups and small companies that market through Facebook extensively, and maybe exclusively, so that they become early adopters and experts at engaging users.

Facebook began as a social networking site but it now generates revenue by catering to businesses. As an author, I market almost exclusively on Facebook through free social networking, paid ads, sponsored stories and sponsored posts. If you spend a few minutes on the site, paying attention to the side bar and news stories in your feed, you'll see a multitude of businesses are active on Facebook. The site's own Business page boasts four success stories:

- State Bicycle Company reported $500k in annual sales from Facebook, with 12 per cent of their traffic coming from the site.
- Hubspot saw a 71 per cent sales increase from Facebook and a 39 per cent increase in traffic from it.
- Luxury Link saw a 100 per cent increase in sales from Facebook, with 90 per cent of purchases from new customers and a 30 per cent increase in site visits.
- Canvas People experienced 3,959 transactions from its Facebook campaign and got 180,000 Canvas People Page likes.

  (August 2012. Read more details at **http://www.facebook.com/ business/success**)

These few companies are examples of huge successes. There are thousands of businesses that may or may not do well, and a large factor in success is how well you utilize all of Facebook's marketing offerings. The true challenge for marketers is to evolve along with Facebook and be an early adopter of new features. First, let's make sure we're on the same page, and then we'll discuss how to maximize marketing opportunities through Facebook's changes.

Whatever your marketing goals are on Facebook, you need to keep one encompassing goal in mind: your company needs to be another friend, not a spammer that constantly pushes products or services. People are on Facebook to interact with friends. There is some kind of passion at the heart of your business, and that's what you can share with people.

How to lose fans

Many pages fall into the trap of promoting to their existing Facebook fans. You don't have to preach to the choir, which will in fact cause fans to 'unlike' the page. As an author, I use a 90/10 per cent split – 90 per cent of posts should be fun, informative or offer something outside my product or service while only 10 per cent of my posts actually promote it. The 10 per cent can include new specials, new offerings or something beneficial to my existing client base. A well-established product, such as Coke, can get away with direct promoting more often because people love Coke. However, if you look at Coke's page, it doesn't push ads. It simply shows photos of people enjoying Coke, with captions such as 'Better with friends'.

How to gain fans

You want to excite your existing fans with the core idea of your online identity. Coke utilizes our feelings of refreshment associated with the drink along with connecting/linking good memories with family and friends.

As I write this during the 2012 Olympics, the Coke page shows Olympians drinking Coke. Another post shows Shawn Johnson holding a Coke and wearing her medals, and it invites fans to post questions for a live Q&A. Coke was hugely popular before Facebook ever came along, so Coke lovers naturally liked the page when it was created. The same might be true for Starbucks, another extremely popular Facebook Page, but I see many applicable lessons on this one. It's very interactive and posts questions on a regular basis. What's your favourite drink? Favourite topping? Favourite location? An app allows users to check in at their Starbucks. There is even an app to reload gift cards for yourself or others. Starbucks uses apps to provide the interactivity that users crave.

Get noticed

What will make people take notice, care and share your posts, pictures and links? Because Facebook is a new medium compared with campaigns in years past, it might be confusing. However, some of the same principles apply. Some of my favourite commercials as a kid were the Coke ads featuring the polar bears. I still have my Coke teddy bear. I also loved the Budweiser commercials featuring draft horses pulling a carriage in the snow. Polar bears don't have anything do to with Coke, except in these ads. Horses have nothing to do with beer either.

You can use this on Facebook when you share photos that link something people like with your product and name. You have the added benefit of including your name, web address or Facebook address on the photo.

When you share pictures, quotes, etc from other pages, it can get likes and shares from your page and take up your 'people talking about this' number. It's even better when you upload a picture so that, when it's shared, Facebook will say Jane Doe shared Coke's picture.

Changes on Facebook

The introduction of Timeline created a tidal wave of user complaints on Facebook. People naturally resist change. However, early adopters found they liked the new features. Yes, it was a bit confusing at first, but resisting and complaining only holds you back from taking advantage of new opportunities.

The cover banner gives businesses a chance to customize their page. Authors are including cover shots of their books. Companies can display product pictures. Everyone can update their cover for new products, promotions and current events. While you don't want to spam the universe with your posts, your cover can. In fact, it should. It connects your Facebook page to your overall marketing campaign by incorporating your logo and/or products.

Coke's cover banner is a close-up of a can with water beads on it. I can feel the chill and imagine the refreshing coolness of a cold Coke on a hot summer day. That's powerful. The Starbucks cover displays the tops of several yummy, frothy drinks, creating an emotional sensory experience of warm, delicious coffee. The banner is your online billboard, displaying the heart of your campaign, while your profile picture, which appears set against your banner, is your identity. It's an awesome way to link your logo with your marketing campaign.

Facebook made a small change in 2012 by adding how many people are talking about a page right after how many likes a page has. It might look good to have 5,000 likes, but not so much if only 39 people are talking about it. This number goes up when you get more likes, when people comment on your page or posts, like your posts and share them. Paying for likes isn't completely new, but Facebook is constantly updating and improving their ads. You can pay for sponsored stories or ads, and a recent change enables marketers to market to friends of fans. This is huge.

Let's say your company is included in a recent news story and you share the link along with a quick tag line. Next you promote the post to friends of your fans. These people can like your page directly from the post.

A Facebook special is a great way to encourage people to visit one of your physical locations. A post on Starbuck's page shows a drink in the foreground with a dock out over blue waters in the background. The post says: 'How are you enjoying that treat receipt? Get a $2 grande ice drink after 2pm with your morning receipt.' There are 788 shares, 23,253 post likes and 487 comments. Only the Facebook person at Starbucks knows if this is a sponsored post, but I'm willing to bet it is. If you sponsor a special or ad, you can get a monetary return on investment.

Embrace change

All the advice and information in this essay will stem from one main idea: embrace change on Facebook. Learn how to use new features and maximize the benefits before everyone else does. Facebook is innovative and makes changes with the aim of helping you advertise and reach more people. This is even truer now that Facebook has stockholders to please. Now Facebook is essentially a business that sells 'connectivity'. It's your job to explore and maximize marketing benefits through their many new offerings.

Essentials of mobile marketing technologies

17

DAVID MARUTIAK

David Marutiak is the Managing Director of the UK office for Scanbuy, a barcode services provider based in New York City. Dave has been in communications for over three decades, with his recent work focused on mobile commerce and social networking applications on consumer smartphones.

The typical mobile marketing campaign takes advantage of the inherent two-way communication path with the target audience. Since mobile readers increasingly have mobile internet connectivity and smartphones for their platform, there has been a general shift towards these in many developed countries. Agencies and brands that want to activate their customer base, build new customer leads, or ultimately to engage their readers in a conversation have a broader set of solutions for that than ever before. A brief overview of their options includes:

- providing a phone number to call a customer service representative or access a pre-recorded audio message;
- providing a short code for readers to text in, with a response sent to the phone's text messaging feature;
- providing a short code for readers to text in, with a response sent via an MMS to the reader's phone;
- providing a URL for the user to manually enter in the mobile phone's browser;

- providing a QR code (or equivalent) that allows the user to easily scan with a common application and be redirected to the phone's browser or to run a command on the phone;

- indicating that the reader should use an image recognition application to scan the advertisement in order to reach the brand or access additional information;

- indicating that the reader should use an augmented reality application to scan the advertisement in order to see the brand's commercial overlaid on the advertisement;

- indicating that the reader should use an audio recognition application to sense an audio track of an advertisement and gain access to additional information;

- indicating that the advertisement has an NFC chip embedded in it along with a prompt for the reader to use a compatible hardware reader in their phone.

There are various advantages and shortcomings of each access method. Some work on any phone, some work only on specific hardware, some require specific software applications, some are language dependent, and finally the very diversity of options makes the decision complex. A quick summary of these (drawn from examples across a wide diversity of suppliers) is shown in Table 17.1. It's worth noting that the mobile ecosystem is always evolving

TABLE 17.1 Strengths and weaknesses of access types

Access Type	Phone Type	Strength	Weakness	Illustrative Service Provider	Magnitude of the Cost Factors
Voice Call	All	Ubiquitous	Time taken	MNO	CSR
SMS Text	All	Ubiquitous	Limited data	IMI Mobile	Per SMS
MMS	All	Widespread	Regional	IMI Mobile	Per MMS
Browser	Most	Widespread	Manual entry	WWW	Monthly
QR Code	Smart	Widespread	Security	Scanbuy	QR Campaign
Image Rec	Smart	Novelty	Prop client	LTU	Image Librar
Aug Reality	Smart	Visual Nature	Prop client	Blippar	AR Campaig
Audio Rec	Smart	Similar Use	Prop databse	Shazam	Campaign
NFC	New	Monetization	Limited avail	ISIS	% Revenue

rapidly, is regionally dependent, and has a number of technology dependencies. For instance, many of the use cases that were once used to justify Bluetooth chips in phones were then used to justify adding WiFi chips to phones and are now used to justify NFC chips in phones. It's also worth noting that smartphone platforms allow users to download new software-only applications readily, while deploying new hardware across a marketplace takes a number of years.

Comparing mobile access types

Network architectures

The basic network architectures of the various technologies are similar at a high enough level. The mobile reader's interactive response is handled by a server, which in barcode technologies is called the Code Management Platform (CMP). The CMP handles the real-time response of answering the inquiry and sending commands down to the mobile phone. There are often additional servers whose roles include the authoring station for the brand or agency putting the campaign together, compiling the data from the campaign and presenting it in a set of friendly analytics to allow the author to tailor the campaign or to compile and organize a variety of campaigns, and then a server or two that process the data from the campaign and (often) dovetail it with the brand's back-end information servers. These back-end servers have the customer proprietary data in them, the billing or CRM information, and the product-specific information (eg specifications for a particular part or design).

Many access technologies are covered by industry standard specifications that allow for smooth interoperability, and common technologies that can be implemented by a wide variety of vendors and service providers. In such situations, the vendor who supplies the client-side technology (that which is within the mobile phone) can interwork with any server-side technology (eg the CMP) from other service providers. Others are built on a proprietary design, where the client and the server have to come from the same vendor. Both approaches are valid and have their own pros and cons, as summarized in the previous section.

Another option is for service providers to cooperate 'behind the scenes' to ensure the transaction. In fact, as discussed above, there is always a mobile network operator providing service to the reader. Sometimes they just carry the traffic back and forth, transparently. Other times they provide the transaction handling themselves in addition to, or instead of, a third-party service provider. These types of arrangements are even more likely to

FIGURE 17.1 Code management

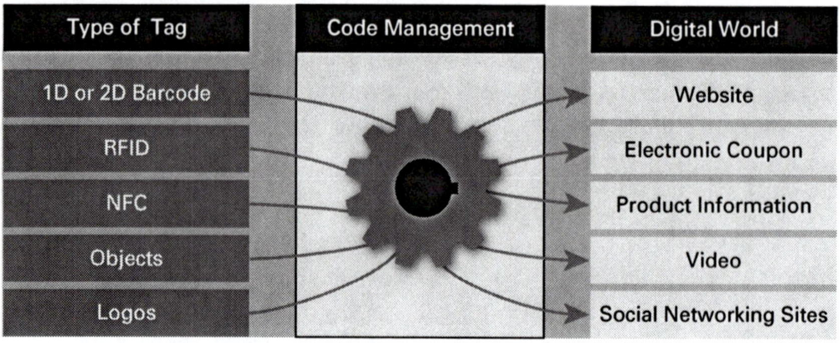

Type of Tag	Code Management	Digital World
1D or 2D Barcode		Website
RFID		Electronic Coupon
NFC		Product Information
Objects		Video
Logos		Social Networking Sites

use industry standards, to ensure interoperability and an open and competitive market for the services.

For the sake of this article, we'll just use the term Code Management Platform (CMP) as shorthand to refer to any server or set of servers that provide interactive mobile marketing services. The requisite features of such a 'CMP' are that it:

- provides a user friendly interface for brands and/or agencies to initialize and administer a variety of interactive mobile marketing campaigns;

- processes a dynamic set of inputs from mobile users who have read about a campaign and want to interact with it;

- interworks with additional servers, services or websites maintained by the brand and/or agencies that contain customer proprietary information;

- provides a flexible suite of analytics to enable the brands and/or agencies to track the results of a campaign, tailor its nature in real time or evaluate its effectiveness.

This last point is worth explaining. The hard work of the CMP is processing the transactions in real time, since the effectiveness of it there determines much of the reader's experience in the campaign. However, the analytics provided to the brand/agency are very much key to the experience that they have with the technologies and vendors involved. A simple illustration might help – Figure 17.2 shows a typical set of analytics from a barcode campaign vendor.

As you can see, the simple act of scanning a barcode and retrieving some product information has provided a treasure trove of analytics to the brand. They know the type of phones being used, the type of software on them, the

FIGURE 17.2 Analytics from a barcode campaign vendor

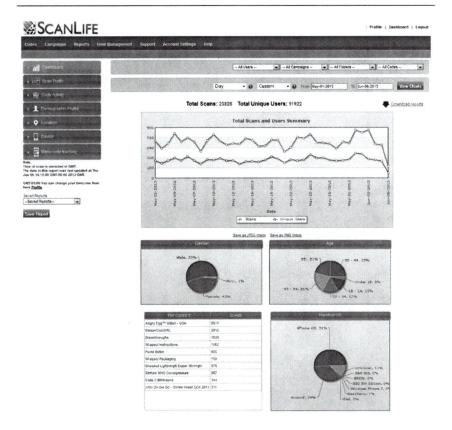

traffic generated by the time of day and day of week, etc. This information is invaluable to the brand or agency in determining the effectiveness of the campaign and the return on their investment.

Knowing that a particular media type (eg posters in bus stops versus ads in papers) is getting more scans than another helps the brand tailor their next campaign. In fact, knowing that putting an ad in a Sunday paper returns more scans than a Monday–Wednesday run of the same ad in the same paper is worth even more. Finally, for a campaign that uses 300 posters scattered around town to get the word out it would be nice to know the locations that are being read most often. Another key facet of many of the technologies illustrated is that they can also provide location information about the reader (subject to their permission, of course). An example would look like Figure 17.3.

Now the brand or agency would know which posters are working and worth using again, and which ones aren't worth the time or investment.

FIGURE 17.3 Providing customer locations

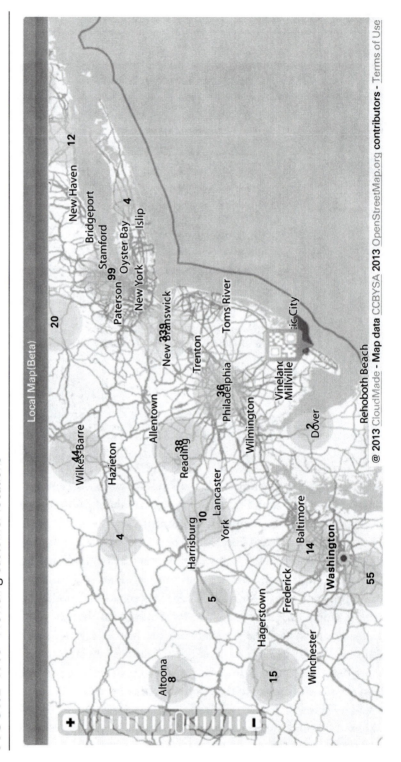

FIGURE 17.4 Tracking the efficiency of signage

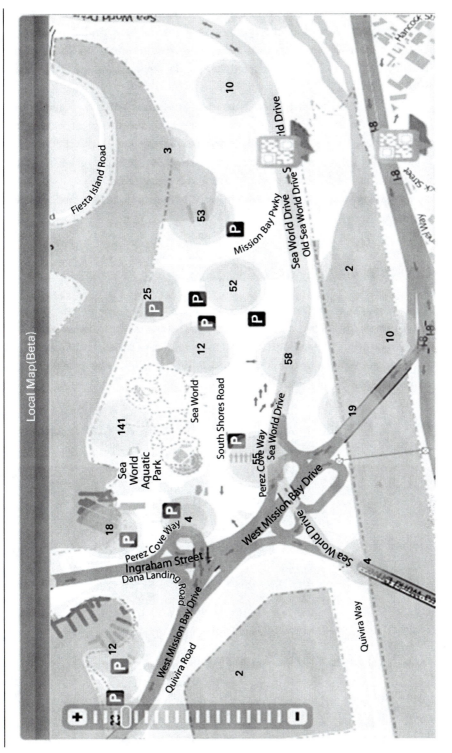

Real-time analytics around the reader's location information are another unique aspect of mobile marketing-based interactions and a powerful tool. For example, the SeaWorld theme park used the information shown in Figure 17.4 to track the effectiveness of different signage around their park.

The desire to benefit from compiled analytics, across a variety of interactive technologies, is a great example of the utility of having a common CMP for them. The insights gained from seeing the differences between the response rate of barcodes versus image recognition, or the number of new sales leads gained from audio recognition versus NFC, etc, can be powerful additions to help tailor future campaigns (or an existing one in real time).

Code action types

It's also important to note that the access method can determine the nature and limits of the response that the CMP can return to the mobile reader. In addition, vendors may support some that are unique to themselves. Table 17.2 gives an example of potential commands that a QR service provider can return to a mobile phone.

TABLE 17.2   Commands that a QR service provider can return to a mobile phone

Code actions	Phone response
Web	Return a URL and launch the phone's web browser to it
Video	Send a video that's optimized for mobile phones
Text	Pre-populate an SMS address and message for one-button Send
Voice	Pre-populate a phone number for one-button dialing
Menu	Send down a web page that provides options the user selects
Contests/lottos	Enter the reader into a contest, choosing winners at random, every 5th, etc

TABLE 17.2 *continued*

Code actions	Phone response
Audio	Send the user to an audio track to play or audio file to download
OS/browser	Send the reader to the right app store for their device to download an app
Note	Send down a note to the phone (eg, use this voucher for 15% off)
Twitter	Pre-populate a tweet for the user to send
Facebook	Allow the user to 'like' your Facebook page with one button
E-mail	Pre-populate an address and message for the user to mail
Contact cards	Download a contact card to the user's phone
Calendar	Insert a pre-populated date in the user's calendar

Note that the commands can be used in a variety of ways. For instance, sending users to a web URL can result in them downloading applications, videos or music for different campaigns. There is a lot of compliance with standards in many cases, but there are a lot of phone and OS specific variations to watch out for. If you want the greatest chance of completing the conversation with the reader, it's important to test many combinations of phones and software while building out a campaign. Finally, most of the information garnered during the scan can be sent up to the brand's own IT and CRM systems for real-time interactions with the customer proprietary information stored there.

Managing a different set of code actions for each mobile access method is another complication of using separate CMPs. While it may not be apparent, managing the variety of digital assets alone can be a nightmare – especially if they're distributed across different regions or subsidiaries.

Illustrative campaign results

- Coca-Cola used the OS Detection code action to direct QR readers to different destinations, based on whether their application was available for download for that specific phone type.

- Taco Bell received over 450,000 scans in a six-week campaign for downloading MTV videos.

- *Stylist Magazine* ran a recent AR issue that received 265,000 users, with 150,000 scans over 7 per cent of publication's readers.

It's clear that both existing and evolving interaction methods for mobile phone users are mushrooming and provide a fundamental part of the interactive brand ecosystem. In fact, the traffic has been growing exponentially for a variety of service providers.[1] It's reasonable to expect mature marketing agencies and brands to be looking at 'multichannel' campaigns just within the mobile channel as a result. The interactive brands will want to facilitate conversations from any potential mobile user, not just ones with a specific phone or software combination(s).

FIGURE 17.5 Campaign example 1

OS Detection linked iPhone users to an exclusive app download and redirected other users to a video on the Snowball Effect campaign

iPhone users   Android and other users

FIGURE 17.6 Campaign example 2

FIGURE 17.7 Campaign example 3

Multi-modal campaign examples

This section provides some near-term, concrete examples of how people are already deploying campaigns based on multiple input technologies.

NFC/QR – Oakland Parking Meters

One natural match is that evolving m-commerce system built on NFC-equipped phones and the wide ubiquity of barcode scanning software on existing smartphones. This is going to be very common over the next three to five years while the NFC enabled handsets make their way into the market in larger quantities. By way of example, the City of Oakland, California, has provisioned its parking meters so they can take either QR Codes or NFC devices alternatively (Figure 17.8).

FIGURE 17.8 Campaign example 4

QR/AR – OnVert

Another natural match is the interplay between the proprietary client/server nature of augmented reality and the open standards approach of QR Codes. OnVert is a relatively new company, specializing in combining QR Codes with Augmented Reality Experiences (Figure 17.9).

FIGURE 17.9 Onvert

Conclusions

As with most interactive campaigns that deal with the mobile ecosystem, the diversity and technical variations are complex. The ever-growing diversity of access methods makes broad spread campaigns more complex, especially for brands that want to reach out to readers regardless of the type of phone or software they may have in their hands when they read the advertisement. There's no need to leave significant quantities of interested readers out in the cold.

However, having entirely different and disjoint technical implementations can only aggravate the marketing agency or brand's problems when it comes to creating, distributing and managing the content and logic of a given campaign. The problem can be managed by building towards a common code management platform (or equivalent) to both handle the variety of access methods and provide a unified analytical platform for the different facets of the campaign and yet a unified view of the overall response and resultant conversations.

In fact, this is also the stated direction for some leading vendors already.

Note

1   Cite recent update to ScanLife statistics – 110 per cent increase quarter over quarter, 60M+ scans a year, etc, and recent update to NeoMedia statistics – 150 per cent increase over last year.

18 How brands can succeed in the local mobile revolution

PAUL BRUEMMER

Paul Bruemmer is the Managing Partner of PB Communications LLC and has a 17-year proven track record improving performance for enterprise organizations in semantic SEO and Google compliance SEO best practices.

As internet marketers, we have a lot in common. We offer our products and services to consumers, and we wish to gain new customers while satisfying our existing customers in the interactive brand ecosystem. To achieve our marketing goals, we employ both traditional and internet marketing tactics, with an increasing focus on the internet. Why? Because the internet is so easy and convenient to use that everyone flocks to the web to accomplish everyday tasks and save precious time. Research shows 78 per cent of US adults (95 per cent of teenagers, 80 per cent of men and 76 per cent of women) use the internet (Pew Internet, *American Life*). Forget the phone book; it's easier to browse on a mobile device – anytime, any-where – to search for local businesses, research products/services, compare prices, purchase online and more.

Over the past 15+ years, marketers have built websites while using online marketing tactics such as display ads, search engines, e-mail, blogs, social media, mobile marketing, social media business pages, local search engines and more. These tactics are now in the mainstream and are gradually replac-ing many traditional marketing tactics. Marketers tweet, and they collect

FIGURE 18.1 Browsing on mobile

'likes' and Google +1s because all these marketing efforts can help a business grow rapidly. The fastest growing marketing tactic in the interactive brand ecosystem is local/mobile search marketing, as mobile users increasingly use smartphones and tablets to accomplish every task imaginable.

Over half of searches have local intent

Yahoo! CEO Marissa Mayer (formerly Google VP) indicated 20 per cent of Google searches and 40 per cent of mobile searches were local in 2009. More recently, it's estimated 53 per cent of searches have local intent (Microsoft, 2010). The 5th Annual 15miles/Localeze Local Search Usage Study by comScore (2012) shows local searches have increased 144 per cent over the last five years, an impressive growth rate. For marketers, local/mobile marketing is the next big thing!

FIGURE 18.2 Search increases over past five years

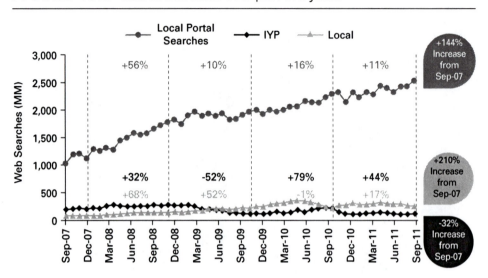

Why you need a local internet presence

In today's interactive brand ecosystem, it's important to have a prominent local presence to get found and stand out from the crowd. Here's why:

- 50 per cent of all searches are local in intent (Microsoft, 2010).
- Local search has increased 144 per cent over the last five years (comScore, 2012).
- 5.9 billion mobile subscribers worldwide with 87 per cent global penetration (ICT, 2011).
- 89 per cent of US subscribers use their devices on a daily basis (Google Research, 2011).

While SMBs can claim a local listing on Google+ Local, Yahoo! Local, Bing Business Portal and internet information services, big brands like GM, Pepsi Cola and other enterprise-level brands must deliver consistent data fidelity in their local listings with, for example, information consistency across the web, mobile web, internet information services, search engines and social pages. Achieving this result requires marketing skills and software automation, along with knowledge transfer from subject-matter experts.

Recent studies also show that 70 per cent of US households use the internet when making local buying decisions and 97 per cent of consumers say they research local businesses before making a decision (BIA Kelsey, 2010).

However, the latest trends indicate Yellow Pages advertising, newspaper advertising and direct mail are becoming less effective as usage keeps going down. While the number of online local searches for products and services is expected to grow at a rate of 33 per cent each year for the remainder of the decade, print business directories like the Yellow Pages are expected to decline by 4 per cent per year.

Another growing trend is the importance of customer reviews. Customers are posting reviews online and sharing their reviews via social media sites like Yelp and Epinions. Reviews rank highly in search results because local search algorithms place more weight on the review quantity. The importance of encouraging reviews was not lost on retailers and merchants, as 88 per cent of respondents to Marketing Sherpa's 2012 Search Marketing Benchmark report said customer reviews are important for achieving marketing objectives.

Local listings are rated 'most relevant' and 'trusted'

Consumers chose local search results almost 2 to 1 over organic results (paid results at the top and side scored lowest) in the 5th Annual 15 miles/LocalEze Local Search Usage Study Conducted by comScore (2012). Customers in local search mode prefer business listing information with NAP (name, address, and phone number) to promotional advertising. Local searchers' post-search contact methods were:

- 38 per cent via store visit;
- 29 per cent via phone;
- 12 per cent via online contact.

Online reviews matter

Consumer online reviews play an increasing role in helping shoppers assess the quality and trustworthiness of businesses, products and services. Online reviews provide subjective information for buyers, allowing them to pre-judge a business or product based on the experience of other consumers before making a buying decision. The 2012 Local Consumer Review Survey by BrightLocal reported the following:

- 58 per cent of consumers trust a business with positive online reviews.

- 72 per cent of consumers trust online reviews as much as personal recommendations.

FIGURE 18.3 Online reviews and customer trust

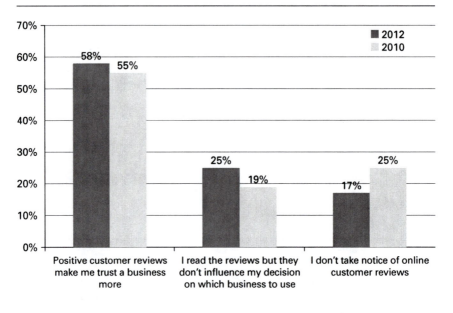

Mobile devices impact local search and buying behaviour

Tablet owners are the most active local searchers and have a higher likelihood of making a purchase (LocalEze-comScore, 2012):

- 64 per cent per cent search weekly for local businesses on tablets.

- 86 per cent made a purchase from their most recent tablet-based local search.

Smartphone users actively conduct local searches from their devices:

- 61 per cent conduct local searches from their mobile device.

- The Number 1 reason for local searches on mobile devices is fast information on the go.

Changes in consumer buying behaviour

Consumers have been finding local business information in new ways, including social, daily deals, couponing, and apps:

- 15 per cent of local searchers found businesses from social networking (LocalEze-comScore).
- 60 per cent are using daily deals (LocalEze-comScore).
- 81 per cent of consumers use coupons (NCH, 2012).
- 49 per cent of mobile and tablet users use apps for local business searches (LocalEze-comScore).
- 82 per cent of local searchers follow up offline via in-store visit, phone call or purchase (TMP-comScore).
- 57 per cent of internet users shop online and purchase offline (NPD Group).
- 61 per cent of local searches result in purchase (TMP-comScore).

How can brands like Ford and Coca Cola take advantage of the upward trend in local and mobile search? Below are some tips for optimizing big-brand, multi-location business for local mobile and organic search.

Create web and mobile web location landing pages for major search engines

Start by optimizing your brand for local search in Google+ Local, Yahoo Local and the Bing Business Portal. While SMBs can claim their local listings, ensuring they are accurate, current and consistent across locations, big brands with multiple locations would be better off with a web/mobile store locator that optimizes their listings automatically and consistently for all their locations as shown below:

- claim the brand's managed listing;
- verify each business location address and telephone number;
- provide enhanced content;
- business hours, directions, reviews, etc;
- payments accepted;
- localized description;
- local categories;

- local images;
- local coupons;
- local phone reporting;
- social network links;
- unmanaged URLs;
- links to store pages;
- links to mobile pages.

Optimize location and mobile landing pages for local SEO

This is more complicated than simply claiming your listings in local search engines. We suggest big brands optimize their landing pages by creating an SEO Scorecard for their digital storefront and mobile storefront to see what is required. There are four web elements to validate and several dozen areas of analysis to document in an SEO Scorecard as complete versus incomplete. For both the web and mobile web, look at these four items in depth:

- Web store locator: 20 variables to meet compliance with search engine best practices.
- Individual location landing pages: five variables to meet compliance with search engine best practices.
- Local page enhanced content: 14 variables to meet compliance with search engine best practices.
- Best practice localized SEO on each page: 10 variables to meet compliance with search engine best practices.

The above features, along with search engine best practices integration and submission to information services and IYP directories are required to optimize location and mobile landing pages for local SEO. For big brands with multiple locations, these features have been packaged into a single, automated solution. An automated solution is required to address the sophistication of achieving remarkable results in local and mobile for today's enterprise-level, multi-location businesses.

The results below were achieved by a national retailer using local (maps), organic (SEO) and mobile (smartphone) best practices.

- 60 per cent+ of total web users click on coupons.
- 22 per cent+ of mobile users click on operating hours.

- 16 per cent+ of mobile users click on maps.
- 5 per cent of total web users click on driving directions.
- 2.7 per cent of web users click 'Shop online'.

The results below were achieved by a dealership network using local (maps), organic (SEO) and mobile (smartphone) best practices.

57.5 per cent of total users call Business Location. Features include:

- call tracking;
- time of day;
- duration;
- demographics;
- missed calls;
- call recording capability;
- specialized service levels by department.

Create a great user experience with multiple conversion tools on your location pages

Compounding the fact that brands may not be optimized for local key-words on the web/mobile web is the fact that brands are not maximizing conversion tools for web and mobile. In order to be found, brands must have a set of conversion tools that provide consumers with the features they expect to find on the web and mobile when looking for local businesses. These conversion tools consist of the data described below:

- business data consistency on the web and mobile web;
- business hours, holiday hours;
- click to telephone call;
- click to map and directions;
- click to shopping;
- redeem coupons: print to web to phone;
- promotions, national to individual store locations;
- reviews;
- gift cards;
- incentives;

- loyalty programmes;
- forms to join/register.

This data is the information consumers like to have handy and in the same place for convenience and time savings when shopping or finding events, restaurants, entertainment and so forth. In today's busy world, time is of essence, and consumers will be attracted to local businesses that provide consumers with all this information at their fingertips when searching the web and mobile.

Conversion tools are features that can be provided by a web store locator and/or a mobile store locator software solution. Such a solution is desirable for big brands with multiple locations and can accomplish the following:

- recognize the user IP address on the web/mobile store locator;
- allow the user to search by city, state, zip and neighbourhood (web and mobile);
- display all the same basic location data to users (web and mobile);
- display the following data: address, telephone, driving directions, hours, enhanced data, local store/office images, maps, join/register forms, local promotions, text to mobile features, social sharing, social check-ins, links to circulars and rich media YouTube videos;
- provide an individual location page for each store/office, dealership or franchise (web and mobile);
- provide all the basic location data, address, telephone, etc, for each page;
- provide enhanced content for each location page (web and mobile);
- provide specific content written for every specific location;
- click to driving directions from the location page;
- provide hours of business operations;
- display enhanced data;
- display local store/office images, maps, join/register forms, local promotions, text to mobile features, social sharing, social check-ins, links to circulars and rich media YouTube videos;
- SEO optimize each location page for local search keywords (web and mobile);
- local title text;
- local keyword tags;
- local description;

- local headlines;
- local ALT image tags;
- local keywords in body content;
- breadcrumbs;
- site map.

Optimize, publish and distribute bulk data feeds to information services, internet Yellow Pages (IYPs) and local maps

As noted by the Marketing Sherpa study, many brands are not fully optimized for Google+ Local, Yahoo Local and the Bing Business Portal. However, to satisfy user intent, your brand's data feeds must be enhanced in the local search engines if you want to take advantage of opportunity on the web. Multi-location brands can do this quickly and easily with web/mobile store locator software. The software would automatically provide:

- updated data feeds;
- updated location data changes;
- updated new store/office dealer or franchise store openings;
- updated closed store/office dealer or franchise stores;
- updated hours of business operations.

Information service providers and IYPs

For complete visibility, brands also must be listed in information service provider directories and IYPs in addition to local maps.

Local maps

The process of local map optimization involves direct management and optimization of the three major search engine map programmes.

- Google + pages direct via bulk feed;
- Yahoo! Local pages via manual feed;
- Bing Business Portal Maps pages via bulk feed.

Optimization of these feeds is the critical path in the overall local search optimization process. Simply providing the basic location data requested by the engines is not enough; several very important fields within the data feed must be optimized.

Internet Yellow Pages

If your brand is not optimized for IYP listings, a web/mobile store locator can optimize your listing in this directory automatically and consistently for all locations:

- Submit enhanced data feeds to IYPs.
- Update the feeds as follows:
  - location data changes;
  - new openings;
  - moves to new locations;
  - closed locations;
  - change of hours;
  - holiday hours.

Local search directories

If your brand is not optimized for SuperPages, Yellow Pages, Merchant Circle and HotFrog, a web/mobile store locator can optimize your listing in these directories automatically and consistently provide for all locations:

- enhanced content;
- localized description;
- local categories;
- local images;
- local coupons;
- local phone reporting;
- social network links;
- URL tracking;
- link to store page;
- link to mobile page.

Local/mobile search information service listings

If your brand is not optimized for local/mobile search information service listings, a web/mobile store locator can do the following automatically and consistently for all locations:

- submit enhanced data feeds to information services and GPS;
- keep the feeds updated;
- provide location data changes;
- update for new, closed or relocated stores;
- update when location hours change;
- add holiday hours.

Local business data aggregators

LocalEze, InfoUSA and Acxiom are local business data aggregators that provide IYPs, search engines and GPS with enhanced local business data. A web/mobile store locator can make their work easier by managing the following automatically and consistently for all locations:

- brand listing;
- address, telephone;
- enhanced content;
- localized descriptions;
- local categories;
- local images;
- local coupons;
- local phone reporting;
- social network links;
- track URLs;
- link to store page;
- link to mobile page.

Conclusion

Your customers and prospects are using online search engines on the web and mobile web to find local businesses; therefore, brands big and small must have a prominent local presence to get found. Local-mobile search has grown tremendously over the last five years, making local-mobile optimization a priority in the interactive brand ecosystem. By using the tactics and technologies discussed above, big brands can maximize their presence on the web and mobile web, ultimately driving more traffic and revenue to their stores and businesses.

Sources

BIA Kelsey [online] http://www.biakelsey.com/company/press-releases/100310-Nearly-All-Consumers-Now-Use-Online-Media-to-Shop-Locally.asp

BrightLocal [online] http://www.brightlocal.com/2010/11/29/local-consumer-review-survey-2010-part-1/

ComScore [online] http://www.localsearchstudy.com/Local%20Search%20Study%202012.pdf

Google Research [online] http://googlemobileads.blogspot.com/2011/04/smartphone-user-study-shows-mobile.html

ICT facts and figures [online] www.itu.int/ITU-D/ict/fact/2011

Kelsey [online] http://blog.kelseygroup.com/index.php/2011/05/25/20-of-google-searches-are-local-40-on-mobile/

Marketing Sherpa [online] http://www.marketingtechblog.com/2012-seo-report/

Pew Internet [online] http://www.pewinternet.org/Reports/2012/Digital-differences/Main-Report/Internet-adoption-over-time.aspx

E-mail: lifeblood of the online ecosystem

RICHARD GIBSON and GUY HANSON

Richard Gibson is the Director Client Services, Northern Europe, and Guy Hanson is responsible for Return Path's Professional Services Consulting Division in EMEA. Richard is a longstanding participant in the Direct Marketing Association (UK) and a past Chair of the Email Marketing Council. Guy is Chair of the UK's IAB Email Marketing Council.

Introduction

History has it that Ray Tomlinson was the first person to send an e-mail in 1971; it took over 30 years for e-mail as a communication method to reach the significant penetration rates.

For marketers it took until 2005 for the volume of e-mail to supplant that of direct mail, at least if the United Kingdom is anything to go by. For the vast majority of both recipients and brands, e-mail has grown to be what it is now, which is the lifeblood of the online ecosystem. For recipients the e-mail address is closest thing to a unique identifier; it is used to log in to more than the inbox – it is the passport to sharing on a plethora of sites, to browsing for information and to transacting.

For most marketers e-mail had somewhat humble beginnings, with newsletters being the predominant type of marketing message. E-mail was initially viewed as an alternative to other communication methods, its growth hampered in part by adoption rates and an slow appreciation of its potential as a channel of choice for users to receive information via e-mail – itself driven for the growth of e-mail as a one-to-one communication channel in both business and personal communication. As those adoption rates quickly rose, so did the levels of learning and sophistication amongst the brands using e-mail. Methods adopted from direct and database marketing including established segmentation techniques such as RFM (recency, frequency, monetary); the importance of testing and looking at the overall value of a customer in a life cycle was realized by marketers looking beyond simply sending the same message to the entire database. Message sophistication evolved to move away from a static form (predominately newsletter and information-led content) to include techniques designed to increase response.

Another important consideration revolves around the way that e-mail is actually being used. While we have typically referred to e-mail marketing, the role of e-mail has actually expanded well beyond this narrow concept. The e-mail mix is increasingly comprising transactional, triggered and notification elements. While doomsayers frequently forecast the demise of e-mail as social media continues to gain traction, the reality is that e-mail is playing new and important roles in linking the billions (if not trillions) of social interactions that now take place every day. It is for this reason that we now refer to e-mail as the 'digital glue' that provides cohesion between all of the other online channels, or we could see it as the medium that lubricates the lines of communication between them.

Any discussion around the growth of e-mail should include reference to the perception of the economics of cost-to-contact. E-mail was seen as 'cheap', and by implication little emphasis was placed by brands on investing in a marketing communication strategy that included e-mail in any significant and meaningful way. Today, while ubiquity is only part of the reason that e-mail has grown to be a dominant marketing channel, the principal reason it is seen by brands as a workhorse is its inherent measurability to drive above average return on investment.

The importance of measurability

One of the main reasons that measurability is so important for e-mail marketers is that it acts as an important enabler for:

- Testing: e-mail marketers can test changes to their programmes, gauge the impact of those changes, and apply those changes that generate performance uplifts, all in a remarkably short period of time – 24 hours is completely viable.

- Execution: because e-mail generates reporting in real time, marketers can respond to 'in flight' behaviour. If a broadcast is generating higher than average spam complaint rates for example, additional throttling can be applied to prevent ISP blocking.

- Improvement: learnings can also be fed back into the e-mail campaign life cycle very quickly. A success factor that was identified during this week's broadcast can be applied to subsequent weeks in order to optimize performance.

In these ways, e-mail marketers can ensure that a continuous cycle of testing, execution and improvement is applied against their programmes – vital in a sector of marketing that is highly competitive.

However, it is not enough to simply benchmark e-mail programmes against a traditional set of metrics, and to assume that all is well with the world if positive variances are being maintained. We have already stated that e-mail is evolving, and this holds equally true for measurability.

The reason for this is directly attributable to spam: high volume, unsolicited e-mail activity promoting cheap 'Viagra', fake Rolex watches and fictitious lottery wins. Spam accounts for more than 90 per cent of all global e-mail traffic, and major internet service providers (ISPs) such as Hotmail and Yahoo! have taken increasingly aggressive measures to identify and block these e-mails.

In doing so, the levels of false positives have increased, as 'good' e-mails have been incorrectly identified as being 'bad' and rejected/quarantined/re-routed as a result. The ISPs have recognized this and more recently have been implementing spam-handling measures that attempt to reward good e-mail senders rather than simply punishing bad senders.

This has resulted in the rise of a new set of metrics that are being referred to as 'engagement metrics'. ISPs are referencing these metrics to gauge how enthused recipients are with the e-mails that they are receiving. Engagement has always been important because of the role that it plays in driving conversions to sale. However, engagement is now also influencing e-mail deliverability, both in terms of inbox placement, and in terms of inbox positioning – how high up in the inbox the e-mail is placed, and how long it remains there.

Typical measurements of engagement include:

- This is not spam: e-mail marketers are used to the principle of monitoring their spam complaint rates and ensuring that they are kept low. Typically a complaint rate of 0.1 per cent or less would be expected of a high-quality e-mail programme.

'This is not Spam' provides an indicator of where e-mails have been inadvertently placed in recipients spam/junk/bulk folders, and they have gone to the trouble of retrieving these e-mails and placing them back in their inboxes. This is regarded as a highly desirable behaviour.

- Deleted read vs deleted unread: e-mail users will often delete old e-mails as part of their inbox maintenance routines. However, there is an obvious difference between deleted e-mails that have been previously read, as opposed to those that are deleted without triggering any read activity at all. The former is a positive behaviour, while the latter is a negative behaviour.

E-mail marketers need to be able to measure these behaviours. They should then deploy enhancements to their programmes that are designed to promote the positive behaviours while reducing the negative ones. By doing so, the programmes have the potential to deliver a double uplift, with improvements in both deliverability *and* responsiveness.

The rise and rise of mobile e-mail

The behaviour of e-mail recipients is also being massively influenced by where they are reading their e-mails. Traditionally this has split between webmail (Hotmail and Yahoo! for example) and desktop (MS-Outlook for example). More recently, the massive rise in the use of tablet and smartphone devices means that more and more subscribers are now consuming their e-mails 'on the move'. Recent research by Return Path demonstrated that almost a third of all e-mail opens are now taking place on one of these mobile devices.

This is creating another important measurability consideration. E-mail marketers need to know what devices their e-mails are being read on, because subscriber interaction with these e-mails will vary widely as a result. Factors such as screen size, image enablement/disablement, and changes in location/ time of interaction are all changing the rules for e-mail engagement.

Many e-mail marketers are now using 'responsive design' techniques that embed code in the e-mail that determines the size of the environment that it is going to render in. For example, a tablet may offer a nine-inch screen while a smartphone only offers a three-inch one. Knowing the difference can then be used to determine whether a multi-column or single-column format is used for the e-mail for example. This is absolutely crucial – the same research that was quoted above also showed that over 40 per cent of European e-mail recipients will delete an e-mail that has not been optimized for viewing on a mobile device.

The day of week is also influencing which devices people are reading their e-mails on. While desktop e-mail clients remain most popular on weekdays, mobile e-mail demonstrates a significant uplift at the weekends. Time of day is also changing, with greater interaction with personal e-mails now happening within a window that was traditionally regarded as 'working hours'. Location is becoming a more important consideration too – the fact that e-mails can now be read wherever subscribers are means that location-specific offers such as restaurant discounts become even more relevant.

Understanding the environments in which e-mails are being read, and the impact that this has on subscriber responsiveness in terms of day, time and location, means that e-mail marketers need to be able to measure these variables and adjust their programmes to reflect these newly identified preferences.

The long arm of the law

In addition to the requirements of their subscribers, e-mail marketers also need to have regard for recent (and future) changes in the requirements imposed by legislation that governs the e-mail marketing industry. Particular consideration needs to be given to:

- The EU E-Privacy Directive: this is the so-called 'Cookie Law' whereby marketers are now required to take a more proactive approach to informing their subscribers about the tracking technologies that are being used to monitor their online behaviour, and how this data is being used. In the United Kingdom, the Information Commissioners Office (ICO) has adjudged that the definition of cookies extends to include the single-pixel image technologies that are used to record data such as open rates and host devices. Lack of compliance will have a negative impact on the measurability of these important metrics.

- EU data protection regulations: changes are currently under consideration that will potentially impact on e-mail marketers, particularly in terms of:
  - a requirement for subscribers' explicit consent;
  - a right for subscribers 'to be forgotten'.

It is possible that these requirements will actually deliver a positive outcome for e-mail marketing programmes. While there will be tougher constraints on new subscribers, the resulting audience will almost certainly be more engaged and more responsive as a result. However, in keeping with the general theme of this article, accurate measurability will be essential to proving whether this is in fact the case.

Lurking inside the crystal ball

All of the issues that have been examined so far already exist. However, there are also a number of new developments that are starting to encroach into the immediate present or will soon do so, and that e-mail marketers are also going to need to take note of:

- Inbox organizers: many e-mail subscribers are now using inbox organizers to automatically identify and categorize specific e-mail message types as they arrive in the inbox, and automatically re-route them to custom sub-folders. This may be a good thing, with all of the e-mails that the subscriber actually wants to receive placed in one easy-to-find location. However, there is also the potential downside of 'out of sight, out of mind'. E-mail marketers will need to start carefully monitoring their response rates in order to gauge the impact of this new phenomenon.

- Spoofing and phishing: while the good news is that spam volumes are coming down, the bad news is that spammers are becoming more clever, taking a leaf out of the e-mail marketing best practices handbook to deliver attacks that are more targeted and effective, and deliver a higher financial return! The potential brand damage is significant – as much as $3,000 per compromised user, according to recent research by Cisco. So not only do e-mail marketers need to be monitoring the performance of their own programmes – they need to start keeping a close eye on pretenders too.

- Web sentiment: e-mail marketers are used to measuring potential signs of e-mail disengagement by measuring metrics such as unsubscribe rates, spam complaints, e-mail address and list quality. All of these are directly attributable to the programme. However, there are important secondary sources for the current health of e-mail programmes, and none more important than the sentiment that is being generated by social media communities on Facebook and Twitter. When this sentiment is positive, it can be harnessed to highly advantageous effect. But when it is negative, the impact can be corrosively detrimental as word of mouth spreads almost instantaneously. Marketers will soon need to be monitoring and measuring the sentiment metrics that their e-mail programmes are generating, and to respond to them at the same speed.

Even without any detailed discussion in this chapter around the consumer perception of e-mail, it is clear that – considering the evolutionary journey e-mail has taken from its beginnings as a method of communication, with a very narrow scope, to its position today of being close to ubiquitous – the challenge for marketers can at times feel nothing short of Herculean.

In this chapter we've outlined what we see as some of the challenges that are present today and the reasons for these challenges – the evolution that e-mail as a channel has undergone as a method of communication, and its use as a marketing channel, means that at the time of writing the landscape is likely to evolve even further, making the current and future challenges even greater. The measures available to marketers to measure their own success have remained more or less identical since the disciplines rise and growth some 15 years ago. Enlightened marketers have sought to understand the importance of new metrics that have an impact on their success, such as reputation, the impact of which directly affects the overall effectiveness of e-mail within any integrated communications strategy. However, with new challenges in play, the measures of success that marketers have used up to today are unlikely to increase effectiveness in the future. The simple hammer and nail analogy (see Chapter 21) applies here and, in a context directly relevant to e-mail marketers: those that are solely focused on measuring open rates and click rates have a very narrow view of their subscribers interactions.

The discipline of the digital marketer will increasingly be one that leverages and utilities additional data and information to inform decisions. Decisions made from rudimentary measures of success are potentially both severely limited and harmful. The intelligence used and employed to interpret and understand the data will pose a significant challenge for some (think: information overload) in the discipline. However, those that understand and leverage the data that is available to them and leverage it to make decisions will have a firm foundation for maximizing their brand's effective use of e-mail within the interactive ecosystem.

Sources

E-mail overtakes print for marketing offerings / FT.com/
   http://www.ft.com/intl/cms/s/0/c5d5ee2a-48e8-11dc-b326-0000779fd2ac.html
   Accessed date 4 June 2013

National Email Benchmarking Report, Q4 2005, Direct Marketing Association UK
   Limited, 2006

20 Integrating search to a multichannel mix

JAMES MURRAY

James Murray is the Digital Insight Manager for Experian Marketing Services. In this role, he communicates the value of Experian data and insight through PR, thought leadership and speaking opportunities, which help to drive customers' multichannel marketing strategies.

Marketing principles: know, get, keep

Marketing is changing. Customers expect a seamless user experience, regardless of the touch-point through which they engage with brands. Whether it is through search, social, e-mail, online or offline advertising, customers now demand a consistent and joined-up experience. As a result, marketing has to respond to become truly multichannel. It cannot just have an active presence across multiple marketing channels but must maximize the strength of each channel to create a synergy that is stronger than the sum of its parts.

As marketing is forced to evolve into a more collaborative, cohesive and efficient machine, the core remains steadfastly immutable and unchanged. Marketing will always be first and foremost about the customer. The goal of marketing is to understand and engage with customers, and increasingly data is becoming the tool through which brands can know, get and keep their customers. Through great data, companies have the capacity to know who their customers are, what makes them tick, and what products and services they are interested in purchasing. Data can help companies get more of their key customers by identifying acquisition channels they are likely to respond to and crafting the best marketing messages that will engage those customers. Finally, once acquired, data can help brands keep those key customers that are so valuable by understanding their current needs and anticipating what they will want in the future.

These three principles are what multichannel marketing is all about. Companies that can execute effectively on all three principles will have a healthy and successful business. They will not only understand how to target new customers to grow their business but also how to nurture and retain existing customers to become loyal brand advocates. Great data is at the heart of these principles, and the bedrock of great data is search.

The growing importance of search

Search has revolutionized the way we find information. Hundreds of years ago if you wanted to find the answer to a question you would have to go to the village elders and ask them. The breadth and depth of knowledge available was restricted to the wisdom of the local guru. As the age of printing evolved we were able to record knowledge and spread it widely, creating libraries to store vast volumes of information. Then came the internet, and the world's information became digital. Invariably now, if you want the answer to a question, you don't ask anyone, you ask Google.

This change in the way we find information has some important consequences for marketers. First, search data has huge volume and is something that can be easily tracked. Online analytics tools allow marketers to see what people are searching for, giving them unprecedented insight into what people want. According to data provider Experian Hitwise there are over 2.2 billion visits to search engines every month in the United Kingdom alone, and 2012 will see a billion more searches made in the UK than were made in 2011. Being able to track the growing number of searches being made online (over 50 million unique search terms a week) gives marketers a phenomenal amount of insight into what people are looking for through the searches that they make.

Second, people are much more honest with search engines than they are when they interact with other people. In face-to-face conversation, nobody wants to appear ignorant, make themselves look stupid or admit to anything that might be deemed unseemly. Even in anonymous market research surveys, when asked a direct question such as 'how often do you exercise?'

respondents often wish to cast themselves in a positive light and so will respond 'one or two times a week' even if the reality is closer to once or twice a month. This type of self-delusion is what psychologists call cognitive dissonance. When asked about something that is socially awkward or unseemly – health issues, falling into debt, looking at adult websites online – people would rather save face and lie than admit to the truth. The beauty of online search behaviour is that search engines are algorithms; they do not judge the searcher, and can answer questions that people would never dream asking their colleagues, close friends or family. To this extent, search gives marketers not only unparalleled access to vast quantities of data and insight but also an honest and true reflection of the needs, wants and desires of their customers, unfettered by the constrictions of social awkwardness or embarrassment.

The importance of relevance

Understanding how and what people are searching for is the first step to acquiring more customers for your brand. Once you know what your customers want, you can start to adapt your marketing strategy to get those customers to your website. Critical to the success of search marketing is relevance. If you know precisely how people are searching for a product or service, you can then align your brand to those search terms in order to get more online traffic and ultimately more sales.

Let's take luxury jewellery as an example. It is a niche market online, yet because of the high value of the products being sold it is an extremely lucrative and competitive one. Top brands dedicate huge resources to rank well online in the search engine results for key terms relevant to this industry. Being a luxury jeweller, you might well think that ranking well for the term 'luxury jewellery' would be a good place to start to building your online brand presence and optimizing your website. However, analytics data from Experian Hitwise shows that when people are searching for luxury jewellery they very rarely use the term 'luxury' in their search.

In fact, when people type the word 'luxury' into a search engine they often associate this word with the travel industry. For Q1 of 2012, 55 per cent of all searches including the word 'luxury' were related to travel. People searched for luxury holidays, luxury cruises, luxury hotels and luxury resorts – what they did not search for was luxury jewellery. In total, there were just 33 unique search variations that included the words 'luxury jewellery' in the first quarter of 2012. By comparison, there were almost 400 variations of the term 'designer jewellery'. The key point here is that even if you consider your brand to be a luxury jewellery brand, that is not how your customers perceive you. Consumers search for luxury holidays, but when they want jewellery they search for designer jewellery or bespoke jewellery, not luxury jewellery. Armed with this knowledge, it becomes much easier to align your jewellery products with the way that people search for them, increasing the relevance of your online content and bringing more visits to your product pages.

How does search relate to know, get, keep?

Search data can be used at every stage of the know–get–keep cycle, helping you to understand, acquire and retain your customers. These are just three handpicked examples of how search data could be implemented to strengthen an integrated multichannel marketing strategy.

Know: market opportunity

Scoping the potential size of a market opportunity is an important step as part of any due diligence phase of market research. Search can be used to identify the size of the prize, and the difficulties associated with growing market share within a particular product category or industry. Let's say you were in the pharmaceutical industry and wanted to launch a new weight loss drug. What is the size of that market in the United Kingdom? How many people might you be able to reach with your new product and who are the competition that already exist?

By analysing search data you can know how big the market opportunity is for weight loss products online. Looking at the total number of searches driving traffic online to the health and medical industry, about 4 per cent of these are searches related to weight loss. That equates to an average of 90 million weight loss searches a year across millions of potential customers. A deeper dive into the search data reveals some very distinct types of people who are interested in weight loss. New mothers trying to get back into shape after pregnancy and women slimming for the perfect summer holiday beach body are just two groups that emerged through searches for 'losing weight after giving birth' and 'bikini diet'. The search data here not only gives you the size of the opportunity but can help to shape the individual campaigns you run to target these individual groups. Furthermore, by assessing where people go after they make weight loss searches, it is possible to see how strong the competition is in this industry and how difficult it would be to break into this market.

Get: fast-moving search trends

Keeping on top of fast-moving search trends can be a great way to acquire customers very quickly by reacting to a change in the market. By their very nature, fast-moving search trends are very difficult to predict and so require a fluid, reactive approach to marketing. By using search data it's possible to stay ahead of the competition and jump on an emerging trend before anyone else.

Travel, perhaps more so than other industry, is subject to very fast-emerging search trends. A natural disaster, somewhat counter-intuitively, tends to cause an influx in searches for flights to the disaster-hit destination rather than a massive drop in interest in travel. For companies able to react swiftly to these unexpected trends there is a huge opportunity to capitalize on more web visits and therefore sales. The Tohuku earthquake in March 2011, for example, caused a 70 per cent increase in UK internet searches for travel to Japan in just one week. This was an unexpected event that suddenly had a huge influence on how people were searching for flights to Japanese destinations. Using search data to get customers at the right time can be massively profitable for companies that can react fastest to changing market conditions.

Keep: customer engagement

Having acquired a customer it's important to hang on to that customer and ensure that they give you repeat business. Often this is handled badly by brands that try to sell to customers at any given opportunity without offering them anything interesting other than the current product being promoted. This hard-sell tactic can be seen as quite aggressive and un-appealing. Giving customers something engaging to interact with is a much softer sell and is more likely to resonate with them. Research from Experian Cheetahmail shows that informative newsletter e-mails are 37 per cent more likely to be opened than normal e-mails, and 49 per cent more likely to receive a click through to a website. People are more engaged with these e-mails because the content is interesting and gives them a reason to open and click through. Search data can help inform the type of content you should be using in your e-mail communications to engage your customers.

Let's take Christmas food as an example. December is the biggest month of the year for online retail, and supermarkets want to make sure customers do their Christmas food shopping at their store rather than at a competitor. Rather than simply sending out offers in e-mail communications for cheaper food, using engaging customer content like Christmas recipes is more appealing and useful to consumers. At the same time this encourages them to buy key ingredients from the supermarket in question. Search data can be used to understand not only which are the most popular recipes being sought after during Christmas but also the changing trends of those searches over time.

Experian Hitwise data showed that for December 2011 the most popular recipe searched for overall was for Christmas cake, but that these searches occurred much earlier in the season than searches for mince pie and turkey recipes. People actually started searching for Christmas cake recipes as early as mid-September, perhaps because good Christmas cakes need treating with alcohol at least a month in advance of eating. In this case, by understanding how people were searching for different Christmas recipes, supermarkets could start sending seasonal e-mails at the right time with recipes in them that encouraged customers to buy ingredients for the food they wanted to cook.

Conclusion

Search is a growing part of the multichannel marketing mix that can be used at every stage of the know–get–keep cycle. As marketing continues to evolve, the core principles of knowing who your customers are, how to get those customers to buy your products and how to keep those customers loyal to your brand will have to incorporate data from many different sources. Search is the biggest source of traffic online, and is the bedrock of data from which effective, intelligent, targeted campaigns can be built. Search can help you assess the size of a market opportunity, jump on emerging fast-moving trends and create interesting and engaging content. These are just three examples but there are many more. Crucially search must be used in a relevant way. There is no use guessing what consumers are searching for; you have to know, and by knowing you can adapt and align your marketing strategy to the needs of your customers.

21 What really counts in metrics

ERIK DECKERS

Erik Deckers is the owner and President of Professional Blog Service in Indianapolis. Erik co-authored *No Bullshit Social Media* (Pearson, 2011) and *Branding Yourself.* (Pearson, 2010). He frequently speaks about blogging and social media.

You know those advertising figures you were given? The ones that tell you how many people read a certain magazine, watch a certain TV show, open a direct mail piece or even drive past a specific billboard? Lies. All of them. Dirty, dirty lies that are told by marketers so they can take as much of your marketing budget as they can get.

That's because the numbers you've been told are based on estimates, best guesses and industry legends that have been handed down from generation to generation without anyone going back to see if they're accurate anymore. In fact, many times, the marketers and ad salespeople don't even know the origins of those numbers; they were given them during their first day on the job, and they've repeated them ever since. Or they're numbers that count something completely different from what is claimed and are fired at you in the hopes that you don't stop to ask what they really count. Here's what I mean.

How would you like to reach 120 million homes?

On its website, the Golf Channel (owned by NBC Sports) tells potential advertisers that their channel is 'available in more than 120 million homes worldwide'.

Oooh, 120 meellion homes! marketers swoon, with their pinkies to their mouths like a well-dressed Dr Evil. Sure, who wouldn't want to have their ad beamed into 120 million homes, where it will be seen by 120 million people. Who can say no to that? Except it's not really 120 million people. It's not even 12 million people. On a good night, it's 1.2 million people.

According to a June 2012 article on the TVbytheNumbers.com website, Round Two of *The Players* tournament in 2011 saw 1.8 million viewers, making it the most-watched programme of the year. Second place was Round One of the *Wells Fargo Championship* with 907,000 average viewers (ie half as much as Number 1).

Other tournaments clocked in around 700,000+, while the Golf Channel's original entertainment programme, *Big Break Atlantis*, reached 349,000 people one time in May 2011. That's not a bad reach, considering the National Golf Federation says there are around 26.1 million golfers in the United States. But that's still not 120 million.

Yet when advertising sales reps sit down with marketing directors to sell ad space on the Golf Channel, which number do you think gets trotted out: 120 million or 349,000? What opportunity are they being sold: the chance to reach a population the size of one-third of the United States, or a population that's slightly larger than Tampa, Florida?

While I'm sure the ad sale reps at the Golf Channel are fine, upstanding people who pay their taxes and love their mothers, I am also willing to bet they don't tell people 'our average viewership for a night is almost 350,000 people'. I would bet their commissions that they say, with a straight face: 'Our channel is beamed into 120 million homes worldwide.'

These are the lies that we marketers are being told – and are telling our bosses and our clients. It's creating some unreasonable expectations, which may end up hurting future marketing efforts, especially as social media marketing becomes an even more important channel.

How thousands are worth more than millions

The problem these lies create for social media marketers is that our clients and bosses are still programmed to expect millions of readers, millions of views and millions of clicks.

'120 million homes?!' they shout. 'We'll take it!'

So you can imagine their disappointment when they see a Google Analytics report that says there were thousands of readers, thousands of views, and hundreds of clicks.

'It's a failure!' they now declare. 'We should have stuck with TV!'

You can see the problem. Social media is used by millions of people. Hundreds of millions. In fact, as of this writing, Facebook has over 1.1 billion users. Twitter is clocking in at over 500 million users.

'So why did only 30,000 people show up at our website last month? How is that not a failure? That's less than 120 million.' The problem with expecting millions of visitors is that it's based on the lies we were told over the last few decades about open rates, read rates, circulation, viewership and every other metric we've been given.

I've heard from many business owners and executives who think that social media should match the same viewership they get from their TV ads, newspaper and magazine circulation, or highway billboard views. They want to measure views by the thousands, just like the other metrics they've measured all this time. And when it doesn't happen, they blame social media for a failure. But they're missing the bigger picture. And that is, on social media they're engaging the customers who are probably the only ones to interact with them anyway.

There are a few problems with the whole 'we need millions of clicks' line of reasoning, some of which you can fix, and some of which will take a bigger educational effort within the marketing industry.

It's not possible to accurately measure most traditional marketing channels

There are a few exceptions, but most people don't take advantage of them. Sure, we're told that 1,000,000 people were watching a particular programme at a particular time. But how many of them saw your commercial, taking account of the number of people who went to the kitchen or bathroom during the break? How many of them flipped channels or for-warded through your commercial? The same problem holds true for radio, newspapers, billboards, direct mail, etc. The numbers only estimate the number of people watching, but can't tell you accurately.

There are a few ways to measure traditional marketing, like using a special phone number that only appears in that ad, or creating a special purchase code that is tied into the ad, or even just asking people 'where did you hear about us?' But those usually take extra effort and are not always properly tracked. It also doesn't tell you which ad was responsible for the sale or store visit, or how many times the customer saw the ad.

You can't target with traditional marketing the way you can with social media

The best traditional marketing channel that lets you target your audience is direct mail. Right now, you can buy a specific breakdown of demographic and psychographic criteria of your potential customers:

'Divorced women between the ages of 30 and 50 with three kids, and a median income of $65,000.'

You can't do that with television, radio, or billboards, because you're reach-ing a large portion of the audience that doesn't fit what you need. Viewers of sports channels may be mostly men, but they may not have the median income you want, or be the age of viewer you want. Or even be men.

You can do this kind of targeting with social media marketing. For ex-ample, Facebook lets you target ads to only show up for those people who meet your target. Google lets you buy ads that only appear when people look for a specific search term. And you can even create an online community that is geared towards your exact audience and let them communicate with each other.

You can also create an e-mail newsletter from your past customers and send it out on a monthly basis as a way to generate repeat business. Thanks to the e-mail metrics tools available, you can even measure open rates, click-through rates and purchase rates. From there you can segment audiences into groups of people who make purchases, click your articles – or who don't even read the newsletter at all.

You can measure social media marketing, and link it directly to sales

Thanks to Google Analytics and your CRM, you can see exactly how and when people arrived at your website, which pages they clicked, when they placed an order and how much they bought. Then you can total up the sales and arrive at a figure: 'This tweet we sent at 2:34 pm resulted in $20,000 in sales.' How many TV ads or billboards can you say that about?

This will even let you determine the pieces of content, the channels and even the times of day that are most effective in reaching your widest – and most profitable – target audience. In contrast, with traditional marketing, you're not reaching the millions of viewers/readers/listeners you thought you were. You also have no idea how many you actually did reach.

You're reaching thousands of viewers/readers/listeners with social media marketing, but you're reaching the right people at the right time; which means you were probably only reaching that many people with traditional marketing to begin with.

Social media marketing is just another tool in the toolbox

This does not mean that you should replace your traditional mainstream marketing efforts with social media marketing. That's not the point of this chapter at all. Rather, you should understand that social media marketing is no longer about teenagers downloading videos from their mobile phones or goofing around on MySpace.

It's about engaging a much wider audience and targeting only the ones you want to receive your message. Rather than using your marketing tools like hammers, and treating your marketing tools like so many nails, use social media as a specific tool that lets you interact with rabid fans, and help them to become ambassadors for your brand.

The final secret about social media marketing

So here's the biggest secret of all about social media marketing: *Your customers do not trust, listen to, or care about you at all.* They get their information about our products from each other. This is actually a stagger-ing piece of news to many marketers, because we've all been told we're special. That our work is important. That the hours we spent as a committee designing that latest brochure mattered. We don't want to be told that the tens of thousands of dollars we spent shooting that commercial were useless. Or that the carefully chosen marketing copy we wrote – and the know-nothing legal department 'helped' with, which we promptly ignored – was ignored in favour of someone's comment on our website.

It's painful to hear, but it needs to be said.

Our customers are talking to each other instead of listening to us. We're the paid professionals. We went to college for this sort of thing. We were told the latest buying theories that told us the right words to say for the right personas, and that everyone would flock to our product if we just found that magic bullet.

Our customers want to hear from people they have relationships with. They trust those people. They're friends, family, co-workers and neighbours. They have a vested interest in seeing our customers get a good value, succeed in their efforts, or at the very least have an enjoyable experience.

That means they ignore the traditional 'Buy This! Buy This! Buy This!' marketing messages. That means that if we want our customers to listen to us, we have to stop advertising and start talking with them on a regular basis. We need to become their friends and trusted resources. We have to stop talking to them like marketers.

It means we have to ignore the millions and reach the thousands, by talk-ing to hundreds. It means finding the influencers in our markets, forming solid, real relationships with them, and then letting them serve as evangelists on our behalf. It means redefining marketing and how we do our jobs, since social media has made it both possible and necessary to do so.

Sources

http://advertise.nbcsports.com/on-air/golf-channel/

http://tvbythenumbers.zap2it.com/2012/06/05/most-watched-may-ever-on-golf-channel/136880/

http://golfweek.com/news/2011/may/09/us-golf-participation-falls-third-consecutive-year/

PART III
Beyond online: how to translate the multichannel ecosystem into revenue

Marketing automation with apps

VILLE MAILA

Ville Maila is the founder and App Director of .PROMO Inc, the app-based marketing automation platform that makes campaign execution as easy as using the App Store. He's one of the most influential advocates of app-based marketing automation in B2C marketing. Ville is also the editor and co-author of the book *Shopper Marketing* (Kogan Page 2009, 2012).

Does marketing need IT projects?

With the emerging multichannel marketing ecosystem, marketing is getting more and more dependent on technology. A Gartner survey (McLellan, 2012) predicts that by 2017 chief marketing officers will outspend their chief information officer counterparts on information technology. According to Gartner there are three key areas in which marketing will spend on IT:

- E-commerce: marketing often owns the e-commerce area, which will mean direct profit-and-loss accountability.
- Social and mobile: marketing is putting heavy stress on experimenting with ways to capitalize on skyrocketing consumer usage of Facebook and other social sites as well as smartphones.
- Campaign and process management: marketing departments are lagging behind other departments in taking advantage of the significant process automation opportunities.

More importantly, campaigns are the bread and butter of marketing and they have already become very technology oriented due to the online, mobile and social dimensions that are part of every noteworthy campaign. With campaigns, however, the IT-project dimension is usually hidden to third parties such as the agencies. This means the marketing department may not even realize the ever-increasing amount it is spending on the technology powering its campaigns. More technology means more complexity, more costs and, on the positive side, more automation opportunities, so campaigns will in fact be a major contributor to all the three growing areas mentioned above.

Furthermore, according to the Gartner survey, CMOs don't have a very positive perception of IT, typically saying no to IT projects and preferring stability over innovation and change because of expensive and slow-moving projects. There is clearly a need for a paradigm change.

Value of technology

Let's face it, unless you are a CEO of an IT company, you would not like your CMO to focus a lot on technology. Marketing's role is to make sure there is traction for the products and services by the means of communications and often by facilitating product development – but not through facilitating IT projects. Therefore, it's no surprise that CMOs are not that fond of the prospect of having to spend their time on things that they are not measured for. It would be easy to interpret the situation so that the focus of the marketing department needs to change in order to be able to invest more of their time on technology. This assumption derives from a common idea that technology would have a value in itself, which is obviously untrue. Using technology is not the goal, but instead is a means to reach the goal. Therefore, one should not require the marketing department to change into an expert on IT-projects, but instead to think of ways in which technology could help them to reach their current goals more efficiently.

The technological challenges facing the marketing department are not simple by any means, but fortunately all of the core areas boil down into a fairly straightforward consumer-centric equation: how to facilitate and measure various consumer interactions with the brand in a way that reduces workloads and costs instead of increasing them.

From IT projects to apps

Enterprise IT has always been complex, which is probably the main contributor to the marketing department's distaste for information technology. Whether it is about databases, CRM, ERP or other enterprise software, there is a long history of complex, resource-oriented projects required for installation and maintenance. Even software targeted for individual users' desktops is still today often so complex that there are not many enterprises in which installation would not require calling IT support.

Fortunately, with the emergence of cloud computing the IT-project paradigm is destined to receive a strong alternative that is, in many ways, ideal for enterprise marketers. Just consider what Apple did to the software paradigm with the launch of iPhone and App Store. Suddenly buying software and getting it installed became easier than buying your groceries. This is the kind of simplicity the marketing department needs instead of enterprise IT projects.

Customization of communications, not technology

Another common mistake often made when speaking about marketing and IT in the same sentence is to think that since every brand and product is unique, they also require unique technology and thus custom IT projects. This is a mistake that marketing departments and agencies become guilty of. Most of the campaigns already today have an online, social or mobile dimension but there are very few marketers or agencies that would actually take advantage of technology as a possible way to reduce workloads and investments. Instead of this, the technological basis required to power the campaigns is commonly built from scratch individually for every campaign as small-scale IT projects. This means a lot of excess investment in terms of human resources and external costs.

Tip of an iceberg

In order to understand the role technology plays within campaigns, one must first break down the structure of a campaign into different components. Figure 22.1 depicts a campaign from a consumer interaction perspective.

FIGURE 22.1 Components of campaigns

Figure 22.1 could be seen as a hierarchical pyramid, or an 'iceberg' in which only the communications part is visible to the outside world and the underlying components all require technological development and are completely or partially invisible below the waterline. When planning and implementing campaigns, the marketing department's main focus is on communications; all the rest is typically left as an add-on task of agencies. The 'rest' however generates the big resource and development requirements of campaigns and often amplifies even simple campaigns into months-long projects.

The participation component of a campaign refers to a participation functionality published on a microsite, Facebook or a mobile site for example. This is where the consumers authenticate themselves. The participation process is typically customized for the brand in terms of visuals and copy. The data submitted by the user is stored in a database and, in more advanced cases, the details of participants that opt in will also be stored into a CRM system.

The reward mechanism represents an incentive that has been tied in to participation, for example a chance to win, earn or save as a reward for participation. As well as the actual mechanism for issuing the reward, this component also includes the technology for the consumer to redeem the reward through providing additional information like a bank account number or delivery address, and possibly tracking the delivery of the incentive. Reward mechanisms range from simple price discounts to instant win lotteries or complex loyalty schemes.

The loyalty platform represents the method by which the brand tracks and motivates favourable behaviour by the consumer. Examples of loyalty schemes include, for example, the loyalty cards of airlines or retailers, code-collections of consumer goods or receipt-based purchase verification. A typical loyalty system includes an account system where consumers must log on so as to access their account and register the points. The loyalty platform is also the component enabling continuity for campaigns through a system that allows marketers easily to publish e-mails or mobile messaging to consumers that have opted in and access their data. Finally, the platform provides consumers with a user interface for opting out and accessing their data.

Campaigns as apps

Mobile apps and the surrounding infrastructure of smartphone operating systems and cloud computing have shown that it is possible to simplify endless variations of complex technology into a package that can be installed and used even by a three-year-old. Thinking of campaign functionalities as apps provides an interesting alternative paradigm for marketers, as opposed to custom enterprise IT projects.

A campaign app is a ready-made piece of software including all the functionalities needed to run the campaign in the online or mobile environment. As opposed to the predominant approach of executing campaigns as IT projects, the app approach means you only need to install the app on the desired environments and you are done. No custom development needed. The same app makes the functionalities available for consumers on the brand's own website, separate microsites, on partners' sites, on Facebook and on mobile sites. The brand's multichannel marketing ecosystem becomes the platform in which the campaign apps are published. This platform could be compared to iOS, Android or Windows operating systems running third-party apps.

Turning campaign functionalities into apps means that absolutely no technological development is needed by the brand or third parties like agencies in order to customize, publish, use or monitor the campaign. All the functionalities are already there and the marketers' task becomes simply to focus on making sure that the campaign app generates desired attitudes and action among the selected target audiences – something quite close to marketing's core purpose, as opposed to IT projects.

The process should be led by the marketer, not by the agency. Since no brands are identical the most challenging task for the marketer is to choose optimal app for the brand and its objectives. Planning online functionalities, consumer rewarding and consumer experience become a similar task to browsing the App Store to choose an optimal app – as opposed to a monthslong planning process with one or more agencies involved.

Once the desired app is selected and the basic settings such as the duration of the campaign and the exact reward mechanism are set, the agency should define the textual and visual appearance of the app and the communications around it. Once this is done, the app can immediately be published on any website, mobile site or within social media by inserting a few lines of code on the site by using 'widget'-technology. In practice this means that the campaign functionalities can be accessed from brand's site for example, but in fact it is running in the cloud.

After the app has been published it resides in the cloud, which means that the infrastructure is there to run the selected reward mechanism and a loyalty platform. User account systems can also be built in so users will have real-time access to their campaign account and opted-in consumers' details will be stored on a loyalty platform that is easy to access and use. Real-time analytics and monitoring are also available. Even a complex campaign with sophisticated set of features could be set up and running within hours instead of within months.

FIGURE 22.2   Difference between app-thinking and IT-project thinking

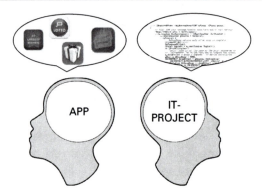

Implications and benefits of the app approach

Within the new paradigm, marketing departments do not have to be involved at all with technology related to campaign execution and can focus all their efforts and budgets on their primary objectives: making sure there is demand for the products or services of the company in the short term and in the long run. The approach significantly reduces the amount of working hours required to create the campaign functionalities because it removes need for custom development and testing, and reduces the risks of technical or user experience issues when the campaign is live. The cost and time savings are considerable, which means the saved money and effort could be invested in creating more campaigns or bigger campaigns, or to other areas such as media. On the other hand, as the lead time for publishing campaigns is reduced from months to hours, the new approach could have major effects on the ways campaigns are run – it would, for example, be possible to start a new campaign every day without significant new workloads, or to react to changes in the business environment, such as a competitor's campaign, by launching a counter-attack within hours.

Source

McLellan, L 'By 2017 the CMO will spend more on IT than the CIO', Gartner webinar, available at: http://my.gartner.com/portal/server.pt?open=512&objID=202&mode=2&PageID=5553&ref=webinar-rss&resId=1871515

23 Using storytelling to build sales

CAM BROWN

Cam Brown is the founder and CEO of King Fish Media. King Fish is a marketing agency that creates content-based marketing programmes to increase sales for clients including Bank of America, Boston Market, Keurig, BBVA Compass and Zappos.

Customers have always been in control of their information sources. Now, however, they have a seemingly infinite number of choices at their fingertips, thanks to a rapidly evolving digital ecosystem that makes it easy to create, store, find and share information on virtually any topic.

This explosion of data sources makes it more challenging for brands to position themselves as a trusted, authoritative information source across all media. In their quest to build credibility and long-term relationships with customers, marketers have embraced content as a key element of customer relationship management (CRM). Companies spent more than $40 billion on all forms of content marketing in 2010, according to research by ContentWise and the Custom Content Council. In a 2011 survey by Roper Public Affairs and Corporate Communication, 84 per cent of CMOs agreed that custom content represents the future of marketing.

But here's the challenge: now that so many companies are practising some form of content marketing, it's becoming even more difficult to distinguish your brand with compelling content that truly engages customers and prospects – and, most importantly, leads to action.

Over the last few years, content marketing has transformed marketers' ability to attract and generate quality leads. They've mastered the art of using white papers, e-books, webinars and other free-content formats to inspire enough opt-ins to pack their prospect funnel and keep sales busy for months to come. This is in contrast to a time, not too long ago, when marketers' toughest challenge and primary endeavour was to generate qualified leads. With this new quill in their caps, however, comes a new challenge: lead conversion. Sound like something that the sales department is better suited to handle? Well, that's the million dollar question...

Many are discovering that there is a grey area between lead and sale. The prospect has indicated interest but is not quite ready to commit. They need to be eased in slowly – courted before being proposed to. And while this ultimate proposal still may be the job of the sales team, the courting is – or, at least, should be – the responsibility of marketing. This is where content comes in.

According to research conducted by the Content Marketing Institute and MarketingProfs, the greatest challenge for content marketers is producing the kind of content that actually engages both customers and prospects. That challenge is important because the organizational goals (after brand awareness) are customer acquisition (68 per cent), lead generation (66 per cent) and customer loyalty (61 per cent). All of these worthy goals require content that build trust and get customers to take an action. Additionally, 39 per cent say their goal for content marketing is for lead management/ nurture.

It is in the area of lead nurture where content marketing can have powerful impact. This takes place after the prospect has been acquired and is now safely inside your lead management or CRM system. It has been estimated by Forrester and marketing automation firms such as Marketing-Profs that it takes five to six high-quality touches to turn a new lead into a customer. If that is the case, then it is critical for marketers to understand how to use authoritative content to move the lead to a loyal customer.

Most brands are good at messaging – but they are not good storytellers. Particularly in B2B markets, content marketing is rooted in traditional lead-generation models, which are based on selling, not nurturing.

The missing link in most content marketing playbooks is good storytelling.

It sounds simplistic, but storytelling is one of the most engaging and immersive ways of delivering content to create an emotional connection with customers and prospects. We've been wired since childhood to understand and assimilate information and complex ideas through the use of stories. Because storytelling is participatory, it enables brands to build a permission relationship with a target audience, across multiple media platforms. This approach helps your customers share your brand and helps them internalize it and fully understand the value proposition.

Marketers must strike a balance between selling and helping to successfully engage with customers and prospects to gain their permission as they progress through the purchase funnel. By helping prospects find the information they need – wherever they are in the purchase cycle – brands will create trust and affinity.

In the business community, narratives such as case studies enable prospects to participate in the story, which makes them more open to internalizing a marketer's messages. Prospects who hear stories place themselves in the process and project the outcome to their situations.

Before they can entertain the notion of becoming good storytellers, marketers first need to rethink how they perceive their customers and prospects. Traditional B2B lead-gen programmes focus on groups segmented by job title, company size or other demographics. Successful storytelling, on the other hand, requires a different type of targeting, with segments based on interests and needs. Instead of thinking about audiences in terms such as B2B and B2C, think about P2P: person-to-person marketing.

Good storytelling can get you in front of hard-to-reach prospects. Copyright Clearance Center (CCC), a global rights broker for the world's most sought after materials, used an innovative video-based storytelling programme to promote its licensing services and special offers to high-level executives who have little time or inclination to open the typical marketing e-mail.

The programme involved an interactive, direct response engagement designed to promote the company's licensing services and special offers. The cornerstone of the programme involved four uniquely crafted, customized video books. The solution was innovative and inspired: a video portfolio wrapped in a custom mailer and co-branded with trusted partners such as the Association of Corporate Counsel, the American Hospital Association and the Motion Picture Licensing Corporation.

The video booklets delivered CCC's case to executives as a compelling package, with the stamp of approval from partners the executives would know and trust. Custom e-mails, landing pages and training for the CCC sales force were put in place to support the unique campaign.

The video book investment, when measured against costly in-person business development calls, was paid back within three months. Sales conversions increased by more than 50 per cent, and the programme generated a forecasted $1 million in customer lifetime value.

'Cutting through the clutter and getting our services in front of new prospects is always a challenge,' said Miles McNamee, VP, Licensing and

Business Development, Copyright Clearance Centre. 'The books' "wow" factor fast-tracked them to the right decision maker.'

Cutting across demographics can expand the market potential and create multiple touch-points, enabling marketers to better target messages amongst customers and prospects. Further segmenting based on where a prospect is in the purchase funnel – awareness, research, consideration, etc – enables more specific storytelling that delivers real value. This is the key to effective lead nurturing, and a step beyond typical lead-gen programmes, which only focus on the wide-open end of the funnel.

Your content plan and schedule must deliver different types of content based on where a prospect or customer is in the sales funnel. Delivering an increasingly deep level of content will enhance your permission relationship with the prospect – the more they ask for your content, the stronger the relationship becomes.

IBM understands this concept. Instead of subjecting IT professionals to an endless stream of stand-alone webinars – a common lead-gen vehicle for B2B media – the technology giant took a different approach with a recent campaign. It launched Eye on IBM, a blog that provides independent news and analysis on topics such as virtualization, social business, mobile and analytics. These topics, of course, are core to IBM's products and services, but nothing on the site overtly sells IBM. Instead, IBM is subtly building credibility on topics that are critical to its business. This approach help IBM generate new leads and nurture the ones it already has. By giving prospects increasing levels of content IBM is building a relationship of trust and leading them to a sale.

To generate prospects and build awareness, focus on creating content that educates and informs. At this stage, most prospects are researching vendors to learn more about a topic or product category. Best practice white papers and research reports can be effective here.

Once prospects identify themselves as a lead – by registering for a download or attending a virtual or live event – you can bring them into the consideration/short list phase. Here, you will want to provide richer content that takes them to the next level and gives them a deeper understanding of your solution. Case studies, testimonials and demos and will show expertise and build trust in your company.

Zmags, a provider of digital publishing solutions, followed this approach in a multichannel campaign to attract new prospects. The marketing team created a series of stories that brought the digital shopper to life for catalogue sellers and other online retailers. Zmags' marketing team commissioned original research that resulted in a white paper. The white paper formed the basis of a webcast, which featured internal and external experts who offered insights on the research and gave the digital shopper a persona that brands could identify with. This is a great example of storytelling. Instead of presenting the research in a dry manner, they crafted a story about the 'connected buyer' and brought her to life. It was now relatable to and easier to learn. The programme helped generate leads and nurture prospects for Zmags.

As they get closer to a purchase decision, you can help prospects build a business case. Provide evidence that demonstrates your product as the right choice and mitigate the risk.

Once a prospect becomes a customer the objective now focuses on retention. The content you create and deliver will now focus on building long-term relationships and turning customers into advocates. Here, it's important to develop content that continues to inspire customers – and convinces them to buy more. Importantly, if you want customers to become advocates, you must design your content to be easily shareable via Twitter, Facebook, LinkedIn or other social platforms.

Marketers have become very good at using content to fill their sales funnel with leads. But the majority of leads generated through content marketing are not sales-ready. Just because a prospect has view a piece of your content it does not mean they are ready to buy. Conversions require more touches – supported by good storytelling and original content.

The ability to nurture prospects and customers with highly relevant content builds trust, affinity and loyalty – and drives sales.

Converting customer dialogues into revenue

24

KRISTIN ZHIVAGO

Kristin Zhivago is a revenue coach who advises CEOs and entrepreneurs. She helps them increase their revenue by removing all obstacles to the sale. Her latest book, *Roadmap to Revenue: How to sell the way your customers want to buy*, provides an in-depth guide to the research process, how to make the necessary changes in the business and how to keep the company on the road to higher revenue.

Marketers always obsess about how to use the hottest new marketing channels effectively. They absorb everything they can about them, and then attempt to apply other companies' successful methods to their own marketing efforts.

The fundamental problem with this approach is that what worked for one company usually doesn't work for another. Every company is unique: what they sell and how they sell it, who they sell it to, the needs and concerns their customers have, what they do well and what they do poorly, what they think matters to customers, how they treat customers, what customers say about the company and its products/services to other customers, and so on. This is one reason that social media results can be disastrously disappointing.

Worse, a new skunk has shown up at the marketing picnic. Companies are losing control of their messages. The new interactive social ecosystem has made it easy for buyers to vent their frustrations quite publicly, in reviews, blogs and discussion groups. New buyers pay much more attention to these customer comments than they do to marketing copy.

Company managers don't realize how many sales are slipping through their fingers due to these stated shortcomings, because they spend almost all their time with internal people, and the turned-off customers never show up on management's radar. There is no way to measure how many potential customers stay away.

'What about social listening?' you might ask. Yes, companies are setting up social listening posts. But the chances of management realizing the seriousness of an issue that's uncovered in a tweet are quite slim. It's one thing to see a few 'they didn't deliver on time' complaints in amongst other titbits of conversation in the social sphere. It's another thing to call seven customers and have them all say, 'The product is good, but they never deliver on time.' The former is easily dismissed as an isolated, special-case incident; the latter is a big red flag that says that something is broken, and is having a serious negative effect on revenue.

Looking at the situation from the buyer's perspective

When you consider your own personal experiences as a buyer, regardless of the channel you use to do your research and make a purchase, you know that most companies make it difficult for their customers to buy. You can't get answers to your basic questions; websites are confusing; instead of a person answering the phone, you suffer through voice-mail hell; salespeople don't call back, and if they do, they don't have the answer; in-store packaging is confusing or missing data. The issues that you, the buyer, care about most are not addressed in the content the company makes available to you, and the company's policies and processes don't make it easy for you to buy.

To increase revenue, these barriers to the sale must be identified and eliminated. Company managers need to understand exactly what their buyers want and how they want to buy it, how they perceive the company, and what their company should do to attract and satisfy more customers.

What's the fastest, most efficient way to do this? The answer is surprisingly simple. Your current customers – those who have already bought from you – will teach you how to sell to your potential customers, if you ask them the right questions, in the right way, at the right time.

Current customers have a lot in common with your potential customers. They approach the buying process in the same way; they wrestle with the same types of tradeoffs; they hold similar perceptions about companies in your space; they expect certain things from you and respond positively when you meet or exceed those expectations. They will answer your questions about all aspects of their purchase experience, including how they used the new interactive channels.

The correct time to interview your customers is after they have purchased from you. They won't tell you what they're really thinking when you're selling to them. Nobody ever tells a salesperson what they are really thinking while they're being sold to, because they are engaged in a conflict. The salesperson is trying to make the buyer sign on the dotted line. The buyer is trying to improve their situation with a purchase, and to avoid making a decision they will regret.

The salesperson is well practised at pushing the positives of the product, and never providing any negative information. If the customer brings up a negative, the salesperson has a ready response, delivered with perfect sincerity. There is no way the customer is going to reveal their inner thoughts while all this is going on. Prospective customers don't reveal what they're thinking to marketers, either. They come to a website hoping for answers; when they don't find them, they simply click away to the next website.

After customers buy, however, they are more than happy to help the company improve what it's doing, because they now have a vested interest in the company's success.

Because they are no longer being pressured by a salesperson, they are willing to reveal what they were thinking, what their buying process was, why they chose that particular product or service, and even what proved to be a challenge as they attempted to make the purchase. And, they will also explain how, when and why they turned to certain interactive channels in the course of making their buying decision.

Company managers assume that their buyers don't have that much in common. Thousands of one-on-one, conversational customer interviews have proved to me that the opposite is true. They have a lot in common, and they always have the most important things in common. These top issues will have emerged by the fifth interview, and they are locked firmly in place by the tenth. What you learn will be so logical and obviously right that you will know that you can bet the company's future on the data.

As tempting as it is to experiment with each new channel when it comes along, if you haven't first found out what matters to your customers, you'll be wasting your budget and market opportunities.

It isn't wise to assume that you know what matters. All company managers always think they know what matters to customers, and all of them are always wrong. Yes, wrong.

I say this with confidence, because every time CEOs brings me in, they start out by giving me the company side of the story. They and their managers tell me: 'Here are the things that matter to our customers, and what they care about when they are trying to buy.' It's a list, and the list always makes sense. Then I interview customers. The customers' list is always different. There are items on the company list that are not on the customer list, and vice-versa. Items at the bottom of the company list are at the top of the customer list.

Obviously, the company's list is what drives the decisions that managers make every single day about products, policies, services, promotion, people and investments. If the list is wrong – and again, it always is – new customers coming in contact with off-target content will see the company as unhelpful, out of touch and unable to solve their problem.

No amount of 'socializing' via new channels will fix this problem. The company will simply be making it more obvious to more people that they're doing things wrong.

Revenue comes from customers who find what they want, like what they see, buy it and tell others about it. If they immediately 'recognize themselves' when they come upon the company through their favourite channel, they will start to investigate further. If they get their questions answered to their satisfaction and are able to move in a straightforward way through each step in their buying process, a sale will be made.

In order for this to happen, you have to know which channels they are actually using, which questions they are asking as they investigate, and the answers that will satisfy them. In other words, you need to reverse-engineer the successful buying process so you can manufacture new sales in quantity.

You can do this by asking current customers a series of open-ended questions, which I have refined and perfected in the course of thousands of customer interviews. The basic questions are:

- What do you think of our product or service?
- What problems were you trying to solve with our product/service?
- How did our product/service help you solve your problem?
- Have you had any interaction with customer service? How was it?

- If you were the CEO of [our company] tomorrow, what's the first thing you would focus on?
- What was your buying process – what were the steps – and what questions or concerns did you have as you were considering our product/service?
- If you were looking for this type of product/service again, and you didn't know about us, what would you type into Google?
- What do you think is a fair price for this product/service?
- What is your biggest challenge right now?
- What trends do you see with this kind of product/service, and in your own industry?
- What do you think of our competition? Is there anything we can learn from them?
- Is there anything I should have asked you that I didn't ask you?

During the conversation, you will find yourself asking additional questions, for clarification and more detail, as they reveal areas that need attention.

Conduct these interviews on the phone; people talk more freely on the phone than they do in person. They definitely will not give you the in-depth answers you need via a survey or an e-mailed questionnaire. It's best to have a curious, courteous and professional outsider make the calls; customers will be more likely to open up. Make sure that the person is completely knowledgeable about your product and industry so they can have a relaxed and in-depth conversation with your customers. It will be obvious to your customer if the person doesn't know what's going on and isn't going to be able to make a difference; if that's the case, they will clam up.

This method is quite different from using a 'checklist' survey, which is flawed from the start because the questions are created from the company's perspective. They don't uncover the customer's reality; all they do is reinforce the company's flawed perceptions of their customers' thinking.

You don't have to interview a lot of people to get the data you need. After 7–10 interviews with a given type of person (such as the main buyer and the approver, or buyers in different markets) you'll see that they are all saying pretty much the same thing. In many cases they will even use the same words and phrases. After you have heard the same thing from 7–10 people, it's completely clear what you have to fix, and how you should be marketing and selling. There will be no doubt in your mind.

Let's see how this plays out in real life.

A business-to-business example

As I write this, Facebook is still the top consumer social channel, and LinkedIn is the top business-to-business channel. Any self-respecting marketer would already have pushed management to establish a presence there. But as I've already pointed out, that may be a mistake.

I recently interviewed customers for a client who sells sophisticated devices that precisely measure the pressure of any liquid flowing through them. They are often used by design engineers to monitor the flow of a liquid through a product they are developing.

I asked these technical buyers about social media, and the role it plays in their decision-making process. It was reasonable to assume that they might, for example, use LinkedIn discussion groups to interact with other research and development professionals. That assumption was dead wrong.

Every single person said the same thing: 'I would never post a question about a product purchase – even something as simple as a question about a certain material – on an online discussion group. The question itself would reveal to my competitors what we were working on. I would be giving away trade secrets, and I could certainly lose my job.'

Instead, they told me, they had come to know people who are in similar positions to theirs in non-competing companies. If they were seeking advice about a product or service they were thinking of buying, they contacted those individuals directly, by phone. They thought e-mail was rather rude; they considered it more polite to ask that type of question one-on-one, via a phone conversation.

None of them had ever used Facebook for any activity associated with their job-related purchasing activities. For this client, investing in Facebook would have been a total waste of resources, budget and market opportunity.

Yes, the client could participate in relevant discussion groups on LinkedIn, and provide useful information. But the interviews convinced us that these efforts should be viewed as secondary. There were more effective ways to increase sales. To start with, the website needed an informed re-design, so customers could quickly find the technical details about the type of flow meter they were interested in. They wanted to have one-click access to the technical documentation for each product. They told us that the best way for them to figure out 'what's going to happen to me after I buy' (which is the question most buyers have, and most companies never answer) was to download the tech manual and see just how complicated or easy it would be to install the flow meter in their own application. They also wanted as much information as possible about the product's ability to handle their particular types of fluids and flow rates.

After the redesign, which makes it easy for customers to find out exactly what they need the minute they come to the site, sales are up. They are now having their second-best-year ever – in a down economy.

- **Before**: Max Machinery does a fantastic job of helping its customers buy and use the most appropriate and efficient precision flow meter for their application. But their home page (Figure 24.1) made it difficult to figure that out from the start; it was more of the billboard approach that many companies have chosen to use. While the buyer knew he was in the right place, he wasn't sure until clicking through that Max had the right meter for him.

- **After**: During our post-research brainstorming and planning meeting, we mapped out the basic layout for a site that would start answering those critical questions the instant the customer came to the site (Figure 24.2). We came up with a capability statement, appearing in the top banner, which said exactly what Max Machinery sells, and the specific needs that their meters meet. 'Technical Docs' is one of the main navigation categories, because customers said that's the

FIGURE 24.1 Early Max home page

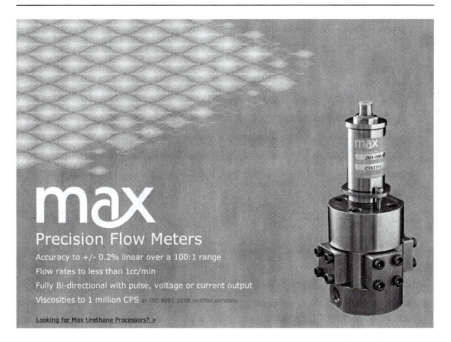

FIGURE 24.2 Revised home page

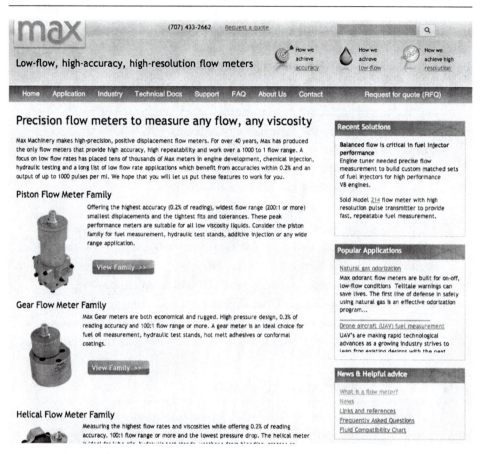

first place they look for answers to the all-so-important question ('What's going to happen to me after I buy?'). Once we agreed on all the elements, Max Machinery's talented in-house web designer created the site. The company's increased revenues are a testimony to what happens when you start selling the way your customers want to buy.

A consumer-side example

On the consumer side, our research for a Newport-based luxury wedding venue convinced us that the company should put more energy and resources into populating eye-candy social media sites such as Pinterest and Fancy, and that what customers really wanted to see was pictures of real weddings – on social sites and the company's website.

This was significant for this particular company, because one of their website designers had convinced them that 'brides didn't want to see pictures of other brides' weddings.' Vendors have personal biases. They often know very little about your particular customers' needs, interests and preferences. Customer interviews will prevent the company from following advice that contradicts what customers really expect and will respond to.

An example of internal thinking

Internal thinking can also make it impossible for customers to do what they come to your site to do. For example, Figure 24.3 shows the Verizon site home page. These three categories – Wireless, Residential and Business – come from the way the company is organized internally. What if the consumer coming to this site is an entrepreneur who does business out of her home, and her main number is her cell phone? She fits into all three categories. How does she know which category Verizon has assigned her to? Further, what if she is coming to Verizon to pay her bill? She cannot get 'there' from here.

Verizon's home page completely ignores the reality of the customer who has come to pay her bill and who falls into two or more of these categories. So their most loyal and important customers are not being served. The first question that any website designer must always ask is, 'What are they coming here to do?' And, I would add, the second driving thought should be, 'How can we make that one-click easy?'

What does this have to do with social media? Everything. If internal thinking has driven the company to miss these important realities about their customers, so obviously exemplified by the website, the company's interactive 'conversational' efforts will be even worse. If you carry out this research process as described, all of your customer interactions will be more effective going forward.

Social interaction is not all two-way. Most of it still involves sending out messages such as tweets, and posting content such as blog posts or posts to a LinkedIn or Facebook page. All of these messages will actually work if you have used effective research to find out who you're writing to and what really matters to them.

FIGURE 24.3 Verizon's home page

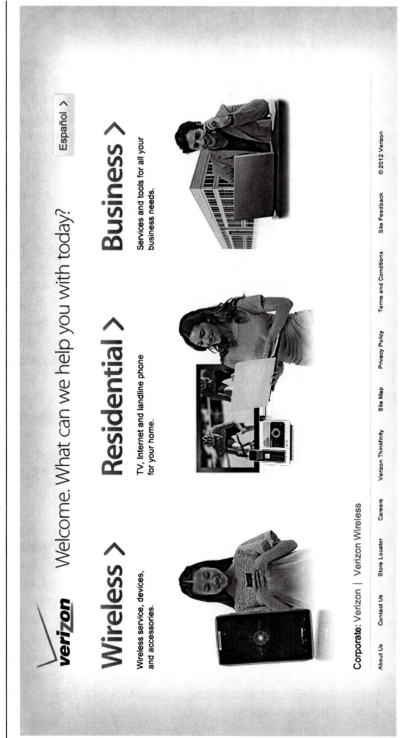

Some executives hesitate to conduct this research because they are afraid of what they may find: that the necessary changes will be more than they can afford to make. In my experience, the opposite is true. The changes are often relatively minor, such as changes to the website or to the positioning of the company and product/service; some internal reorganization or process improvements that make sense and work better for all involved; or changes in how management communicates with employees about what is important to customers. The increased revenue from easily made changes will make it possible to afford the more difficult changes.

The cost of not doing this research is the higher cost. If your channel selection and your messages don't match up with your customers' channel usage and point of view, the people who come upon your messages will simply click away – even though they could have, and perhaps should have, become customers.

The customer's reality is what drives your revenue. Fortunately, your own customers – people who have already bought from you – will reveal that reality to you, and you will be able to use what they tell you to build your own roadmap to increased revenue. You will get the fundamentals right, and you will be able to apply those fundamentals to each appropriate interactive channel.

25

What comes after social media

LON SAFKO

Lon Safko is a remarkably creative person. Among other things he has founded 14 successful companies, has 18 remarkable inventions in the Smithsonian Institution and authored nine books including *The Social Media Bible,* a Number-one hit on Amazon in both their Marketing and Business categories.

As many of you know, I am the author of the best-selling book, *The Social Media Bible.* My newest bestseller is called *The Fusion Marketing Bible.* It is about 'What's next': what comes after social media? Fusion marketing is actually an entirely new form of marketing.

I discovered Fusion Marketing as a result of constantly being asked in interviews 'So, what comes after social media?' Social media has changed the way the world markets, sells and communicates forever. And, it has caused us to change at speeds we have never seen before with technology, and I think you want to know what's next?

I decided to take that question on as a challenge. I asked myself, 'Where will marketing and sales be in say, five years? How will we be treating traditional, digital, and social media marketing?' That's when I realized that Traditional Marketing + Digital Marketing + Social Media Marketing = Fusion Marketing!

I realized that even now, if you are still calling yourself a 'social media expert' then you're announcing to the world that you have been left behind. If you're an expert in Facebook and Twitter, then you're trying to build a entire marketing strategy restricted to using only one or two tools from all of the marketing tools available today. Facebook is not a strategy. Twitter is not a strategy. They are only tools.

If you're still stuck looking at social media as a stand-alone marketing technology, then you've been left behind. Today the term 'VP Social Media Marketing' sounds normal, but it is already as obsolete as VP of Billboards. Companies that recognize social media marketing as one set of marketing tools out of many will be ahead of the curve.

Fusion Marketing is the next generation of marketing that brings together all of our 6,000 years of traditional 'push' or 'monolog' marketing, the exciting digital marketing tools of the internet, and social media or 'dialog' marketing, and fully integrates them into one seamless toolset that will accomplish every objective you set at no additional cost! Fusion Marketing is such a totally new concept of 'interconnecting' all of your marketing tools that it has been accepted by the United States Patent & Trademark Office as 'Patent Pending'.

As part of the Fusion Marketing concept, I also invented a tool to help you implement your Fusion Marketing, called the Safko Wheel. This tool is available for free with the pre-purchase of the book at **www. TheFusionMarketingBible.com,** or you can make one from scratch.

This article is about how Fusion Marketing works, how the Safko Wheel works, and how you can use these tools to discover hidden ROI opportunities in your marketing. Fusion Marketing is a 12-step programme and here's how it works!

The Fusion Marketing Safko Wheel: 12-step process

Traditional tool analysis

Go to **www.TheFusionMarketingBible.com,** get the book and download your free $25 Safko Wheel Marketing Toolkit or just make one yourself. An example the wheel is shown in Figure 25.1.

Step 1 – Select your traditional tools

In Step 1, we will start by selecting (or creating) the traditional cards (red), for the traditional marketing tools you used last year, then place them around the wheel or... try working with all of the cards at first to see how powerful Fusion Marketing and this wheel can be.

FIGURE 25.1   An example of the Safko Wheel: traditional marketing wheel

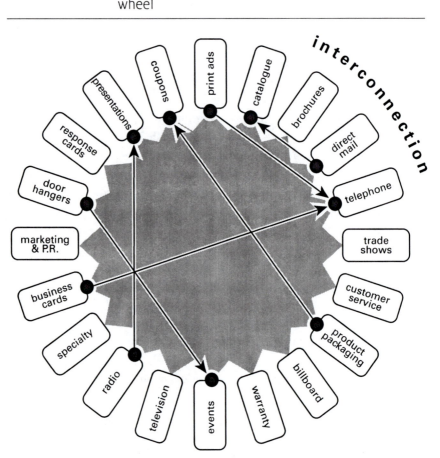

Step 2 – Perform Fusion Marketing

Fusion Marketing is about 'fusing' all marketing tools together to create new opportunities. To begin, select one tool from the wheel. Study that tool for a moment and understand how it really works. Then, randomly select a second tool from the wheel and study it. Then connect Tool 1 to Tool 2.

Now, ask yourself the question 'How can they work together?' For example, if I chose 'coupon', what if you 'put a coupon on the back of your business card' or 'put a coupon on your brochure'? We know that business cards represent a strong interaction, face-to-face, and most likely, you 'touched' the other person in the form of a handshake.

If you put a coupon on the back of your business card, that person – prospect – after meeting you, might exercise that relationship more readily by purchasing. Would putting a coupon on your brochure make a customer more likely to purchase while holding or viewing your product brochure? Of course it would!

Let's look at another example. What if you put the information about your next trade show on your business card with a QR barcode that said 'If you are in Atlanta on May 23, stop by booth 2103 for a demo and free gift!'? What if you did a radio promotion about an event you were putting on and during the promo you mentioned your event, and where to find a discount coupon?

Make multiple connections

The next step is to keep Tool 1 and move around the wheel connecting it to different tools and discover the hidden opportunities. Move completely around the wheel keeping the first tool and connecting it to a different tool. When you have completed this, repeat the process with an adjacent tool and write down all of the discovered opportunities. Can you see how many different opportunities that can be discovered by looking at your traditional media in this way?

Make reverse connections

Once you have gone around the wheel making the one-way connections, now you can make reverse connections. Start with the first toolset (Tools 1 and 2) and 'reverse' the connection to identify additional opportunities. Move around the wheel again making reverse connections such as 'put your personal contact information on your coupon', or 'put a QR barcode on your coupon to view your product brochure'. What if at your present-ation you mentioned the radio station that promoted you? What if on the coupon it had the call letters of the radio station that promoted you? It would all allow you to negotiate free radio time!

If you had a 'person' – someone to speak with, an individual who repre-sented your company with their personal contact information – on your coupon, would that make a prospect more likely to exercise that coupon and convert from a prospect to a customer? It would!

Digital tool analysis

Step 3 – The trinity of social media

Start with the Trinity of Social Media: blogging, micro-blogging, and social networks. With only these three tools, you can accomplish 90 per cent of the total success social media has to offer. Next, add in other digital/social

FIGURE 25.2 An example of the Safko Wheel: digital/social media marketing wheel

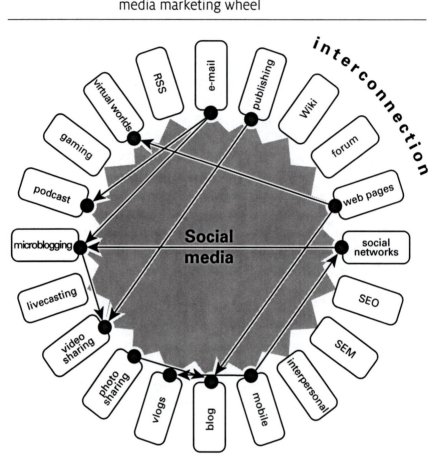

marketing tools such as SEO, SEM, Facebook (social networks), YouTube (video sharing), e-mail, etc. Tools that you wish to incorporate into this year's plan or you can look at all of the tools, first. If you aren't familiar with all 20 categories, please read *The Social Media Bible* (**www. TheSocialMediaBible.com**).

Step 4 – Perform Fusion Marketing

Refer to Step 2 above and repeat the process of fusing all of your digital/ social media tools together to discover new opportunities. How many can you identify?

Business cards and almost everything

An actual example of how this affected me was when I began thinking about my traditional marketing in a completely different way. I realized that my business card represented a personal relationship that had impact. I then put my business card information on my brochure. Rather than just having a corporate name and telephone number, customers could contact me directly. I immediately saw an increase in activity.

By putting my personal contact information on my event (seminar) flyers, I saw more people calling in asking questions and signing up to attend. It's the personal contact that is increasing the brochure's effectiveness. Having a personal relationship with a person is always better than trying to build a relationship between your customers and your company.

Fusion Marketing analysis

Step 5 – Create a TraDigital toolset

In this step, you combine the traditional marketing tools with the digital/social media marketing tools you have selected and place them around the wheel to create a custom tradigital toolset. And start making connections once again.

Step 6 – Perform the cost of customer acquisition (COCA)

You will quickly see that there are just too many possible connections. None of us have the time or resources to pursue all those opportunities. Actually, with the 20 top traditional and the 20 top digital/social media tools, there are 8.15×10^{47} or 8 with 47 zeros after it. We have to trim it down somehow, someway that makes sense.

To do this, we will perform the cost of customer acquisition on each tool (campaign). Start by listing all of the traditional campaigns you performed last year on a white-board, yellow pad or spreadsheet. List every expense, and be sure to include all of your overheads. Total the columns for those expenses. Estimate the number of new customers each campaign generated. Finally, divide the totals for each of the expense categories by the number of new customers. This is your cost of customer acquisition (COCA). These numbers will surprise you, some in a good way and some in ways that will cause shock and dismay.

Step 7 – Eliminate and prioritize

Here we eliminate campaigns that were ineffective; the ones with the poor ROI. This will provide new human and financial resources that we can use later. Prioritize the remaining tools you will use for this year's Fusion Marketing plan. Add in any new tools (cards) you wish to incorporate this year.

Step 8 – Perform Fusion Marketing

Once again, refer to Step 2 above and experience the process of fusing all of your tools together to discover new opportunities.

Second Life and web pages

These connections amazed me! When I looked at two random tools and how they could connect, I first chose Web Pages and Second Life. For those of you who aren't familiar with Second Life, it's an on-line three-dimensional world that people use to meet other people, do business and just explore. I use Second Life for business.

I have two 'real' stores on my property where I sell 'three-dimensional internet advertising', and my educational CDs, DVD and books. I also hold international meetings and interviews and teach virtual classes for universities around the world. I can even do a PowerPoint presentation to a group of avatars. In this example I'll choose virtual worlds and web pages to start with because I felt that they had the least in common. Second Life is what they call a 'thin client' or software run from your computer, and we all know how web pages work.

By using the Safko Wheel and connecting these two 'unconnectable' tools, I suddenly realized that, on every one of my web properties, any mention of my participation in Second Life was missing. Nowhere did I mention that I am marketing and participating in Second Life.

I went to my virtual office in Second Life, grabbed a screen capture of my avatar, and placed the image along with a link back to Second Life. Within 24 hours, I saw a 400 per cent increase in my visitors in Second Life! I am driving all of my website traffic to my virtual store in Second Life.

The next task I had was to promote my websites from within Second Life. So I created a large framed image that I hung on the wall in my virtual store that read 'Mention Second Life with any purchase and receive a free $50 DVD!'. Guess what? I saw a significant increase in traffic and revenue in my e-commerce web store. There are 16.5 million members on Second Life that I am now driving to my web properties. Fusion Marketing really works!

Strategy, objective, tool and tactic development

Step 9 – Define strategy

In this step we will define 'strategy' and create all of the strategies you will need to build a successful Fusion Marketing plan. Strategy = Objectives + Tools + Tactics. A strategy is the outcome, not an item.

Create objectives

Let's begin by creating five objectives that you want your marketing to achieve this year (goals), such as: 'increase e-mail list', 'drive more attendance to presentations', 'perform more webinars' or 'develop more product awareness'. Write them down.

Step 10 – Work the wheel

Now it's time to work the wheel by placing one of your objectives from above in the centre of the wheel. Select each tool, one at a time, and ask, 'how can I use this tool to achieve that objective?' Move around the wheel connecting each tool to that objective. These connections are your tactics. Try making multiple connections, using two tools to connect to the objective. Continue around the wheel. Record every tactic. Repeat with the next objective until you have fully developed all five objectives.

Step 11 – Prioritize your objectives

Next we will prioritize each tactic for each objective, then prioritize each objective, because you can't do everything. Remember, now that you have performed your COCA in Step 6, and have eliminated campaigns with a poor ROI, you now have human and financial resources to accomplish additional objectives. If you settled on only 20 final tools and developed five objectives, then you now have 100 tactics!

Step 12 – Finalize your Fusion Marketing plan

It's the combination all of the tools and tactics for each selected objective that becomes your final list of successful strategies. Combine all of your final objectives, tools and tactics to form your new strategic Fusion Marketing plan!

EXECUTE WITH SUCCESS!

By utilizing fusion marketing and the Safko Wheel process, you will only spend resources on your most effective tactics, on your most effective

FIGURE 25.3 An example of the Safko Wheel:
strategy–objective–tactic-tool wheel

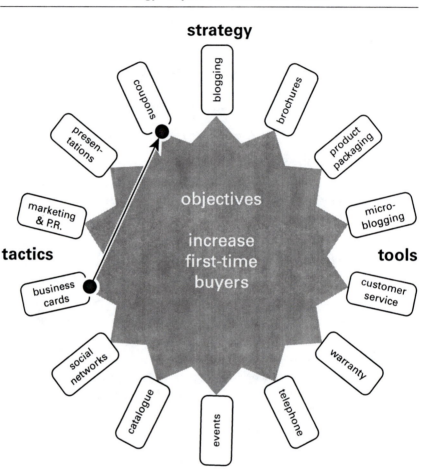

strategies, using the most effective traditional marketing tools combined with the most effective digital marketing tools.

That's fusion media marketing!

Fusion marketing is about looking at all of your tools, campaigns, objectives, conversion strategies and everything you do in marketing in a completely different way so as to identify hidden opportunities to increase your ROI without spending any additional money.

For more information on Lon Safko go to **www.LonSafko.com**, to learn more about fusion marketing, and to get your free Safko Wheel Marketing Toolkit download, go to **www.TheFusionMarketingBible.com**.

How to spell marketing in 2015: product development

26

MARTIN DEINOFF

Martin Deinoff is a Senior Vice President at Creuna – the leading digital agency in the Nordics. Martin has vast experience in digital strategy, digital concept development, project management and process improvements.

It is better to be great than to say that you are great. That is an obvious fact, or isn't it? Companies and corporations often act like this is the news of the century, which it actually is in many ways. Today there is a big unexploited potential for most companies to be great, to add more real value to customers instead of trying to charm them with loads of advertising.

This struggle to be great is not new, but the drastic increase in the potential to improve and the effects it has on marketing sure is. Digital technology and the internet are the driving forces behind this trend, altering the rules of the game for all players in the market.

The consumers of the new world – connected, informed and determined – have new demands. The companies of the new world – flexible, open and fast – are creating new competition. To be able to keep or win market shares in this environment, companies and organizations need to focus all their resources on improving their products and services, to add real value to customers instead of hiding behind old-fashioned advertising. The way to spell marketing in the future will be: product development.

Today society has truly moved beyond online. Digital technology is so deeply integrated with all aspects of our lives that we can no longer treat it as a field of its own. There is no e-marketing, just marketing. No e-strategy, just strategy. However, there is an ongoing shift in how companies do business and how people live their lives that has only begun. When it comes to how successful a product will be, the development is being pushed forward from two directions simultaneously. One is the new pressure that classical marketing is under – the control of information and media is now in the hands of consumers, rendering many old marketing ideas obsolete. The other is the rapid development of products and services as companies are starting to utilize the full potential of digital.

This article will describe how these two areas, marketing and product development, will be affected, changed and finally merged by the effects of the digital ecosystem of today. Let's begin by looking at marketing.

Marketing

The old advertising system was built on a number of flaws, imperfections that made advertising work. The main flaws were information asymmetry, communication obstacles, and control over media and tools.

Information asymmetry exists when companies with their great resources know more than you do. And also important – they know that you don't know. They can then use this asymmetry to create messages that are very biased and that cannot be controlled. In much plainer words – they can lie. Lies have been a cornerstone of advertising, whether the ad-industry like it or not.

Communication obstacles prevented consumers from spreading information in larger groups and across long distances. If a brand did not deliver what it promised, there were few ways for users to spread the word.

Also, the control over media and tools put the power in the hands of the companies. By controlling the production of the content and the channels in which this content was consumed, companies were able to tailor the total experience to fit the needs of advertisers.

Without these flaws we would not have had the marketing we've mostly seen through the years. Well-informed consumers that easily could communicate with each other and that could control and create media by themselves would not have been so easily persuaded. But it was not the disappearance of the flaws that first challenged the marketing situation but something that came from marketing itself – the fact that it was so easy and rewarding to shout out advertising messages.

Blur

When companies realized that mass media advertising was profitable they all wanted to jump on the bandwagon. More and more started to send marketing messages to an audience that did not grow proportionately. It is easy to understand that the situation quickly got out of hand. All advertising needs to get the recipients to stop what they are doing and instead focus on the advertising. If not, the ad will have no effect. So all of these advertisers needed to interrupt users to tell their story. In the beginning this was quite easy as an information – and even more entertainment – hungry audience often liked the advertising. Who remembers getting to the cinema in time not to miss the commercials?

Today there is no information – or entertainment – shortage. We have a practically unlimited supply of information and entertainment in a myriad of parallel channels, most of them online. There is an extreme over-abundance of even the best and most exclusive content. No matter if you like films, series, news, games or something else – there is a far larger supply than anyone can consume. Even if you just choose the best of the best there is not time. All this media consumes attention, and that resource does not scale well.

Marketing today does not only have to compete with all other marketing; it has to compete with all media, information, entertainment and communication – it is a daunting challenge.

Advertisers do all they can to cut through the noise. They place messages in all kinds of imaginable and unimaginable places – like the bottoms of glasses, the backs of receipts or even in toilet bowls. Or they turn up the volume: make their messages louder, bolder, more extreme. As soon as one player manages to be heard over the noise there are 10 others who copy the idea. It never ends.

Power to the people

The advertising that manages to pass through the blur, through the competition of our unlimited supply of high-quality content, and the filters we set up to get rid of all the unwanted interruption advertising, is still not in the clear.

The flaws in the system are no longer present – today there is no information asymmetry, no communication obstacles, and easy access to tools and media means that all users have the ability to create and broadcast almost in the same way that large companies do. Users are fundamentally different from before because they can instantly determine if the messages are true and if they deliver value or just steal their precious time. This means that the advertising that manages to reach the customers must balance on the edge of a knife – between effect and bad will.

Value

So what to do? Well, if the main problems are that users can avoid most unwanted advertising and judge the rest both morally and factually, the only way to win is to make marketing that users want – that adds value.

Marketing needs to be perceived as something that users want – something they will not filter out, something that makes them happy, that makes their lives easier and better. In a world where the users have the power, it is only this type of marketing that can get users' attention, be accepted and give effect.

To be able to provide real value companies need to focus on building better products, but before we discuss how this can be done I will provide three pieces of advice for the modern marketer.

Information before storytelling

Much marketing is all about telling a made-up story. As the competition for users' time gets fiercer, the challenge to create a story that can compete with other, non-commercial content is very hard. The users of today are often searching for information by their own will – mainly online. In this case a story may get in the way of the information a user is seeking. The skip-into button has never been more sought after.

In non-interactive media the messages should dare to focus on a few core messages that point the user towards a digital resource to find out more. Try to give customers as many ways as possible to find the information they may seek, on and offline. Once they get the basic information they may very well be ready to spend time on longer and more story-based messages.

- Solve the users' need for information before you tell a story.

- Trust that your product is interesting in itself – if not, make it interesting by developing it.

- Information does not need to be boring – make your communication effective and to the point, but still enjoyable and interesting.

Ask permission

Most marketing is based on interruption, which in its core is the very opposite of asking for permission. Such marketing has huge problems, as we discussed above, and the solution is to get the customers' permission. Most will of course reject our invitation, but those who accept will anticipate a message and be less likely to filter it out. If the message is relevant or even personal, it will probably provide value and the customer may very well take the first step towards a relationship with you. The hardest part is to get past the filters to ask for permission – and this is one of the few times when broadcasting may be a solution. Personally I believe more niche marketing efforts are the best way to get the first contact – like PR, product placement or events – but as long as you get a chance to ask for permission it is ok. The spontaneous interest that well-known brands or categories can get should not be forgotten – Google and other search engines are the permission marketer's best friend. Listening to social networks like Twitter is also a great thing – what can be better than if the customer initiates the communication. Once a contact is established, asking permission can be quite simple. General questions like 'may I send you this', 'would you like to try that' or, even better, personal questions like 'I believe that you might like...' or 'others with your profile have...' may go a long way.

- Respect the customer's integrity; to interrupt, annoy or disturb is not often a positive thing.
- Anticipated and relevant communication has a much better effect than one that is not – try to focus on this rather than fancy or loud commercials.
- Take care of a customer's confidence; don't gamble with the permission that is given.

Provide incentives

Customers need incentives if they are to give their interest and time. They need to trade the things companies want for something they want.

One important thing to think of is that very few incentives appeal to everybody. It is far easier to target small groups than to reach wide audiences. It is also important to make the incentive clear. Because it is this incentive that will get the customers on the hook, they need to be clear what is in it for them. Incentives are also important later on, but by then the company has a longer time to tell their story. If we cannot clearly explain the value for the user of engaging in the communication, we might need to rethink our approach. In a world where time and attention is very scarce, the one that can explain the benefits often wins. A well-defined value is always better than a vague one.

The actual incentive can vary a great deal. Information is the easiest; if the product is interesting enough this can be all that is needed. The trick is to get the users to understand how important the information is. A personal approach is often key to a perceived value. Using competitions and games is a common trick to get the customers' attention. Rebates work well for products whose functionality is commonly known. Product samples are great if the brand is unknown but the product category is something people want. To be part of a panel or test group can be interesting if the product can give a social value. The most radical incentive is to pay for the attention. What works varies from time to time and user to user – when it comes to incentives one size sure doesn't fit all.

- A clear incentive is better than a vague incentive.
- Most incentives need to be targeted to a specific group to be relevant.
- Invest in a relationship early to get payback in the future.
- Create incentives that are as close to your product as possible – giving away cake to get someone to buy porridge is probably not a good idea.

Future marketing

There are many more things to think of if you are to make great modern marketing. The three points above are however, in my opinion, the most important and the ones that traditional marketers have the most problem in listening to. Things like continuous improvement over quick campaigns, user collaboration, context over content and the creation of owned channels are also important – but can be handled once you get the basics right.

So how can these rules affect the great challenges that marketing is facing? How does one succeed in marketing in a world where the blur is getting worse all the time and users have so many possibilities to evaluate messages? By clear incentives, asking permission and quickly getting to the point, you show respect. By trying to constantly improve and listen to users, you show a willingness to help. By being honest and speaking with a natural, human tone of voice, you can come across as someone to trust.

Most important is to add as much value as possible through the marketing – no matter if that value comes from marketing or the product itself. It is much better to be great than to say that you are great.

As I mentioned, marketing that is not perceived as marketing at all may be the absolute winner. If you can develop the product in a way that also takes care of the needs of marketing, much is won. In doing this one important aspect is to focus the marketing and communication efforts not only before the purchase, but afterwards – when the product is in use. That way the messages have a good chance of reaching the user and being both relevant and personal. Users today are connected and can be a very good marketing resource, if you can get them to spread information about the product. Also, many products today generate a lot of information when they are used, information that can be great content. For example, the Nike+ products generate information about people's running that can be used to reach both people connected with the customer and a more general public.

Product development

For most companies, the products constitute the core of what they are, the raw, unpolished offering that they go to the market with. A lot of companies have added so many layers on top of that offering – stories, financing, package deals, clubs or campaigns – that it often is hard to tell what they actually do. Nevertheless, the products are still the most important element. As we can conclude from the previous section about marketing, products will be more important in the future as marketers will continue to face more and more obstacles. The companies that focus on deliver solid and clear value will be the winners.

We will also see that product development will be more important as most products will be more complex and made with more and more information. All development follows technical advances in society, and this applies to product development in particular. Right now digital technology is the flavour of the month, but around the corner wait developments such as nano-technology or gene-technology whose effects we can only guess.

The good news for product developers today is that there is a huge potential for most companies to add value. Traditional products that are mostly based on physical elements often reach a point where further development is very hard. Of course all products can be improved, but the rate of improvement gets slower and slower as the physical forces of nature get in the way. Digital technology, and even more the virtual services that spawn from this technology, are very young and the rate of improvements and inventions is steadily accelerating.

Kilobyte outweighs kilogram

In order to exploit this potential, companies have to digitize at least some parts of their offering. This can be done by transforming something that is done by physical means today and do it digitally instead, or to add a digital service to an existing physical product. Where value can be created by either virtual or physical means, a company should always choose virtual.

Digital technology is already integrated in many products. Small chips that control and handle data are built into many of the things we use every day – like our car, TV, heating system or burglar alarm.

If a product has digital integration or if the whole product is virtual, then it can be developed by adding services. The service process the data the product produces or consumes connects it to other users, products, services and systems. The digital hardware is often a tool, like a saw or a hammer, and the service provides new or increased value. A loudspeaker can play sounds, but a service can control what it plays, how loud and which loud-speakers should be used. A physical lock is needed to keep a door closed, but a service can control who can open it under which circumstances, and keep track of who has opened the lock, and when. A refrigerator keeps food cold but a service can give information about how cold it is, when it was opened last and if it needs service. It may be integrated with food containers so that it can give information about what is stored there, and possible recipes I could cook with those ingredients. Physical laws do not bind these services, nor have they reached any point where development is impracticable. On the contrary services are easy to develop as they can use the network to connect and integrate with other services.

Overabundance

Today we live in a world where we often have far more things than we need, at least in the rich parts of the world. Our basic needs were met a long time ago and we often feel that we would like to reduce the number of things we have rather than adding more. If companies can meet the demand for smaller and less obvious products that meet our needs, they can be winners.

When it comes to digital content the situation is different. I'd rather have all the music in the world than half the music – and the same applies to movies, games and encyclopaedias. Digital services and content can also quite easily be tailored to our specific and personal needs, and with a global market the demand for niche products may very well be high enough to enable the craziest stuff to be sold.

Be part of the network

The obvious advice is to digitize and make the product a part of a network. Move both information and functionality online to draw upon all the benefits that the virtual world provides. This is done in two distinct steps. First digitize – that is, connect to a network. Products that are already virtual don't need to bother with the first step.

Does the technology need to be baked into the product or can the product connect with a virtual service to perform the same task? For example could a car information system be handled from a web page instead of some hardware built into the car, and managed from a smartphone or tablet. Can the technology be made less visible, and focus more on the actual usage.

Services connected to a product are often best when on a network. Here they can use the exponential growth of value that comes from connecting many nodes or forming groups and sub-groups. Connecting to different networks gives different advantages. Social networks are good for connecting to user groups with information created by the product or the context in which the product exists. In aggregating networks, information can be gathered and compared, sorted or shared. A camera manufacturer could for example connect to Flickr or a hotel manager to Tripadvisor. In a functional network the focus is more on the core value the product delivers. Often these networks let technology talk to other technology to create better or new functionality or experience – like two cars talking to each other to avoid collisions.

- If you can deliver a value virtually or physically, always choose virtually – do all you can to find possibilities to digitize.
- Start by adding supporting information to the network, continue with information the product produces and finally information it consumes.
- If part of the network you are part of increases in value, your product increases in value.

Optimize the business model

As the digital revolution continues, companies need to look at the business model and adjust it to the new demands and opportunities on the market. This may be less urgent for typical bricks and mortar companies, but for most it is critical. If you believe that your company is part of the digital eco-system, then your business model will probably need some adjustment, no matter what you do.

The production costs of digital resources are generally much lower than for physical products. The way the costs develop over time also varies a great deal, with almost all the cost of a digital product occurring in its initial development; after this the second or the millionth copy probably costs the same – often zero.

Companies need to understand that when they add digital services as an important part of their offering, they also need to work with new business models based on other aspects than production costs. On the internet most things are free, and payments often come from a complex weave of exchange of value between different actors.

One of the results of the digital revolution is that we will own less and less – renting, leasing and hiring will be more common. In the more service-oriented market, what is actually sold will be much more complex – a product that is often specifically tailored to a customer's needs, which change over time and which interact with the digital ecosystem of other products, users, services and systems.

- Most companies need to base their business model on something other than the production cost of their products.
- Try to differentiate the offering and charge for the value that is provided. This is often easier for a service than for a physical product.
- Be aware that new business models will come and go – stay flexible and make sure that you can adjust to what is working best right now.

Open up

A connected product can become even better if it opens up and lets others add to the value. Online, many services can draw on resources from each other to create new and higher values. The more people who use your product to create value, the more value can come your way. The trick is to be as generous as possible without violating your business model, to make it easy and appealing for others to integrate with and use your particular product or service.

Traditionally, demand and supply were closely connected. Now they might not work together as we usually think. A product in a network might be more popular when there is the more supply, and more users will mean more value.

If many users, companies and creators use your product and build it into their systems, there is a great possibility that they are marketing it in a way that can be really valuable. If the product is put into a personal and relevant framework, it may be discovered and appreciated by a crowd that you could otherwise not have reached. Also the services that arise from mashups of your product and other products, services or systems may be your greatest hits, others may actually do the product development for you.

- There are more bright people outside the company than inside it; use this fact.

- Be open to letting others use your stuff, and use others' as often as possible; if you create value and usage the reward will come.

- Support and reward interest in your product; care about those who care about you.

Future product development

The basic principle of product development is the same as for marketing: to add value. But instead of facing new challenges, product developers will find new opportunities. The increased intelligence of the products probably makes it more interesting to talk with our products than about them.

The added value will to a large extent come from new technology. Companies must learn that technology is not mainly a tool to reach an established strategy – it is the foundation for the strategy they will set.

It is a good idea to prioritize tests and trials, tear down old walls of structure or communication. Don't be afraid to develop new products, even if they make your star product of today obsolete. Make products smaller, faster and cheaper. Don't worry about computer power; the development is so fast that it will be available when you need it.

27 Smarter checkouts: beyond the transaction

MATTHEW OXLEY

Matthew Oxley is founder and Managing Director at Truly Digital, which provides excellent yet affordable digital marketing solutions to businesses. Matthew has a wealth of experience in digital, primarily in paid search (PPC) and natural search (SEO).

Introduction

So your brand has finally made it online – the website looks perfect, the brand has lots of traction in social media, there's traffic coming in from the search engines (or probably just Google) and all is well – except your customer just doesn't buy from you.

Beyond price and product, few things matter more in digital marketing than the buying process – although it's wrong to look at the process as pre-post checkout, it is often the case that, at some stage, the checkout process of a website comes under scrutiny.

We've all seen what happens next – questions get dropped, pages disappear, what you thought were vital steps in the customer journey are suddenly discarded. Create an account? Who wants to do that? And product upgrades? Nobody seems to bother doing that anyway. Why ask all those personal questions? Let's just get their credit card details and take the money!

If you're a true marketer at heart, the above process will probably make you weep, but the reality is that the above sort of simplification has been happening to shopping baskets, checkouts, quote facilities and the like for years, and the trend is gathering pace. What starts out as a genuine effort to improve the effectiveness of a website, all too often ends with a soulless, empty, money-grabbing attempt at transacting with the customer that cheapens the brand and, just as importantly – reduces revenue.

Contrast this for one moment to the offline 'checkout' process and it suddenly seems illogical. On a typical visit to Marks & Spencer's, instead of a being able to beeline to the cashier, I'm made to zigzag my way past an assortment of snacks and other potential impulse buys until I make my way to the checkout where I'll be quizzed (hopefully in a subtle way) on whether I want to upgrade my credit card to an M&S credit card. I'm not saying that process is ideal from a customer's point of view, or that it can't be taken too far, but the potential of the brand to cross-sell high-margin products, or deepen their relationship with the customer is simply greater than the cost of the customer spending 10 seconds walking round the planned obstacles.

Ultimately there has to be a compromise – some (many) customers are in a hurry and want to do things quickly, while others have a little more time to spare for making a more meaningful interaction. A good process – online or offline – allows for both scenarios. Just think: many of the offline stores like the one I highlighted above also have self-service checkouts now.

The logic behind checkout optimization

Despite the negative way in which checkout optimization can be implemented, the logic for it cannot be escaped. The conversion rate – the percentage of visitors who buy from a given website or campaign – is one of the inescapable metrics associated with digital marketing, and for good reason. It usually beats return on ad spend, reach, saturation and all the other potential metrics that digital marketers obsess about.

It's a fairly simple principle that, the better a website can convert a visitor, the more profitable any given campaign will be. Since it's also usually the case that a profitable campaign is likely to be renewed and/or extended, it also follows that more campaigns can be run, generating more profit, if a website converts well. This example holds especially well for pay per click (PPC) based marketing – such as Google Adwords – the advertiser pays for every click, so the conversion rate is often the main limiting factor determining how much the advertiser can bid. An advertiser who can convert twice as many customers as their competitor can probably afford to outbid their rival, securing the higher spot.

To a large extent the obsession with reducing conversion rates has been driven by technology – especially the cheap availability of analytics software. Free software such as Google Analytics is now considered to be among the leading solutions despite being free when a brand doesn't want to own the data. Analytics software can accurately pinpoint aspects such as drop-off in the conversion process, often in quite stark ways, and, more importantly, can measure the impact of changes. When combined with a/b or multivariate testing, which allows the marketer to create multiple versions of the same process and divert only a portion of the website visitors to the 'experiment' pages, the rationale for testing improvements becomes even more compelling.

Finally, in the modern age of social networks and dual screening, it cannot be argued that any process simple enough to survive distractions just long enough to get a purchase is undoubtedly worth pursuing.

Just whose checkout is it anyway?

Part of the problem besieging checkout optimization as an activity is just who should own the process. At first glance it's now obvious that:

- Marketing feel they should drive the process, because they are responsible for the customer journey, and most probably for the budgets involved.

- IT feel they should drive the process, because they have ownership over the website – it's essentially a technical exercise.

- The data agency see the task as all about data collection, so they want a say.

- The media agency (or specialist agencies such as search agencies) wants ownership, because they send the customers to the website in the first place. An improvement in the checkout conversion rate positively impacts the ROI of everything the agency does.

There are many potential stakeholders, and each of the above entities can be subdivided, often along commercial and non-commercial lines. The project may have unbalanced, or in some cases entirely disjointed, goals.

The process doesn't always play out as a tug of war but, more often, in larger, matrixed organizations, it is a case of different parties making contributions at different stages. IT make the checkout process more secure one month, but marketing reverse it later down the line. Because an online checkout (despite its importance) is rarely owned by a single person in a company, the route to authorization is opaque and can easily be circumvented.

In reality, when a serious attempt is made to overhaul the process, it is nearly always driven by those with a commercial remit – and more often than not it's an in-house acquisition team or an agency provider. Creative, brand and CRM teams lose out to number crunchers, and the process narrows towards a single common goal – converting more customers.

Diet or tone?

Slimming down the checkout is the general perceived wisdom, as already articulated, but it's often only part of the answer.

Smarter checkouts achieve better conversion rates while gathering better quality insights from the customer, allowing for an all-round improvement for the business.

Consider somebody who wants to get in shape for their summer holidays – one approach would be diet, but another would be build muscle – but ultimately, if the goal is athletics, then they would look to achieve good muscle tone, accentuated by a slimmer body frame. Your goals for your checkout can be thought of in a similar way – the end goal is to make the checkout more effective, but there are multiple ways of getting there, and not all involve shedding fields, pages and questions.

Having your cake and eating it

This ultimately leads us to the Utopia that we all seek – how to improve the conversion rate of a checkout while not taking away the crucial input needed to make it a 'good' transaction – in other words, how to have your cake and eat it.

When viewed as a mission to improve the overall effectiveness of the checkout (as opposed to just slimming it down) it becomes easier to identify such possibilities.

Register an account?

Perhaps one of the most well-known aspects of online shopping controversy revolves around the requirement of the user to 'create an account'. The idea of creating an account is fraught with problems for the user – how long will it take? Is this really a retailer to share this kind of information with? Will the items suddenly drop out of the basket? The reasons for avoiding having to register an account are plentiful, with few apparent benefits to the customer.

In recent years, retailers have moved away from forcing the user to create an account, with a number of alternatives, most of which involve removing the requirement altogether, or otherwise giving the user a choice to create an account or not (the worst of which involves taking the user to a page dedicated only to this choice).

The main problem with both these approaches is that customer accounts are very useful to the retailer (aiding repeat purchases amongst other aspects), and dissuading customers in any great number is a problem. Why not simply make the account process a lot easier? Better yet, why not make it almost transparent to the process of buying online? The single mandatory piece of information necessary to creating an account to the user is a password.

Smart checkouts have now started integrating a password field into their forms, with a small note informing the user that, while the field is optional, it'll help them checkout in the future. The user specifies a password, and is able to return to the website in the future using their e-mail address and password – simple, effective and the best of both worlds.

Saving the best till last

There are lots of things you'd like to know about your customers in an ideal world, but how do you go about getting the info? Questions on your checkout add to the process, and, even when marked as optional fields can cause some customers to drop out.

Saving form fields till after the customer has checked out can be a good way of getting information that might otherwise have held up the transaction. Consider a financial services business – most of these companies will, of course, post the customer a written agreement that the customer needs to fill out anyway. Questions that aren't essential in calculating the price can be asked at the end of the checkout, and if the user omits them they can be included in the documentation sent to the customer.

Adding personality

In a world of faceless corporations, people are wary about what they want to share, and to a large extent care little about the entity they are transacting with. So when you give people optional fields on a checkout about them, their natural response is to skip those questions – whether the motivation for doing so is fear or simply not caring enough to spend the extra time, the result is the same.

I recently came across an excellent checkout however, which prefixed a small section of questions with a funny note saying how the following questions were not mandatory, but that they (the brand) were a little bit nosy and would love to know.

This is an excellent approach on many levels – first, it makes it clear to the customer that the section is voluntary, meaning those who are time constrained will ignore it and proceed as necessary. Others, however, I suspect might be more inclined to answer – the checkout had ingeniously brought personality into the process, subtly telling the customer that they'd be doing somebody – a real person – a huge favour by filling out a few simple fields. Most people who are having a good shopping experience won't mind doing somebody a favour, and that's a powerful thing to have on your side.

28 Making money with metrics that matter

CHRIS PERRY and ALEX STEER

Chris Perry is the Joint CEO and Alex Steer is a Senior Strategist at the creative technology company Fabric Worldwide. Chris has been running digital agencies for the last 16 years and Alex has vast experience in marketing technology, consulting and advertising agency environments internationally.

Not long ago, big data looked very small. At least, it played a very small role in the day-to-day work of most marketing departments. Data typically existed in pockets throughout organizations, and access to analytics software was normally confined to a few individuals. Over the last few years that has changed. CIOs, CTOs and research buyers have made a push to put their businesses' high-volume data – especially online behavioural data – on a more consistent footing. This has increasingly spelled an end to a world in which a brand's big data resources depended on a password sticky-taped to a computer monitor. Data is increasingly likely to be brought onto common platforms, in standardized formats.

But as big data has become more prominent within organizations, there has also been demand for it to become more important. And as it has got into the hands of marketers who are keen (and under pressure) to demonstrate measurable results and a return on investment, the limits of even well-organized data have been tested.

We've started to hear a common message from marketers, analysts and technologists working with big data on behalf of brands. It's that simply having more and more data isn't enough. You need to be able to do something with it.

This attitude – it's not what you've got, it's how you use it – is right, and is the first step to brands taking a more considered approach to unlocking the value in large-volume data. But many marketers have found themselves frustrated and less than impressed with the results of their first efforts to use data to their advantage. In part this is because of a tendency to assume that 'we should do something' means 'we should do anything'. So data is applied in silos, to small pilot projects where they can do little harm but little good. The admirable 'test and learn' approach can often become 'test and give up', especially when the alternative to spending on data pilots is to put budget back into the kinds of activities that deliver stable results and are easy to measure. Because data tests are kept in these 'safe spaces', they often lack strategic focus and the kind of rigorous measurement that they should make it easy to see. Big data, for all its potential, becomes a sideshow that never made it to the main stage.

In this chapter we look at some ways in which brands are pushing their use of big data past the experimental phase, and using it to unlock insights and value that support their core business strategies, and even start to re-define them. The best brands aren't just looking to do something with data – they're looking to do the right thing. They are constantly asking: how can this make us money?

Finding the finish line

Very simply, online data – especially at the level of volume and detail that big data provides – lets us measure more. In particular, as so many parts of the brand and customer experience shift online, it lets us see and connect the points in a customer's journey, and identify the paths and patterns of behaviour that lead to success. Suddenly we can move from looking at data in a series of isolated pools, to seeing an entire brand ecosystem and all the moments of interaction within it.

This can be a shock as well as a blessing. After all, there's something comfortable about being insulated from hard financial reality. But a way of seeing that focuses on the connections between customers' interactions with a brand has the effect of bringing the bottom line into sharp focus. In a genuinely connected system, where we can measure and monitor customer journeys, we can draw close links right the way from the first point of contact a customer has with a brand (an online video, a branded game, a post on a social network), to the moment of truth where that customer decides whether to spend money with you or not. By seeing enough customers, the ways they behave and their outcomes, we can identify the contribution of all the interactions we measure towards the end result. Though it's not perfect, the more touch-points we can measure, the more accurate our picture will be.

Improving the bottom line means focusing on the finish line. A good digital strategy consists of the ability to take a set of commercial objectives and identify what role digital channels and tools will play in helping the business reach those objectives. A brand's ecosystem of digital assets (eg sites, mobile apps, social channels, e-commerce portals) should work together to improve the chances of a successful interaction between brand and customer. Each ecosystem will differ. Some will serve only to take new customers and provide them with information or offers so they will consider the brand at some future purchase occasion. Others will walk customers right the way through to the point of purchase (and beyond, in the case of after-sales support).

In any case, a good data strategy should successfully translate that digital marketing plan into a series of measurable indicators that show how efficiently and effectively the digital channels are getting consumers to whatever 'finish line' has been set. Sometimes these will be literal indicators of commercial value – in cases where purchase and payment are part of the measurable digital journey. Otherwise, marketers should set proxy indicators – the digital activities that suggest the highest likelihood to purchase, or highest degree of brand bonding or loyalty, that it is possible to reach online. (In the case of an automotive brand, we might assume that sending a message to a dealer to book a test drive would be this kind of proxy.)

Defining 'finish lines' is not just about knowing the raw percentages – that, say, 40 per cent of your customers reached the goal, 60 per cent didn't. It's about being able to look back from there, because you measure every touch-point, and see: What made the difference? What were the campaigns, touch-points, dates and times and places and user types that typically led to success or failure? From this kind of knowledge you can see what you need to do differently. You can build segments of users – not the traditional pen-portraits of attitudes and values (useful though these are), but clusters based on shared behaviours and outcomes. For these you can define what's needed to turn failure into success, and work to find the marketing opportunities to improve the likelihood of a good result in future.

For this to work and make money, though, the stakes have to be high enough. Marketers need to be capturing, analysing and applying big data on digital assets that matter to their core business. This doesn't mean betting the farm. A 'test and learn' approach is still best – but the test should be set on a meaningful opportunity or a difficult problem, closely aligned to the basic strategy of your business. Like any experiment it should have a well-defined 'finish line' and a measurable outcome.

Beyond the 'guesswork economy'

Marketing necessarily thrives on educated guesswork. The ability to take a limited set of information about consumers' attitudes, values and behaviours, and extrapolate that into a real plan of action, is what makes it a creative as well as an analytical profession.

It's hardly worth saying that big data offers more certainty – the opportunity to move guesswork and inference, and identify real observed behaviours which can often differ markedly from claimed ones. It's also true that there is an immediacy to big data which can correct the tendency to find an insight once and assume that it remains true.

But big data also lets us be surprised in a way that is more difficult in a world of educated guesswork. When mined for patterns, it can yield insights that have little to do with what we thought our customers were doing – or even who we thought they were. We recently worked with a personal care brand that was targeted at young women, and spent money and time immersing itself in the lives and values of that target market. We showed that half of its online visitors were young men – a segment it had never thought to investigate, that provided a growth opportunity that would have gone untapped.

So big data offers something genuinely new and powerful – but the challenge is to act on it as marketers, and as a business. Many organizations that have access to big data are still structured as if they don't, and with the exception of a few individuals they continue to make decisions based on occasional information. The 'guesswork economy' – the money spent on decisions not informed by certainty – remains huge.

Let's not underestimate the challenge of going from being an organization that has big data (and road-tests it occasionally) to an organization that is responsive to behavioural insights at scale. It means becoming a business that has customer insight at its heart, keeps that insight fresh, and organizes itself around it.

The best first step is to set metrics that matter – the markers that help you measure your customers' progress towards the finish line. These can be led by marketing, but should be agreed on throughout the organization – and talked about widely. Marketing's internal role is a difficult one, to keep that relentless customer focus alive and interesting, and to build a culture of data that is accessible (not complex or intimidating), lively and focused.

From optimizing to innovating

Even where big data has been used in focused, measured ways by marketers, the trends of the last few years has been heavily towards optimization: monitoring existing marketing activity, seeing the results, seeing what works and changing your next move.

This is admirable, but the culture of testing and fixing has often been confined to digital advertising and media, the important peripherals of marketing. They rarely reach through to the core of how a business organizes its marketing strategy, where they have a chance to reconfigure the entire ecosystem to grow value. As a result we have a world in which online ads use increasingly sophisticated algorithms to understand and segment their audiences, only to use that knowledge to re-target them with simple sales messages. Anyone who has had the experience of being followed around the internet across sites by the pair of shoes or garden shed they once looked at, will know that this does not exactly feel like the frontier of insight-driven consumer engagement.

More than anything, it risks diminishing returns. As consumers are bombarded with ever-more digital advertising, they get smarter at screening it out, and the strategies needed to get any of it to stick have to become increasingly ingenious to get the same results. It's a little like juicing a lemon: the harder you have to squeeze, the nearer you are to the last drop.

Putting big data at the heart of your ecosystem – not just using it to tweak the edges – is hard work. Many business are not set up to collaborate around data, and it is a long process to go from beginning to understand and share insights, to using them to rethink quite fundamentally how your business should serve its customers. Beginning that process, though, can be an inspiring as well as a tough process, creating opportunities for new types of collaboration around data and insight, and conversations that would never otherwise have happened. Above all, a focus on common goals and metrics that matter, that are understood and talked about throughout an organization, drives an appreciation of the bottom line. This creates a shared conversation about customer value, drives business model innovation (not just marketing optimization), and sets businesses up to profit now and in the future.

Customer currency: contextualized data insights

SAUL STETSON

Saul leads client strategy for Exponential UK, helping brands to provide a more relevant and more engaging advertising experience for their customers and maintaining Exponential's position as thought leaders in the industry. Exponential is a leading global provider of advertising intelligence and digital media solutions to brand advertisers.

As Bob Dylan once famously sang, the times they are a-changing. Without entirely realizing it, marketing strategy has become more technical, more intricate and more sophisticated than we have ever seen before. Change has been gradual and adoption has been fairly slow but the digital age now appears to be in full swing. Those who truly embrace digital and the benefits that it will come with will be the clear winners and those who stick with traditional marketing strategies are likely to be left behind.

While there are many aspects of digital that should be considered as relevant for any modern marketing organization, this chapter will focus on the growing importance and availability of data, significantly on how high-quality data should be collected and used to inform all aspects of a marketing strategy both online and offline.

The internet really is a weird and wonderful place. Information of all sorts, shapes and sizes is at our fingertips, whether through a computer, smartphone or tablet device, and we take full advantage of that. The statistics will vary depending on which article you read but the story is the same. If we are searching for product information, film reviews, travel advice or just general knowledge, the vast majority of us will turn immediately to the world wide web in the hope that it will satisfy our craving for knowledge. The result is a very revealing digital footprint that, when tracked effectively, can offer more insight about customers than any data they would voluntarily give you. When this footprint is fully contextualized, we start to understand customer behaviours in what has become their very native digital environment.

What is contextualization?

The first question to answer is: exactly what does data contextualization mean? Contextualization is the methodology that categorizes – in precise detail – specific areas of content with which users are engaging. The web is full of unstructured information, with a massive variety of content on all sorts of sites. Contextualization technology is able to scan a web page, understand its content, and assign it a pre-set category that will sit within a more general category chain. When the data is then analysed, it is well structured for interpretation (Figure 29.1).

As consumers navigate their way around the net on a day-to-day basis, the consumption of that category of information can be added to an anonymous user profile. When these user profiles are aggregated around a central seed like a visit to a brand's website, a model can be created that offers the statistical likelihood (in comparison with the average) of that brand's customers consuming information in the categories highlighted. This is referred to as the behaviours 'lift'.

Of course much of this depends on the quality of the contextualization technology itself. Does a page talking about Paris Hilton contextualize in a 'Travel' or 'Hotel' category, or does it correctly categorize under 'celebrity'? Can the technology understand images and photos on the page that may improve the categorization? Can this technology be applied within a mobile, social and even connected-television context to complete the digital picture? These are all important questions; some have been answered and some remain a focus for various technology companies who are taking an individual approach to answering the others.

FIGURE 29.1 Data contextualization tree

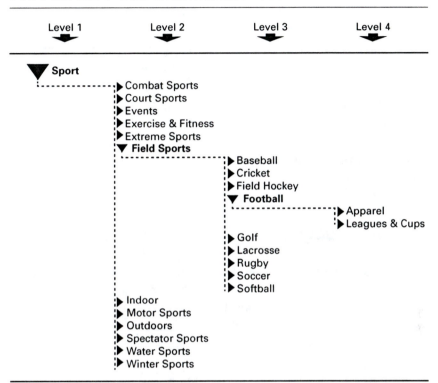

Practical and actionable

We've seen significant investment in the collection of data from customers but question marks remain over its relevance and usability. By fully contextualizing the collection of data and building both individual user profiles and aggregated behavioural models, we can go a long way to answering possibly the most important 21st-century marketing question: how effectively can data drive actionable marketing insights?

Creating an audience for a campaign needs to be scientific and should always start with a true understanding of who your customers are, what else they like doing, and subsequently where and how you can best advertise to them and others that look a lot like them. The logic is simple; if, when aggregated, your in-market customers are interested in certain content and digitally behave in certain ways then it is likely that your ideal target market will also have a similar digital footprint.

Figure 29.2 is a behavioural model built of the in-market customers of a utilities provider, and analysis of the higher-interest behaviours offers a fairly clear indication of a key marketing segment. A dominance of furniture, home improvement, mortgage/personal finance and other household utilities would suggest a clear home-mover segment. Utilities are often something that customers are reluctant to change because of the complexity and hassle that is sometimes involved. When people move home, however, it is often taken as a good opportunity to look for a better deal. Tailoring the creative, the offer and the targeting both online and offline would be clear actions that are derived from understanding the story that sits within contextualized data.

Scientific segmentation

Market segmentation is of course a crucial element of an organization's marketing strategy. Market research will be taken into account; product specifications are often important but for many companies intuition can be the key driver for segmenting their target markets. Contextualized data gives marketers a chance to be far more scientific in determining who their ideal customer is likely to be and what that customer looks like.

Take for example a car insurance provider. Their fundamental segmentation model was that the more affluent customers would be able to afford a fully comprehensive policy and so this would be their most likely purchase. The less affluent customers would probably want to reduce monthly outgoings and therefore be more likely to purchase a policy with a more limited cover for a lower cost. By building an aggregated behavioural model based on the customers who had already purchased one of the two different insurance products online, the digital footprint could be compared. When this was done, the comparison showed that the company's segmentation model was flawed. In fact, those who had purchased the fully comprehensive policy showed high levels of interest in content like family products, cookery and football, suggesting a more family-budget-oriented profile. Conversely those who had purchased the lower-cost, limited insurance policy showed high levels of interest in consumer electronics, designer fashion and other luxury products, suggesting an affluent, cash-rich profile.

After further qualitative analysis, the contextualized data began to tell a logical story. In reality, those who either have or are starting a family prefer an insurance product that gives them budget certainty. The extra cost is

FIGURE 29.2 Aggregated behaviour model for utilities provider (Q2 2011)

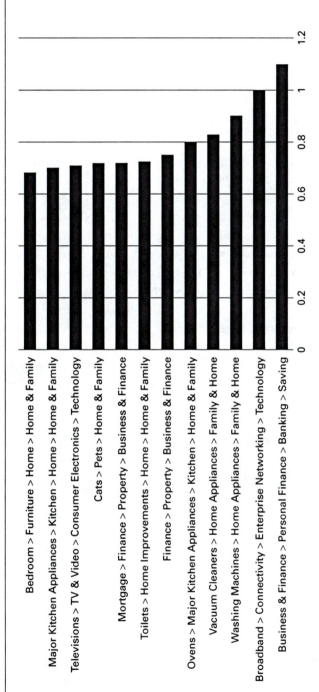

acceptable for the peace of mind that a fully comprehensive policy offers. Likewise, if cash flow and financial planning are not important then you are perhaps more likely to take the risk of a third-party-only policy. Immediately, two distinct segments can be defined that are each attracted to a different proposition.

Questioning assumptions

It is always healthy to question existing marketing assumptions, and as we move further into the age of data our ability to do this improves. As products and markets mature, often the originally intended target market will change as new market information is available. Take for example a DVD mail-order rental company, whose obvious initial assumption would be that their customers were likely to be movie lovers. However, a contextualized behavioural model of their existing customer base revealed a very different story. After aggregating the user profiles, the high-interest areas were baby supplies, cosmetics, women's health and also video games and consoles. This suggests that in reality, while movie lovers would obviously remain an important segment, their current customers fitted the profile of people who wanted and needed to be entertained at home. This includes mothers who are trying to keep themselves and their children entertained along with gamers who naturally enjoy staying in.

While contextualized data makes interpretation far more practical, it is still of course open to interpretation. Nonetheless understanding customers from a contextual perspective will always give marketers the capacity to develop new ideas and drive new propositions to market. In many respects, even if contextual data insight merely confirms marketing assumptions it can be a valuable exercise. This may enable an overall strategy to be more streamlined, with budget allocation being more focused on true target segments. Regardless of whether the data confirms or changes assumptions, the value it offers is clear.

Seasonal strategy

Once the principles of contextualized data insights are grasped, its practical uses are limitless. Comparing data sets from interest in different products, purchase of different services and the consumption of varied information offers marketers an answer to more specific questions.

FIGURE 29.3 Aggregated behavioural model for online retailer (Q4 2011)

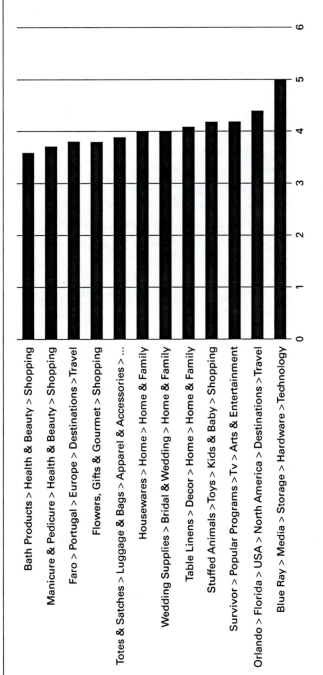

Online retailer play.com used contextualized data insights to better understand the changing nature of the visiting customers profiles throughout the year. When two contextualized behaviour models from Q2 and Q4 were compared, the insights gained told a compelling story. Throughout the year the high-interest behaviours were for gadgets, sports and other masculine indicators. However, in the run-up to the Christmas period, the dominant behaviours aggregated were teddy bears, house ware, family holiday destinations and other feminine indicators, suggesting their Christmas shoppers are more likely to be female heads of households who are perhaps looking to buy their family presents in an efficient way.

In a market of switchers and generally low customer loyalty, it has never been more important to be dynamic. If data suggests that there are certain timeframes in which to differentiate yourself to a specific segment then your marketing strategy should be nimble enough to reflect that. The more quality insights that can be derived, the more proactive the strategy can be.

Data as a true international currency

The fact remains that data has become such an important part of the international business world that organizations will even start to discount products as a ploy to capture some customer data. We're consistently offered free trials, special offers and many other clever incentives in return for our personal information, suggesting that data capture is in some occasions more valuable than actually charging. Membership of loyalty programmes that require 'registration data' often entitles consumers to a reduction in the cost of the item or service. Furthermore, to the untrained eye Facebook remains a completely free service, although cynics will be aware that we are in fact trading a significant amount of personal data in order to really use it. Are all of these initiatives an indirect first stage of creating a different price for those who are willing to pay partly with their personal data?

Put simply, high-quality data has become something that every organization should want and will need in order to survive in the global marketplace. It's become a true commodity and the business logic is undeniable. The more data you have, the greater understanding you will have of your customers and the more relevant you can be throughout your entire brand's experience.

Relevance is the name of the game in the modern consumer market. Power has radically shifted from the big organizations to the consumer, and with so much variety and choice we only have to buy the products and services that we truly believe fulfil our needs. Contextualized data will become a key mechanism as we glide further into the digital age. Aspects of consumers' day-to-day lives are increasingly being lived out digitally where previously they weren't. Contextualized data from a cross-platform digital network is an easy way to learn more about who your customers are and what they like to do, and then derive practical and actionable insights from them that should inform the holistic marketing strategy.

One final note: interpretation remains key

Regardless of the granularity and quality of data that is now available, data is and will always be open to interpretation. It's crucial to have somebody within the organization who is able to read between the lines and make practical sense of it, and contextualized data makes the task that much easier. However the fact remains that the data merely facilitates the insight, whereas the individual who is able to make use of it will always be the one who actually derives it. The old saying that two heads are better than one seems appropriate for this function. The reality is that we're unlikely to ever get to the stage of understanding our customers exactly or knowing exactly who they are and where to find them. Marketing will always maintain a trial-and-error approach, so developing new insights and ideas will continue to be valuable contribution, and you can never have enough people in your organization who are able to do this.

30 Introduction to predictive marketing

BRENT CHATERS

Brent Chaters is the author of *Mastering Search Analytics*, published by O'Reilly, and has worked or consulted for multiple Fortune 500 companies, including HP, Intuit, Target, Chrysler and John Deere.

> *Be where the puck is going to be, not where the puck is.*
> **WALTER GRETZKY**

Great marketers will be where the customer is. Digital marketers on the other hand have no excuse to not be where the customer is. Today digital marketers should be held accountable for the impact on sales, units sold, revenue driven and other hard financial measures such as cost per acquisition or return on ad spend. Digital marketing today should be a blend of traditional marketing, sales and technology. To be successful at marketing you need to be smarter and faster than your opponents.

Digital marketers must leverage social media, search, display advertising, video streaming pre-rolls, mobile messaging, e-mail, SMS texting and a barrage of other digital channels to market effectively. To maximize the usage of these technologies you can tie it all back through data. Data that can provide predictive insights to who your customers are, what they need and when they need it, through predictive marketing.

There are examples of companies that are pushing the trends in predictive marketing; not surprisingly two of the biggest are Google and Facebook, both of which have come under fire for changes in their privacy policies to share data across applications, websites, or third parties. Most of these changes, for better or worse, were put in place to deliver more relevant ads or user experiences that push more relevant content that will engage the consumer or users of the their products.

Google's push in this space was to leverage what they know about consumers based on data from search, their display advertising network and anonymous data from other web properties they currently own. The end game is to develop a 360° view of their customer (Figure 30.1). But more than that, it is to understand where their customer will be next in that 360° view, and what exactly the customer will be or is looking at, so as to better target advertising to them.

Predictive marketing begins with the consumer. More specifically it begins with the consumer taking an action. Every action can be measured and monitored. Once the action is captured you can begin to make assumptions about a consumer based on aggregate data from other consumer actions and behaviours. The more data you have on both the collective as well as the individual, the more accurate predictions you can make as to what a

FIGURE 30.1 360° view of the customer

consumer is likely to do next; this is a very simple and linear approach, as shown in Figure 30.2.

FIGURE 30.2 Linear approach to predicting customer behaviour

The ability to track, measure and understand what consumers are doing is where leading edge brands such as Target are placing their bets. They aim to become smarter on where, when and what they message their consumers, but also about the optimal amount of money to spend on that messaging. On 16 February 2012 *The New York Times* published an article on Target and their predictive marketing tactics. The article explains how predictive marketing can move beyond the digital activities of an individual and drive direct mail, point of checkout offers and other real-time behaviours that happen in the physical world. All it takes is a unique identifier and you can begin to track the habits of individuals as well as the patterns of larger groups.

What is predictive marketing?

Predictive marketing is the use of data to drive decisions to better understand not only what your customers are doing but what they *will* do. The most sophisticated systems use big data to make real-time decisions, but even the simplest solutions can leverage free tools, with some clever thinking.

What separates predictive marketing from regular marketing or even personalization is focusing on the intent of the customer. It moves away from blanket advertising to a message that customers may not even be asking for yet or even know they have a need for, but the message aligns quickly with a need they will have. It is like being the concierge at a five-star hotel that always has what you need on hand at any given time, even before you know you need it. Anticipate what your customer will need and you will be the first voice in that conversation, making it much easier to close a sale or opportunity.

Wal-Mart has recently introduced semantic search, which they have code named 'Polaris'. The ultimate goal of Polaris is to not only provide consumers with what they want but also to suggest items based on their interests and intent. Site search, which most companies take for granted, can become a highly profitable opportunity to better understand both your customer and the opportunity to up-sell at the right time the right products. Predictive marketing through searchendising can drive incremental dollars simply by providing relevant content based on user and group behaviours.

Why predictive marketing is critical to success

Traditionally most marketers have thought of the typical purchase funnel and how consumers think and are engaged at different points through this funnel has determined the media type and message that is crafted. Figure 30.3 shows what a purchase funnel looks like.

Most marketing spend for larger companies will fall into the Awareness category, simply because the feeling is you have to keep the top of the funnel full in order to drive the bottom. TV, radio and print are mediums that typically have calls to action, but are more focused on getting the message out. Experience has taught me this is typically the case because it is more difficult to measure the impact these mediums have on driving sales. Digital marketing, however, allows you to market and measure success much more

FIGURE 30.3 A purchase funnel

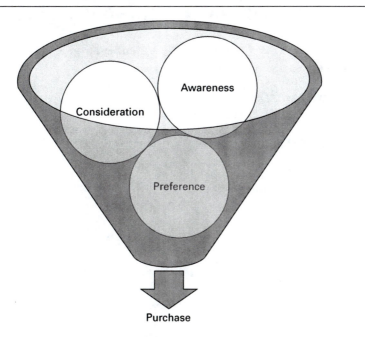

Awareness

Consideration

Preference

Purchase

easily, and because of this digital marketing is being held accountable not only for driving awareness but also for consideration and preference.

Further, by being able to measure and understand the funnel you can realize exactly where most effort should be placed to maximize value. Simply speaking and assuming everything stays the same, 1 per cent in the top of the funnel should yield 1 per cent out the bottom. This however may not hold true for everything in between. Bottlenecks may result in that extra 1 per cent in the top being squeezed down more than it should be. Through data analysis and predictive marketing, you should be thinking about how to message through the entire funnel process so as to eliminate these bottlenecks. Google published what they call the 'zero moment of truth', a decision that happens after the stimulus (the awareness stage) and 'first moment of truth' (the purchase stage).

This is the moment when predictive marketing is most effective. This is where your digital ecosystem needs to be honed and sharpened to deliver timely and relevant messages to your audience to deliver your biggest wins. Developing digital marketing that delivers not only on getting your message out, but on getting your message to people who have a need or interest in your product, service or offering. By quickly iterating through messages and content that get smarter and more relevant, you get a better understanding of your customer.

How to better understand your customer

As a digital marketer you should have a number of options at your fingertips, including some or all of the following:

1 company website;

2 paid search;

3 social media;

4 mobile content;

5 display advertising;

6 digital video;

7 data.

The last point, data, is perhaps the most important and crucial weapon. Every company, no matter what size, will always have access to some data. Data will be driven from items 1 through 6 on the previous list. This data

FIGURE 30.4 Options for the digital marketer

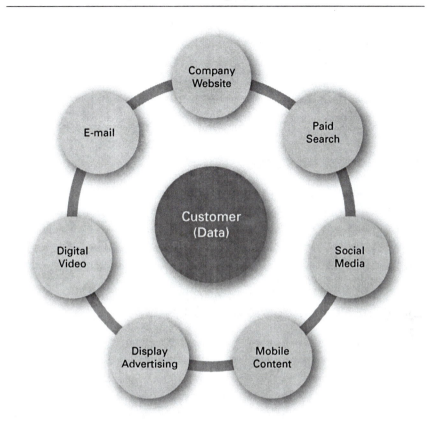

is what is required to deliver and develop a predictive marketing model. It doesn't require you be proficient in R or any other data-modelling application or software. What it does require, however, is that you spend some time with it to understand not only your digital ecosystem but the impact each element has on the consumer experience.

There are several types of data you can use for predictive marketing.

One-to-one personal

This is where you collect personal data on an individual, such as name, address, e-mail or anything else that can be used to personally identify that person. This typically requires a login to a system at some point. Facebook for example can use personally identifiable information to present some content to you.

One-to-one anonymous

This is where you don't have any personally identifiable information on an individual but you track their behaviour so as to display something to an individual. For example you may decide that every individual who adds a certain product to their shopping cart will be displayed complementary product. The data is used based on what they did, but the outcome is the same for everyone.

Many-to-one personal

This is where the activity of many individuals is projected to a single individual. For example Amazon does this when you login and have made several purchases. They look at the items you have bought as well as the items that others have bought, and make recommendations based on both your personal preferences and the choices the larger community has made.

Many-to-one anonymous

This is when an individual is presented with information based on the activities of many people, but the system does not know specifically who you are. For example, on Amazon when you browse a book, regardless of whether you are logged-in or not, they will often show you what other books people have bought who have viewed this book. They do not assume that they know who you are, simply that you are looking at something others have, and then project what others have looked at and purchased afterwards. This content is dynamically updated as more and more information is collected, and unlike one-to-one anonymous, where content is usually static or driven by a system administrator, this content updates every time another data point becomes available.

Knowing these four types of predictive marketing can show how simple or complex a system can become. The easiest and simplest is one-to-one anonymous, where you generate rules and do not require users to login. Systems as simple as WordPress and those as complex as Tridion SDL or Adobe CQ usually have the features or plug-ins to enable these features. If you are not taking advantage of some sort of targeting on your website today, you are probably missing great opportunities.

Evolving predictive marketing

While direct marketing on your website is an excellent start to predictive marketing, it doesn't really leverage your full digital echo system. While we can create rule-based behaviour triggers based on actions taken on our sites, if we consider the larger spectrum of digital marketing, we can look at how we leverage what we know based on users action off our site as well.

There are a number of targeting solutions available today that can leverage information from third parties or from referring data. Adobe has Test & Target, and there is also Autonomy, Interwoven, Optimost or BTBuckets, which is a free solution. These all offer the ability to target a user based on the geography they appear to be in, the type of technology they are using or even the traffic source.

For example knowing that a user is a Mac user may mean sending a different message that may appeal more to a Mac user's sensibilities than to a PC user. Even more interesting – and where the tying of technology comes into play – is understanding the keywords a prospect uses to arrive to your site. Say for example I searched for 'car quote'. I could be redirected to a page that provides car quotes, instead of a generic page that discusses the car quotes, or suppose that any time a user arrives at a website by searching for the term 'free', I position trial versions of my product instead of starting a hard sell.

This is using the concept of one-to-one anonymous data but tying it to other elements within my digital utility belt to create a better customer experience. Delivering the right content to the right customer. This requires neither large budgets nor big teams. What it does require is for you to sit down and think about how you would better engage with your customers. To think about what you need to say to customers based on what they are doing. These decisions should all be data based, which ultimately comes down to a simple implementation of web analytics on your company website. Google Analytics, the most popular and free choice for many sites, can often provide enough insights to give you a better way of thinking about your customers.

Simple reports in Google Analytics such as the keywords people arrive to your website on or the referring domains may give you a better idea of how to better target or market to individuals. You don't need to have a hardened analyst but taking time once a month to look at what pages are receiving the most views, and how are people getting to those pages can open up ideas on how to better engage with your customers. Think of the questions you want answered then look at the data to see if you can find the answer.

Where predictive marketing is going

While we have focused on how to use predictive marketing on your website as a whole this is growing through the entire digital world. DMP service providers such as BlueKai are offering targeting solutions for display advertising by leveraging both aggregate data and data about your customers to better target and display ads. Leveraging technologies similar to what Google and Facebook are developing to understand users behaviour and patterns better to provide relevant content on third party websites.

Chango and Magnetic are companies that are leveraging search keywords to re-target ads to users based on the users' intent. Much as I discussed how we can use targeting software on site to look for certain keywords, they are using this same approach to target users on third-party sites with display advertising.

In fact, search is potentially the biggest weapon in your marketing arsenal that you have probably not fully tapped into. Search is not only a medium to drive traffic to your site; it is the only medium today where users are actively telling what they are looking for.

A study by Jackob Nielson on the negative aging effect of a user on a web page shows that a user who spends 10 or more seconds is much more likely to engage with your content or the rest of your site. The simplest and easiest way to push time on a page to those critical 10 seconds is to deliver relevant and worthwhile content. Perhaps, the most critical moment is to establish that relationship digitally with your costumer.

As predictive marketing evolves it will likely incorporate Weibull Hazard Functions, as Nielson discusses, and focus on elements that provide customers the most optimal experience. And likely it will be a blend of technologies. It may include Google Analytics, BTBuckets, BlueKai and Chango technologies to not only deliver the right content to the right customer but also deliver the content at the right time. Understanding not only who the customers are but what they need, and better serve them.

Sources

Google Inc [accessed 9 December 2012] <http://www.zeromomentoftruth.com>
Nielson, Jackob [accessed 16 December 2012] How long do users stay on web
    pages? [online] <http://www.useit.com/alertbox/page-abandonment-time.html>
Wal-Mart [accessed 16 December 2012] <http://www.websitemagazine.com/
    content/blogs/posts/archive/2012/09/04/is-walmart-s-semantic-search-
    an-amazon-killer.aspx>

INDEX

NB: page numbers in *italic* indicate figures or tables

Also available from **Kogan Page**

Find out more; visit **www.koganpage.com** and
sign up for offers and regular e-newsletters.

CPSIA information can be obtained at www.ICGtesting.com
Printed in the USA
BVOW04s1134091013

333315BV00003B/3/P

9 780749 469627